Best Wishes

Bul Leaf

The Art of Perception

The Art of Perception

MEMOIRS OF A LIFE IN PR

ROBERT LEAF

Atlantic Books

First published in hardback in Great Britain in 2012 by
Atlantic Books an imprint of Atlantic Books Ltd.

Copyright © Robert Leaf, 2012

The moral right of Robert Leaf to be identified as
the author of this work has been asserted by him in accordance
with the Copyright, Designs and Patents Act of 1988.

All rights reserved. No part of this publication may be reproduced,
stored in a retrieval system, or transmitted in any form or by any means,
electronic, mechanical, photocopying, recording, or otherwise,
without the prior permission of both the copyright owner
and the above publisher of this book.

Every effort has been made to trace or contact all copyright holders.
The publishers will be pleased to make good any omissions or rectify
any mistakes brought to their attention at the earliest opportunity.

10 9 8 7 6 5 4 3 2

A CIP catalogue record for this book is available from the British Library.

Hardback ISBN: 978-0-85789-002-3
E-book ISBN: 978-0-85789-959-0

Printed in Great Britain by the MPG Books Group

Atlantic Books
An imprint of Atlantic Books Ltd
Ormond House
26–27 Boswell Street
London
WC1N 3JZ

www.atlantic-books.co.uk

Contents

Introduction

It was 1970. Nixon was in the White House. Brezhnev was running the Soviet Union, and the Cold War was in full swing. The Russians had recently invaded Czechoslovakia and had an iron grip on the nations of Central and Eastern Europe. So it came as a great surprise that the government-run advertising agencies of Romania, Hungary, Czechoslovakia, Poland and Russia were all interested in hearing about the latest trends in advertising and public relations. I was invited, along with two publishers and another senior executive, to go on a seventeen-day lecture tour around Eastern Europe culminating in a visit to Moscow.

Much to my surprise and delight, we were treated like royalty nearly everywhere we went. We were generously entertained, taken on trips around the region and talked to with incredibly sincere honesty. This was not what I was expecting from our cold war 'enemies'. One of the key local executives proudly told me that his son had translated *One Day in the Life of Ivan Denisovich* by Aleksandr Solzhenitsyn into Romanian. The book had been outlawed in the Soviet Union and Solzhenitsyn had been expelled from the Union of Soviet Writers for having written it.

The men and women I met were fascinated by our stories about advertising and public relations in the United States and what it was accomplishing there. You would have thought the cold war was a figment of some politician's imagination. . .

In Czechoslovakia, though, the mood was very different. In Prague, you could still hear the firing of cannons in the outskirts of the city where Russian troops were stationed. Presumably the soldiers were taking artillery practice and reminding the Czech citizenry of their presence – and who was boss. Our hosts, who had invited us to their beautiful city, seemed wary of being too close to us Westerners. And who could blame them? Our meetings had a formal air and, unlike all the other countries we visited, there would be no hobnobbing or social activities after the formal discussions were over.

In Moscow we were met with a high degree of cordiality, and were taken as guests to the opera, ballet and numerous museums. We were given English-speaking guides capable of answering our questions. It was obvious that our hosts really wanted us to enjoy their city, and there was a great deal there to see.

Yet, in spite of the warmth and cordiality extended to us, it was obvious that there was still a belief among many Russians that Western marketing techniques were tools of capitalism and thus open to question: should they be used in a communist society, and if so, how? This attitude became increasingly apparent to me during informal discussions I held with some of the audience before a talk I gave at a conference. Even though the audience of government officials, academics and business executives was engaged in advertising, it was still considered an unappealing tool of Western capitalism.

I was the final speaker and gave a presentation on what carefully considered advertising was able to accomplish. When I finished, the floor was open for questions. An academic who I had been talking with before the conference began, asked: 'Mr Leaf, how can you justify any social good in advertising?'

I paused for a long moment while I studied the audience. After some careful thought I replied, 'Let us say you are trying to sell harvesters you manufacture in Soviet plants to Egypt. And at the same time, Americans are also trying to sell them American-produced harvesters. If the Americans succeed in making the sale, the profits would usually go to individuals in private companies who can use the money in any way they see fit and for their own pleasure. But if you sell the harvesters, you can use the money to build hospitals, improve roads and provide a better life for the more impoverished. But to be able to do this first you have to sell those harvesters. And if it is your advertising that helps you to accomplish this, there is no question that it definitely has a social good.'

The professor immediately replied, 'Mr Leaf I can accept that completely.' Looking out at the audience, I got the feeling that he was not the only one who bought my reply.

I've often thought about this meeting in later years and my response to the learned Russian gentlemen's question and what it accomplished. I became more convinced than ever about a strong belief I had always held – about the key to successful communications, no matter who the audience is. That key is the need to manage perceptions and that belief is that the public relations business is, in reality, *perception management*.

The fact that one good answer could change the mind of a very learned man steeped in a particular ideology and change his attitude towards what he saw as a pernicious practice of Western capitalism – that showed what changing a perception could accomplish.

My belief is underlined by the fact that my encounter led to a significant client assignment and gave us a chance to create a closer communications tie between the East and West during the cold war. As a result of the conference, I was later able to negotiate a deal for Burson–Marsteller (the public relations firm of which I was the international chairman) to represent Vneshtorgreklama, the Russian state advertising agency who hosted our trip to Moscow. The relationship then led to our parent company starting the first Western advertising and PR firm in Russia.

One had to get used to the fact that different perceptions existed there, especially among publishers of trade magazines. If you wanted to place an ad in April, a publisher might schedule it in June or even refuse it on the grounds that there was no need for that particular product. On advertising, the Russian encyclopaedia says something very reflective of local thought on the matter: 'Methods of capitalist advertising are different, but they all clearly show the character of capitalist trade. Commercial enterprises often advertise useless goods and sometimes goods of poor quality.' In Russia, things were very different.

I have found my belief in the importance of perception management to be true from the time I started as the first trainee at Burson–Marsteller in New York (they had only six executives at the time) to later when I became international chairman and helped grow the company into the largest PR firm in the world. Throughout my entire fifty-year career in PR, I constantly saw that the way we managed perceptions was a significant factor in our success and also the success of our clients.

The importance of perception management proved true for nations, politicians, companies, executives, religious leaders, doctors, lawyers, and even private individuals. I found it to be true as I lived and worked in New York, London, Brussels, Hong Kong, and elsewhere around the world. Perception is what counts anywhere and everywhere. But it is equally important to recognize that perceptions can differ dramatically from market to market.

What do Barack Obama, Vladimir Putin, Pope Benedict XVI and the Taliban all have in common? They need to create the perceptions in their key audiences that they feel benefit them the most. Some do it better than others and, as President Obama – especially – has found out, perceptions can change dramatically and very quickly. Think about the way the Barack Obama of 2008 was perceived, compared to the Barack Obama of 2011.

During my career, I have watched public relations change dramatically. In the course of this book, I will describe what it was like to be both a catalyst and an observer of these changes. First and foremost, the business has expanded dramatically, and the growth continues as I write these words. Public relations firms of all sizes have mushroomed around the world: there are more than two thousand in China alone. In-house PR executives have achieved a stature unimaginable when I started. Mobile phones, digital cameras and the Internet ensure that communications are instantaneous worldwide and have prompted the need for PR professionals to react immediately to events. Corporate Social Responsibility programmes, non-existent when I started, are not only necessary, but have become the norm. The digital revolution has created a whole new world of communications, and relationship marketing has emerged as Facebook and Twitter have become vital tools for today's PR professional. Websites, of course, have become the key public face for many organizations, a face that must constantly be reviewed and changed when necessary. Many companies, unfortunately, do not understand this.

1   How I Got Started

Years before I joined Burson–Marsteller and later established offices throughout the world, I learned how important it is was to understand that people in different countries can differ dramatically in their attitudes and reactions to everyday events and situations. What we communicate and how we communicate has to be adjusted similarly if we are to be effective.

In 1955, I was serving as an information and education specialist in the US Army, stationed in Orléans, France. My responsibilities included giving a weekly lecture to the troops, based on Department of the Army pamphlets, covering subjects important to these peacetime troops, including how to behave while on leave abroad. These lectures were supposed to reflect the various different cultural attitudes influencing the natives' perception of our soldiers and their presence in these countries.

I explained that when on leave in France the men should always wear civilian clothes, never a military uniform. Having a history of military invasions, the average Frenchman did not like the sight of foreign uniforms, even those belonging to allies. This advice was especially important for any soldiers hoping to meet up with local women. I told them that if they tried to pick up a girl in a bar while in uniform, it could lead to a brawl.

On the other hand, attitudes were very different in Germany. I strongly advised the men to wear their uniforms while on leave there, one that was spit and polished. This was ten years after the end of the Second World War, and the German people still had a great respect for discipline and authority; in this part of the world, a well-uniformed soldier would earn respect instantly.

And then there was England, a place I had not yet visited but where I was destined to live for more than forty years. The British, according to the information I was given to tell the troops, were a very private people by nature, particularly with strangers. I told the soldiers that they should seriously avoid any discussions about politics, religion and – especially – sex by all means. When I finally set foot in London for the first time and decided to visit the pubs for which the country was famous, I found that the army's official word was dead wrong. I engaged in all sorts of interesting discussions with the locals on politics – and sex, too. Upon returning to base I seriously modified my lecture, except when I was being observed and graded by a senior officer. In those cases, I would keep to the official line when dealing with the British.

It was 1948, and it was time for me to attend a university. I selected the University of Missouri. At the time, Missouri housed the most important Journalism school in the US. The J–School had been founded in 1903, making it the world's first Journalism school. Joseph Pulitzer, the newspaper baron best known for the Pulitzer Prize that he later founded, was involved in its establishment. At the time, it was the only school that granted a Bachelor of Journalism degree.

I initially thought that I would like to build myself a career as a journalist, probably as a sports writer. Then I decided that I should be a creative writer, and later still an advertising executive, as that business needed people with writing skills, which I thought I possessed. But after my first few years in school taking general studies, I changed my mind. I decided that I would pursue a degree in Journalism after all but would major in Public Relations, a field still in its relative infancy. The reason was simply that I found the Public Relations courses particularly interesting because they underlined the importance of developing the right messages and presenting them in the best possible manner to any audience, whether a government or political party, a business or association.

I did not know a great deal about public relations back then. I thought its primary role was to get individuals, companies or ideas better known. In some cases it was linked to advertising, but advertising was already a major industry, while PR was still a small business. Even in my PR coursework, the emphasis was on how to ascertain what would be of news value, and to write about it in a way that would make it appealing to the media.

When I finished my bachelor's degree in 1952, the Korean War was still on. Since I was registered as 1-A by the draft board, it meant that I would be inducted into the US Army immediately upon graduation. But since I felt, at 6'3", that I was too big a target for the Korean sharpshooters, I decided it was best to remain in school and go for a Master's degree, a pursuit that would allow me to postpone my induction until I had finished my studies.

Since I now had a degree in Journalism, I decided that I didn't need a Master's in the same subject and switched to History, focusing on the period from 1871 to 1945. I believed that knowing the history of this modern period would be beneficial no matter what I eventually decided to do. I found world history so interesting that I even began to toy with the idea that upon leaving the army I might become an academic.

Switching to History turned out to be a smart move. Later, I was engaged in public relations in many different countries around the world and I found that being knowledgeable about a country's history – sometimes more so than many of the locals with whom

I was working – I was able to gain a much greater degree of acceptance in the local marketplace. People saw that I had a personal interest in their country.

To obtain my degree, it was necessary to write a thesis. The choice of subject was the student's, unless his professor felt that the topic was already covered in too great detail already. I chose to write my thesis on Father Charles Coughlin, one of the most controversial priests in American history. He started as a very left-leaning prelate, attacking the financial community as a major precipitator of the Great Depression. At that time, he was a great supporter of President Roosevelt, even stating at a congressional hearing that 'God is directing President Roosevelt.'

Father Coughlin started a magazine and even had his own radio programme. Known as the 'Radio Priest', he became one of the most famous people in the United States. At the peak of his popularity, he received 80,000 letters a week – second only to the president – and one third of the American public listened to his radio show.

Inexplicably, he began to embrace extreme right-wing political positions, even talking favourably at times of Hitler and Mussolini. When the Second World War began, his magazine was banned from being shipped around by mail. It was ruled that, while freedom of speech allowed him to say anything he desired, the American postal service was not required to deliver any post it felt was detrimental to the country's interests. His radio programme was then outlawed and, finally, the Archbishop of Detroit and head of Coughlin's diocese, the Most Reverend Edward Mooney, told him to end all involvement in politics or risk defrocking – he chose the former option. When I wrote to him to request an interview so that I could accurately portray his thinking, he replied that he was not permitted to give interviews. This study of Father Coughlin proved to be of great value to me in my career. It showed me the power of both the print and broadcast media and how one man could dramatically change the perceptions of thousands.

As I leisurely worked on my thesis, I received a number of letters from the Department of the Army asking when it would be completed, so that I could be inducted into the US Army. I kept replying that I was working on it steadily but couldn't give a definite date. Finally, they decided that my academic career had been going on long enough and I was notified that I should report for induction in New York a week later.

This turn of events meant I had to get my final draft to my professor for grading before I left for the service. Instead of hiring a professional secretary to type it up – which was what most graduate students did – I typed it up myself. Not being the world's greatest typist, I made more than a few errors. I had no choice but to send it, errors and all, to my professor. Then I headed back to New York to let my mother know there was now going to be a soldier in the family.

Soon after my induction, I got a letter from my professor with my grade and some comments. He wrote that as far as style was concerned, this was the worst paper he had ever received. But because he thought so highly of the content, he was giving me an 'A' overall.

It could not have come at a better time. I was going through the least enjoyable part of basic training: cleaning rifles, washing dishes, guard duty all night. I was also learning that answering: 'Yes sir! Yes sir!' with enthusiasm was key to surviving. My professor's letter made me feel more like a general than a private.

While I was not looking forward to a two-year hitch in the military, I honestly believed that it was a national necessity. During my last year at university, while I was still working on my thesis, I was interviewed by an officer in the Central Intelligence Agency at the recommendation of the Dean. He wanted me to consider going to Officer

Candidate School upon graduation, thus becoming a Lieutenant. He explained to me that as a Lieutenant I could lead an exciting and glamorous life. He went so far as to explain that if the war was still on, I might be dropped behind enemy lines in a black parachute, possibly becoming a national hero in the process.

I thanked him kindly and said I would give it very careful consideration. It didn't take long for me to decide I'd be better off going in as a private and avoiding anything that looked like a parachute, regardless of colour, especially while the war was on.

Upon induction, I was sent to Fort Dix, New Jersey. In the army, everyone was assigned a 'Military Occupation Specialty' (MOS) and, because of my academic background, I was made a clerk typist, making it probable that I would land an office job.

After finishing my basic training – quite a change from life on the Missouri campus – I was sent to Fort Eustis, Virginia. After a few months, a very friendly major who was my commanding officer asked if I would like to go to a special training school in New York so that my MOS could be changed to 'information and education specialist'. Then, I could give weekly talks to the unit on a variety of topics and also work on a unit magazine. I, of course, agreed and spent a very relaxing month in New York City learning how to be a government PR man.

Then came the break that patterned my future career. Even though the war was now over, every American base had to supply a number of soldiers to be sent overseas. Divisions were sent lists of the MOS's that were needed and the commanding officer of each division would select which soldiers with the requested MOS's would be chosen to go abroad. Fortunately for me, the man who picked which divisions would be assigned which MOS's was a staff sergeant who was a good friend of mine and a fellow poker player.

During our weekend poker games I had won a good deal of money from the sergeant. He didn't want his wife to know, so I told him to pay me whenever he wanted with any amount he wanted. In appreciation, he came to me and said there was a need for an information and education specialist in Europe. I was the only soldier with that MOS in my division and, should he select me, the major would have to send me abroad. 'Would you like to do this?' he asked.

I sure did. I immediately asked him to go ahead. I was excited by the prospect of visiting countries I had studied, whose history I knew despite having never set foot there. My luck didn't end there – it was just the beginning. The sergeant was familiar with the ship that would be transporting me. When you were shipped overseas the voyage usually took six to seven days. You were assigned a job, and you had to perform it for the duration of the entire trip, whether it was kitchen police, guard duty or cleaning decks. The best assignment was to be one of the chaplain's assistants, and it so happened that the sergeant knew the ship's chaplain and arranged for me to meet him. After he interviewed me, I became his assistant, and my main role was to help run the religious services and even play the organ at these services. Since playing an organ was not one of my great skills, I asked the chaplain if he had any other assignments. Fortunately, the chaplain was also in charge of the ship's daily newspaper, and because of my degree in Journalism he changed my role to editor of the ship's paper.

When we arrived in Germany my luck continued. When we got off the boat we had to join one of a number of lines where we were to be interviewed and then assigned a location in Europe, typically for our entire time abroad. Fortunately one of the people giving out assignments was a soldier I had become friendly with at Fort Dix. I joined his line, and he asked what I would prefer. The choice wasn't difficult. I could either go to one of several forts in Germany where most of the time was spent out in the field, or go to headquarters in France, a beautiful new base in Orléans in the Loire Valley, where they needed an information and education specialist.

No contest. I happily went off to Orléans where the commanding officer assigned me to an orderly room where I acted as a secretary, opening all the mail, directing letters to the right people, answering the phone, taking messages and basically doing anything the major asked me to. My main two jobs, though, were giving weekly lectures to all the troops, and giving out weekend passes and leave certificates. . . and carefully making sure that there was always a weekend pass for Robert S. Leaf.

And the breaks continued. Among my room-mates was an artist, Bill Kohn, who had studied at Washington University in Missouri and had won five scholarships – the last one granting him the freedom to go and paint anywhere in the world. He chose Paris and was there for more than a year. Later, when he was drafted by the army, he ended up back in France.

We spent nearly every other weekend in Paris and Bill was the best guide to the city that I could ever have. We lived with the artists and students he had met during his scholarship year. They shepherded us around the churches, museums and other key points of interest, and I developed an appreciation of the Paris that Ernest Hemingway had described in his writings.

My lectures, meanwhile, consisted mainly of aspects of American history, the military and its operations, and world organizations such as the UN and NATO. Other more memorable topics included 'The best way to avoid venereal disease' and 'The advantages of re-enlisting'.

I never would have imagined that I would really enjoy my army career. I had only had one unhappy moment during the entire time I was stationed in Orléans and it concerned a photograph I failed to take. In April 1956, the beautiful American actress Grace Kelly married Prince Rainier of Monaco. Though I was stationed close by, somehow they had forgotten to invite me. . . but I wasn't going to let that stop me. I took some leave and went to Monaco on my own, hoping to get close to the action. The tiny country was lit up like a dream-world, especially the harbour. The night before the wedding, there was a spectacular fireworks display that was probably unequalled anywhere at that time. I felt like I was in a magical kingdom.

On the day of the wedding only one reporter was allowed to attend the ceremonies in the Cathedral of Saint Nicholas. The rest of the press were assigned to a room nearby where they could watch the ceremony on television. I decided I would try to get into the press room so that I could also watch what I knew would be a memorable event. When security challenged me and told me to leave I pretended that I couldn't speak English, French or German and didn't understand a word of what they were saying. So they decided I must be a reporter from some other foreign country and let me stay to watch what was a truly exciting event. I remember Prince Rainier was a little nervous and had trouble putting the ring on his bride's finger, so Grace helped him.

The weather was perfect and when the ceremony was over, the Prince and Grace got into an open Rolls Royce to drive through Monaco to the royal palace. By then, the officials were convinced that I was a photographer, as I had my camera with me, and they let me join the other photographers in the press corps. We were taken to a place where we would be able to get the best shots of the newly-married couple as they left in their open Rolls. As we waited to photograph Grace, I looked through my camera's viewfinder to get a feel for taking the picture. The procession had started more quickly than I expected. Suddenly, Grace came into view. She looked so stunningly beautiful that I put my camera aside so that I could really see her. I stared and stared – and never snapped the picture. To this day, I regret missing the opportunity to take what could have been a historic photo. The memory of that moment is still there, and the sight of her is as fresh in my mind's eye as though I had seen her just yesterday. She was that beautiful.

Fast-forward fifty years. Recently the Victoria and Albert Museum in London held an exhibition of Grace Kelly's clothing and, as my wife is a guide at the V&A, I decided to attend. In addition to the clothing, the museum was showing a series of filmed highlights of her life. One highlight was the wedding, including footage of her leaving the church in the open Rolls Royce near where I had been standing. I saw again how beautiful Grace Kelly was, and I relived the moment, easily understanding why I couldn't pull my gaze away from her in time to snap the picture.

Soon after the wedding, my military career came to an end and I moved back to the United States in 1956. It was time to go out and earn a living. I moved in with my widowed mother and started to scan job offers in the various papers, especially the *New York Times*. One ad that particularly intrigued me was from a show business publicist who was looking for an assistant to help him prepare material about his entertainment clients for public dissemination.

After an initial interview, I went along to the publicist's office with nine other candidates. The publicist explained who was on his client list. He told us all to go home and write interesting and funny material that was good enough to appear in the columns of the leading newspaper writers of that period: Walter Winchell, Leonard Lyons, Jimmy Cannon and Robert Sylvester. He told us to make up some funny stories involving his clients that would be suitable for the columns.

His clients turned out to be entertainers like Milton Berle, the father of American television, Eddie Condon, a famous jazz musician, and the singers Pearl Bailey and Tony Bennett. He told us that it didn't matter if the facts in our stories were all made up. He just wanted to see the style and approach and to estimate our capacity to reach the audiences he was interested in. I was very impressed with his enthusiasm and how he sold the job. He made us feel that our future was going to be limitless if we were selected. I went home hoping he would choose me and it would be the beginning of an exciting future.

A few days after I turned in my material, he called to say he had been very impressed with my work and that the job was mine. I would start the following Monday. When I arrived in the office for my first day of work, we reviewed my boss's client list in depth, discussing what these entertainers were like and what they wanted the press to say about them.

Thus, my first professional paying job in PR meant spending each day making up stories about things the clients supposedly said, things they had supposedly done and, in most cases, creating an interesting context for things that they really had said or done. I also had to be in early to answer the phone as my boss generally didn't arrive until around noon. When clients asked for him, I was instructed to say he had just stepped out for a few minutes. He did not want them to know he could run the business on a half-day basis – in case they felt the fees they were paying for his services were too high.

On the Friday of my sixth week on the job my boss called me into his office for a serious conversation. He said my output had been slowing down and that I was nowhere near as fast at turning out material as when I started. I said I should be able to pick up my output, but he replied that it didn't matter as: 'This is your last day and I wish you luck. I have selected a replacement for you starting next Monday.' I was disappointed but not surprised as I had already come to the conclusion that this was not the organization where I could build my future.

My soon-to-be former boss then sent me to the post office to get some stamps. While I was gone, he went through my desk and took all my notes, apparently assuming that anything I had written while on his payroll was his. A few months after I had left the company, I read in Robert Sylvester's column in the *New York Daily News* that, at midnight soirées in Buckingham Palace, Princess Margaret mainly played Tony Bennett records. This was something I had made up entirely when working for this publicist.

Now that my budding career as a publicist was over – at least for the time being – while living at home with my mother, I began to look for new employment. This time around it was easier. A friend of the family who ran a one-man marketing company with a few clients needed an assistant and felt that I would be the right person for the job. He was a man I really liked and respected, in contrast to my previous employer. This new job was like finding the promised land.

There was a major problem though. His business was growing faster than even he had anticipated and in reality he needed someone with far more experience than me to deal with senior people in his clients' organizations, especially when he was away travelling, which was quite often. I began to feel that he needed someone better than I was at this stage and I told him so. He was exceedingly nice and said he was sure I would learn and that he would be pleased to keep me. But feeling this wasn't fair to him, I said I would stay until he found a more experienced replacement.

As part of his appreciation, he said that I should write any letter of recommendation that I wanted to present to possible future employers and that he would sign it regardless of the content. So I wrote a letter which pretty much gave the impression that when I told him I was leaving he wanted to publicly disembowel himself with a samurai sword, and that there was no doubt I had the potential to become the president of the United States or, at the very least, governor of New York.

Armed with that letter, I was off job-hunting again. This time I decided I would stay away from entertainers and deal with companies. PR was growing fast and I had met some impressive people working in that field. I went to a directory of public relations firms and listed about fifteen of them. I added fifteen large corporations that I felt would consider public relations important and needed a large internal staff.

I sent each of my targets a letter with a résumé (but not my letter of recommendation, which I planned to save to present at the interview) along with a stamped self-addressed postcard with a place for them to put the time and date when they could see me. I received a good number of replies and ended up with some excellent opportunities.

I was impressed by the people I met, especially at IBM where they wanted an editor for their in-house magazine. They told me that the chairman studied every single article before it was published so that if he believed the material I prepared was good, I would be assured of a future at 'Big Blue'. They gave me some tests and I was told afterwards that I came in second among applicants. Number one already had experience writing for in-house magazines, so they had picked him.

Hill and Knowlton, which was then the largest PR firm in the world, called me in, and their interviewer spent a long time talking to me. They had no openings at the time but said they would stay in touch. They contacted me soon after I joined Burson–Marsteller and offered me a job with one of their clients with the understanding that I would eventually join them.

I knew nothing of Burson–Marsteller when I initially wrote to them except that it was a very small firm. In fact, if they had listed their clients in the directory I was using, as did most of the other PR firms, I wouldn't have applied to them. Their clients would have made them appear as a 'business-to-business' practice, as they were all industrial firms using PR to sell their products to other businesses. This was the area of PR I had the least knowledge of and, at that time, the least interest in as well.

Burson, when I walked through the door for my first interview, had six executives in New York and was a small branch of what was then known as Marsteller Gebhardt & Reed – the largest industrial advertising agency in the country. Burson's business was picking up, and they were looking for their first trainee.

My interview was to be with Elias (Buck) Buchwald, the company's executive vice president and Harold Burson's original partner. We immediately hit it off. But there was one major problem, they were looking for a trainee and felt that I was far too qualified. They wanted someone to open the mail and paste captions on pictures for client releases to the press, as PR mailing houses did not yet exist. Buck told me that I could easily get twice the money they were able to offer anywhere else, and even if they raised the salary a little it would not be enough for someone with my academic background and work experience such as it was. So this very unlikely job interview went like this:

'You are far too qualified for this particular job.'

'No I'm not. I'm new in the field and so just starting out.'

'But even starting out you could start at a higher level.'

'But this is the perfect job for me at a place where I can learn from the bottom.'

'But you'll soon be bored and want to earn more money elsewhere.'

'Right now money is not my problem as I live at home with my mother, and she doesn't charge rent or board.'

Little by little I felt I was winning Buck over, but one serious problem remained. When I arrived at his office, I had put my spectacular letter of recommendation – the one I had written and which my previous boss had signed – on the table where we were sitting. I had intended to use it as the coup de grâce, revealing it at the proper moment, ensuring that I'd get the job.

Now I was thinking, 'If Buck reads it, I'm on my way out.' They certainly didn't want as a trainee someone a previous employer thought could someday be president. So while I continued talking, I started to slowly and nonchalantly slip it off the table top and onto my lap. There, it remained out of Buck's sight for the remainder of the interview. Thirty years later, I showed Buck the letter while we were having lunch. He said that if he had read it back then, we wouldn't be having lunch that day. There was no way he would have hired me after experiencing that encomium to my virtues.

The interview ended and Buck said, 'Harold Burson isn't here right now but will be in tomorrow. Come in during the morning to see him and he can make the final decision.' The next day, leaving the letter at home, I went back to the Burson-Marsteller offices and met with Harold Burson. He gave me a warm greeting, said Buck had been impressed, and asked me to sit down. We had a good discussion.

People continually ask me what Harold – whom *PR Week* was to later name as the country's most influential PR figure of the century – was like back then. All I can say is that Harold back then was much the same as Harold today: friendly, soft-spoken, a good questioner, but an equally good listener.

His parents had originally emigrated from Russia to Leeds in England, and then came to the US and settled in Memphis, Tennessee, where he was born three months later. At the age of twelve he was a copy boy on the *Memphis Commercial Appeal*. Harold then attended the University of Mississippi where he was editor of the school paper and was also the school's publicist.

While at the University of Mississippi he gained some renown when he obtained one of the rare interviews given by William Faulkner, one of America's best-known authors. After graduation he went into the army and while writing for the military newspaper, *Stars and Stripes*, he covered the Nuremberg war trials.

We talked for about an hour and at one point he said, 'What is it you are really looking for? What is it you want to do?' I explained that I thought public relations was in its relative infancy and had a great future. I told him that I really wanted to understand it, to learn what it was able to accomplish and to build my future around it.

This conversation took place on a Friday and Harold said, 'If that is what you want, you can start working for Burson–Marsteller on Monday.' Little did I think that I would still be there some forty years later.

2 Early Years at Burson–Marsteller

On 1 July 1957, when I arrived all smiles at the Burson–Marsteller office in Manhattan to start my career, I figured I'd probably be there for a year or two before moving on to a larger company. Little did I envision the roller-coaster ride that would ensue, but fortunately it was one that defied gravity and went upward 90 per cent of the time. It was a ride that would lead to my becoming international chairman of the world's largest PR firm; starting offices in nearly all the major parts of the world; living in Brussels, London and Hong Kong over the course of forty-five years; advising companies such as IBM, General Motors, Coca-Cola, Johnson & Johnson, Citicorp, McDonald's, American Express, Unilever and hundreds more; dealing with governments as diverse as Argentina, Egypt, Saudi Arabia, China and Russia during the cold war; and navigating through levels of corruption in Asia that I had no idea existed. All the while I witnessed (and helped bring about in my small way) the dramatic change in public relations as it reached a level of importance that even the most ardent advocates would never have anticipated when I signed in for my first day of work.

The term public relations was still somewhat new then, supposedly first having appeared in the US in the 1897 *Yearbook of Railway Literature*. What public relations stood for in the most simple terms was managing relationships with various publics. Publics could include the government, the local community, the financial community and possible investors, other businesses, employees, customers or potential customers and, in the case of politicians, the public in general. It concerns anyone you want to create a specific perception with, that in turn will benefit you in some way.

But the practice and importance of PR in its most essential meaning is nothing new. Even if it was not then called public relations, the need to reach out to key audiences has always been significant. And it was something people did intuitively from the beginning of time. The ancient Egyptians didn't need a PR firm to tell them that they should be on the good side of the pharaohs, priests and generals. And Ptahhotep, the advisor to one of the ancient Egyptian pharaohs, wrote of the need for communicating truthfully, addressing audience interests and acting in a manner consistent in what is being said – and this back in 2200 BC.

When I joined the industry, PR as a business was basically an American proposition, though some PR firms were operating overseas, the best of them probably in the UK and Australia. But public relations in its present form was born in the US. Two Americans – Ivy Lee and Edward V. Bernays – are generally given credit for being the co-fathers of PR.

Ivy Lee, along with his partner George Parker, established one of the world's first PR firms in 1905. And, rightfully or wrongfully, he is credited with developing the modern public relations campaign when in 1913 he lobbied the government on behalf of the Pennsylvania Railroads. He was opposing Theodore Roosevelt who was then blocking many of the railroad's efforts and, finally, he helped win the right to a 5 per cent freight charge increase.

Lee is by far most famous for his long time association with John D. Rockefeller and his family. He developed the idea of having Rockefeller Senior hand out money to the poor, dramatically improving his image and reputation as he was not considered the king of generosity. Lee is also credited with the idea of giving the family name to the giant real estate project they were developing in Midtown Manhattan. Initially, some members of the family were against calling it the Rockefeller Centre.

Ivy Lee fought for companies to be more open and accurate – a pioneer for what is now called transparency – and for PR to go beyond hucksterism. Many consider him a force in raising the level of public relations counselling to a degree of importance and professionalism it had not seen before.

But while most of Lee's history and contributions were looked on favourably, not everything he did was. The famous author, Upton Sinclair, nicknamed him 'Poison Ivy' and accused him of completely altering, on behalf of a client, the true facts of how miners were killed during a coal mining rebellion in Colorado known as the 'Ludlow Massacre'. It was known as a massacre because the Colorado National Guard attacked a tent complex of striking miners, killing nineteen people, including women and children. He was controversial in other ways: shortly before he died in 1934, the US Congress was investigating his work in Nazi Germany on behalf of I. G. Farben.

Of the two men, Edward Bernays probably more rightfully deserves the moniker of 'Father of PR'. He did more to get PR known than anyone. He was the first to teach a course at university in Public Relations in 1923 at New York University. His book, *Crystallizing Public Opinion*, which was published that same year, outlined the theory and practice of public relations for the first time.

His client list, which according to his records ended up numbering 435, included General Motors, General Electric, Allied Chemical, Philco Radio, Mack Trucks, American Tobacco, Cartier, the New York Philharmonic, Mutual Benefit Life Insurance, CBS, NBC, *Fortune Magazine*, *Ladies' Home Journal*, *Time Magazine*, Waldorf Astoria,

R. H. Macy, The Union of Electrical Workers, The Brotherhood of Railroad Trainmen, America's Brewers, the author Eugene O'Neill and the artist Georgia O'Keefe. To his credit, he also worked for dozens of charitable organizations at no cost.

He was the nephew of Sigmund Freud and remained very close to his Austrian uncle. Some of his uncle's thoughts on what motivates people obviously impacted on his thinking about how to use PR. And he was very active in promoting his uncle Sigmund in the US. Bernays's ego was legendary. He was quick to take credit for anything he was even tangentially involved in. But, faults and all, when he died aged 103, he was considered by most observers to be the true founder of modern public relations.

In his excellent book on Bernays, entitled *Spin*, Larry Tye quotes Harold Burson as saying: 'While Lee clearly came first and was a superior tactician, from a theoretical standpoint and on an organizational basis, I'd have to say Bernays was the father [of PR]. To my knowledge no one came up with anything better. We are still singing off the hymn book he gave us.'

But even before public relations had its official name, its key role was getting publicity (for some clients the same remains true today). And while many people throughout history had the skills to accomplish that, the man many consider the greatest publicist of all time was P. T. Barnum.

Barnum would do anything to get coverage. He had his own museum featuring exotics, including albinos, giants, midgets, fat boys and exotic women. He was not against using hoaxes such as the Feejee mermaid – a creature with the head of a monkey and the tail of a fish. And later, the man-monkey – a black dwarf who spoke a mysterious language Barnum had conveniently created for him. By 1846, his museum was drawing 400,000 visitors a year.

But by far what earned him his title of the greatest publicist was his development of Tom Thumb. He found this young boy in Connecticut who had stopped growing at twenty-five inches and weighed fifteen pounds. He named him Tom Thumb after a character in English folklore, made up all sorts of stories about his background and brought him to New York where he performed a variety of roles in plays, including that of Napoleon.

Barnum's greatest accomplishment, the one he is known for to this day, was his trip to England with Tom Thumb. The publicity around this tour was so great that it led to his being asked to visit Buckingham Palace to meet with Queen Victoria and her family. Tom put on a complete show for her, and the Queen took him by his hand and led him on a tour of the palace. The Queen saw Tom two more times and the resultant publicity led to huge successes for Barnum and his show, not only in England, but in other European capitals. He and Tom even met with the Tsar of Russia, Nicholas I.

Upon their return to the US, Tom Thumb remained a dominant figure and Barnum kept up his exploitation. When Tom married another small person, Barnum promoted the wedding so successfully that it led to lines of people stretching from the doors of Grace Church down Broadway on the day of the ceremony. The couple was even invited to visit President Abraham Lincoln in Washington during their honeymoon.

The reason I am giving so much emphasis to Barnum and his brand of publicity is that when I began my career clients mainly paid fees to get publicity. In my early years at Burson–Marsteller, once I had been promoted to account executive, publicity was my main responsibility.

From the beginning, I found Burson–Marsteller the ideal place to learn the public relations business. Both Harold Burson and Bill Marsteller did everything possible to help all of their staff – no matter how high or low they were in the organization – to learn as much as they could. Their office doors were open to everyone at all times.

They were very different people from each other and maybe that contributed to the company's great success. Harold was short and very soft-spoken. Bill was tall and very dynamic. He had worked for a newspaper, a life insurance company and at Rockwell Manufacturing as advertising manager where he rose to become vice president. They became a major client when he left to form his own agency.

Harold by nature was comfortable being in the background until he had something he wanted to get across, and when he did decide to speak, almost every idea he expressed was a good one, soon accepted by his listeners. Bill had a tendency to dominate discussions and meetings. At new business pitches he answered too many of the prospect's questions, not allowing the people who would be handling the account to take the lead. But he began to realize what he was doing and developed the habit of taking a pencil and putting it into his mouth so when a question came up it would help prevent him from jumping up and providing the answer.

Both men were incredibly caring about staff, their interests and their problems. And they were generous. We had an older mail-room clerk whose one great love was baseball, especially the New York Yankees. And one year when the team was in the World Series, Bill got him the best box seats at the Yankee Stadium to see some of the games. No gesture could have had a greater meaning to that clerk.

Bill and Harold first got together in 1953. Harold had his own small PR agency and Bill was head of Marsteller Gebhardt & Reed, then the biggest industrial ad agency in the US. When a number of Bill's advertising clients began to see the need for some publicity, Bill questioned people at the *New York Times* and the *Wall Street Journal* for the names of PR men he might use, and Harold's name came up with high recommendations. When they met, they immediately liked and respected each other and together formed Burson–Marsteller in 1953 as a very tiny adjunct to the advertising agency. Bill kept his headquarters in Chicago but came to New York frequently.

Even before they formed Burson–Marsteller, Bill knew he had made the right choice when one of his biggest clients, Rockwell Manufacturing Company, was looking for publicity about their line of power tools. Harold went to see them and soon after arranged for a three-page article in *Life* magazine about their products. Bill's other major client, Clark Equipment Company, then the largest manufacturer of forklift trucks, decided they needed some professional help in putting out an earnings release and contacted Bill Marsteller. He sent Harold to meet the chairman who was a very tough, outspoken engineer. Harold interviewed him and got the necessary information. The chairman asked Harold who he would have write the release, and Harold said he would do it himself and came back the following day with a draft.

Clark got far better coverage than they ever anticipated as a result and the chairman called Bill Marsteller to say: 'That small man you sent to see me whose name I can't remember – I looked into his head and I very much liked what I saw.' That was enough for Bill. From the beginning, Burson–Marsteller was treated as a completely separate company and was never considered part of an advertising agency. This helped contribute to its growth.

Both Harold and Bill were excellent writers. Once I started writing releases I always sent my copy to Harold to edit. He was invariably able to make it about 20 per cent shorter without losing any of the important messages and could change the wording of the lead in a way that would attract any editor.

In those days, the average PR man was a better writer than today. Writing was a major part of the job back then, whereas today writing a release or feature is usually a very small part of the PR executive's total activities. A number of editors have told me and even shown me examples of material they have received in the mail from PR firms and in-house departments that was so bad it was embarrassing. And possibly because, back then, PR people had more time than in today's far more demanding and competitive world, they read much more and so had more factual data on which to base their releases.

Bill always sought perfection. One of his greatest speeches was entitled 'The Pursuit of Excellence'. He constantly sent out memos to the staff on the need to be on time, the need to be neat (he even had rules on what women could wear), the need to protect the client's security and how to ensure one got a promotion or a raise.

He was unique in his love of words. One of his greatest memos and later the title of a book based on his speeches and memos was 'The Wonderful World of Words'. To him, words were like people coming in all sizes and colours, each unique.

'There were,' Bill wrote, 'tall words, short words, fat words, skinny words, boy words, girl words', and so on. As a brief example: 'title', 'lattice', 'latitude', 'lily', 'tattle' and 'intellect' are lean and lanky words. And some nice short-fat words are 'hog', 'yoghurt', 'jar', 'pot', 'bonbon', 'acne', 'plump' and 'slobber'. Masculine words are 'bourbon', 'rupture', 'oak', 'cartel', 'steak' and 'socks'. Feminine words are 'tissue', 'slipper', 'cute', 'squeamish', 'flutter' and 'gauze'. Words can have the same meaning and still be of the opposite sex. 'Naked' is masculine, but 'nude' is feminine.

Bill also put out a memo to all staff called 'The Boy Scout Oath' listing twenty-seven pieces of advice, such as:

1) Quit worrying about your competition. The only real competitor you have is yourself.
2) Look for the best in others and remember all of us have more weaknesses than we see in ourselves.

3) Reserve your opinions of people, good or bad, until you've observed them and lived with them long enough to know you're right.

4) If you have problems, doubts or suggestions about the management of this business, go to the management with your comments. Not to the guy at the next desk. He can't do anything about it.

5) Other people like a compliment as much as you do.

6) Take your triumphs home to your wife and tell your troubles to the bartender or keep them to yourself.

7) Never lose your sense of humour.

8) Don't waste your abilities – write articles, make speeches. Stand out from the crowd or be lost in the crowd.

9) Don't get discouraged. Look back at your progress, account by account, job by job, person by person. Thousands of good novels were never written because the author got bored or discouraged after the first chapter.

Bill Marsteller was unique. When he passed away, Harold wrote a memo to staff, most of whom had never met Bill, describing him as 'larger than life. . . a giant among men'. 'But these phrases,' Harold continued, 'would have brought denial from Bill. They would have suffered his scorn. After all, he hated clichés; he rallied against banality.' I will talk more about Bill later as I reported directly to him when I was put in charge of the company's PR.

When I started my job, Harold had said to me: 'Bob, if you want to learn the business from the bottom there is no better way than beginning as a trainee.' And he was right. I had the opportunity to gain a general understanding of all aspects of the public relations business. I also acted as Harold's assistant. Going over his mail taught me a great deal. I learned what clients liked – and what they didn't like. Harold was very patient and would always answer any questions I had.

Another of my responsibilities at this time was building up and maintaining our media lists. In those days there weren't the professional mailing houses of today that specialize in disseminating news releases. We used to do all our own mailings from the office, and I was in charge of getting releases out. I soon learned the importance of relating specific stories to specific types of media, even to specific journalists. I also learned the value of multiple placements and the art of maximizing the facts available – meaning including subjects that would be of the greatest interest – to get the most coverage in the most media.

The firm was growing rapidly and soon I was promoted and given an assistant. One of my early assistants was a girl named Mary Travers who later became better known as one third of Peter, Paul and Mary, one of America's leading singing groups. Occasionally, Mary would sing in the office, but being partially tone deaf, I would not have been able to predict her future. She left Burson–Marsteller to join Peter and Paul and sing at the Bitter End, a club in Greenwich Village. A few years later, as they became increasingly famous and toured the US universities singing five or six days a week, *Look Magazine*, then a leading consumer publication, sent a reporter to travel with them. His article described their tours and mentioned the kind of fees they were earning. It turned out that my former assistant was then making more money than Harold Burson and Bill Marsteller combined.

Soon I was assigned my first account work promoting lubricated plug valves. I had never heard of lubricated plug valves, nor had I ever seen one. But after immersing myself in the company literature I quickly learned that there was a large number of industries and people working in those industries who could benefit from using one. I wrote dozens of stories – the lubricated plug valve and its use in the food industry, the lubricated plug valve and its use in the paper industry, the lubricated plug valve and its use in the chemical industry, the lubricated plug valve and its use in the petroleum industry. Much to my surprise, all of my stories appeared in major trade magazines. The client was ecstatic. Further to my surprise, these stories not only created interest – they led directly to sales. Somehow, there was magic in a well-publicized lubricated plug valve. The value of a carefully defined public relations programme was now apparent to the client and I learned early that public relations programmes – whether product, corporate, financial or any other type – can have an impact on the bottom line.

At this time, the company was mailing out news releases to hundreds and hundreds of monthly trade magazines throughout the United States and Canada. While these were of interest to the editors, they had no urgent news value, and it didn't matter in which issue the material was used. Yet we were mailing them all first class. One day I suggested that from now on we should mail all such releases second class because it didn't matter if they arrived a few days later. This was not rocket science, but it saved the company in one year much more than my total salary, and these results brought me to management's attention in a very positive way.

While moving up the business ladder I also moved up the social ladder: I gained a wife, and that is a story in itself.

One evening at home I received a phone call. The voice on the other end asked if I was Bob Leaf. 'Did you go to Joan of Arc Junior High School?' the voice continued. I had, but just for one year when my family moved to Manhattan from the Bronx when I was twelve years old. When I replied that I had, the response was: 'You won't remember me but I was in your class and my name is Adele Ornstein.'

'Of course I remember you,' I responded. 'You were the prettiest girl in the class.'

'No, I wasn't, Nina was,' she answered.

'Nina was the brightest girl in the class [which she was] but you were the prettiest.'

The reason Adele was calling was that I had filled in a form saying I would attend a charity fundraising event that had been held the night before. At the last moment I had decided not to go and now the charity was calling all those who hadn't attended to ask for donations. Adele had been given the people whose name started with the letter 'L'. My name not being common, she remembered me from class, though we hadn't seen each other in fourteen years.

We talked a little bit and she asked whether I would make a donation. I pleaded that I had very little money. She explained that they accepted as little as five dollars and that I would have a year to pay. 'If I contribute five dollars, will you go out for lunch with me?' I jokingly asked. Her comeback was a pretty good one. 'Will you make it ten dollars then?' she said, half in jest. I agreed, a lunch date was set and we enjoyed our time together. We started dating but we were also seeing other people. About four months into the relationship, I had gotten us tickets for a Saturday night to see *Utopia Unlimited*, a very rarely-produced Gilbert and Sullivan operetta that had not been shown for forty years in New York. On the Friday night she called and said she would have to cancel the date. I asked if she was ill, and she said, 'No, it's not that. It's just that I'm getting engaged this weekend.' Since she was not getting engaged to me, I thought her cancelling the date was an excellent idea.

Three months later the phone rang and it was Adele calling, this time to ask if I would buy tickets to a charity dance. I explained that she should know better, as we had gone dancing when we were dating. She knew first-hand that this was a skill I lacked. I guessed that she probably still had bruises on her legs to back this up. Then I asked, 'How is your fiancé?' After a small pause, she replied: 'He's gone,' for reasons she later explained to me. I immediately asked: 'Do you want to go out Saturday night?' She did. And neither of us saw anyone else after that night, and we've now been married for more than fifty-three years. She keeps renewing my option every six months, so I think it will last.

When we became engaged, I wanted her to meet Harold Burson and his wife. I was planning to take them to dinner at a Chinese restaurant – it seemed like a perfect occasion to introduce her. The minute we walked into the restaurant, she recognized Harold. She had met him a few years back, even before I had. It turns out that she had once dated Harold's doctor and had accompanied him to a house-warming at Harold's new home. She got on amazingly well with Harold and his wife Bette, and a few years later the Bursons, concerned about what would happen to their children if they were ever jointly killed in a plane crash, made us their guardians, should the need arise.

That dinner had another impact, because it drew Harold and I even closer. When the dinner ended, as is the custom in Chinese restaurants, the fortune cookies arrived. Bette opened hers and it said: 'Your child will soon be toilet-trained.'

'Harold,' she exclaimed, astonished, 'this is a miracle!' As a matter of fact, they were having a problem training their youngest child. Then Harold opened his, and it said: 'There will be wild parties this summer at 260 Beverly Road.' This address happened to be their home, and they had plans to be away for the summer and were allowing someone from the office to live there in their absence.

'Bob, you son of a bitch,' Harold said. 'You had them fix the fortune cookies!' Of course I had. That act sealed a friendship that over the years has gone way beyond just business.

Burson–Marsteller kept growing, and my major clients – Rockwell Manufacturing Company and Clark Equipment – kept increasing their budgets, so my role at the firm became more significant. A few years passed with continuing success, and I was given added responsibility by being put in charge of getting publicity for both Burson–Marsteller and Marsteller. I reported to both Harold and Bill, but in reality Bill acted as the day-to-day client.

It proved a very worthwhile post as I spent a great deal of time with the press that covered the public relations industry. And it underlined to me that a proper PR programme, even for a PR firm, can be very beneficial. I was fortunate in the fact that both Burson and Marsteller were very good writers and speakers and the top people under them were as well, making it easier for me to achieve excellent results.

For example, I arranged for Buck Buchwald, the executive who first interviewed me for the job at Burson, to give a speech on a business topic he specialized in, outlining the problems and opportunities that would face a client in this area. More than four years after he gave the speech, he took a call from a potential client who said, 'Years ago I heard you talk, and we are now facing the problem that you discussed. Can I come in and see you?' We were given the account without them talking to any other agency.

Bill Marsteller tended to behave more like an actual client than anyone in the companies I was working with. Whenever we reviewed an account, he was far more difficult and demanding than any of them. He was a perfectionist and was especially tough on you if he liked you and saw you as a key person for the firm's future. He reviewed every release or feature I wrote in very great detail. It was sometimes painful, but I was grateful for his interest and attention.

One feature I had written for *PR Journal*, intending to have it by-lined by Marsteller's creative director, was entitled 'Think Visually'. I went into great detail about how PR men do not think visually enough when preparing stories for the press, arguing that a better use of photographs, cartoons, drawings or charts to accompany a story increases its chance of publication. I thought that it was one of the best things I had ever written, and I had shown it to the editor of *PR Journal*, who readily accepted it.

Bill read it, studied it, read it again, nodding his head every now and then, looking as if this piece had really met with his full approval. I readied myself to receive a nice compliment from my boss, but instead – and this is the whole truth and nothing but the truth – he returned it saying, 'It's missing two commas.'

I got angry, which was rare for me. So angry, in fact, that I threw the article back at him and stalked out of the room. Bill must have felt that he had gone too far that time because he went much easier on me after that. Oh, and thirty years after that article appeared, the creative director whose by-line it appeared under got a letter from a publisher asking his permission to use the piece in an anthology.

The situation that I described in the article hasn't changed much. I still feel that even today PR executives are not being creative enough in their use of photographs or other graphics in order to ensure greater coverage.

Of course, there are exceptions. One of the best examples I know of was a release we put out for Gardner Merchant, the British catering organization, later bought by Sodexo, one of the world's leading caterers. Among Gardner Merchant's yearly clients was Wimbledon, for whom they provided strawberries. Of course, this is not an earth-shattering piece of news that the press is dying to learn about. But one year, using an extremely creative photographer, we took a picture of the chairman of Gardner Merchant, Sir Garry Hawkes, very early in the morning standing in the middle of a strawberry field. We were fortunate that the light during that time of day and the perfect weather conditions contributed to creating a photograph so beautiful that it looked like a painting. We sent the picture with a basic release. The photograph ran for three columns in the

Financial Times with a story about Gardner Merchant. The chairman still has the picture hanging on a wall in his home.

By now Burson–Marsteller had offices throughout the US and was no longer just an industrial PR firm. We were becoming active in corporate, financial, governmental and consumer PR. And I had been made a vice president.

When I look back on fifty years in advertising as well as PR, I can see a lot of differences between then and now. Many people ask me whether the business back then really was as it is portrayed by the US TV show *Mad Men*, which is tremendously popular in Europe as well as in the US. And the answer is yes. Many heads of agencies, such as David Ogilvy, whom I met a few times, and Bill Marsteller, who had an exuberance about him that convinced others that he was top of his league, dominated their companies and the agency's personality was theirs. Today, most agencies are much more group-oriented, with no individual dominating as these men did. And though there are exceptions, most agencies try to promote themselves *in toto* rather than focusing on a specific individual.

Was there more drinking back then? Definitely, yes. I remember one executive who had three Martinis every day at lunch, a lunch that could last three hours. But he always went back to work after lunch, stayed late and got his work done. There was also far more drinking at client lunches than there is today. Part of the reason was that in those days it was helpful in building a close relationship with the client which was important for business. That's not the case anymore, as today's client-agency relationships are not as personal and close as they were back then. And it's true that back in those days far more people had bottles hidden in their desk drawers than today.

The drinking culture existed for a number of years before fading away. It never existed in England. In the early years the head of Burson–Marsteller London was visiting the US and went out to dinner with Marsteller's CEO. The American ordered a Martini for the Brit, a drink he had never experienced before. After tasting it he said, 'Isn't this a bit strong? How many of these can you take?' The CEO turned to him – this is gospel – and said: 'Martinis are like breasts. One is too few. Three are too many.'

What about all the sex we see on *Mad Men*? Back when I was a young man, attitudes about sex were far stricter than they are today. I grew up in an environment where if you put a hand on a girl's breast there had to be an engagement ring in the other. If you put a hand under her dress, her father had already selected the wedding date. But this had already started to change. While I never took a poll, there appeared to be more intra-office affairs in those days. Back then, there were not many women executives, an issue I will cover later. The jobs women were doing put them in closer proximity to their male bosses in both a business and personal sense. A closeness developed that could easily lead to a more intimate relationship.

But then, as now, personal relationships with clients were avoided if at all possible. These were always considered no-win situations. One day, one of our few women executives came to me and said she had a problem. She was putting together an event on a Friday for one of our biggest clients with whom she had been working for some time. She really liked and respected the man. The client had called and said after the event was over he had arranged for a place for them to spend the weekend. She had no desire to take up the invitation but didn't know how to tell him. This was her only major account and without it she might not even have a job.

I suggested that she had to get out of the invite in a way that would allow the client to save face. Making a joke out of it would be the best approach. She should say something along the lines of, 'I really appreciate your offer, but I discussed it with my fiancé, who's a sumo wrestler and with whom I planned to spend the weekend, and he said it wouldn't be a good idea.' She followed my advice and the client took it well. She went home after the event instead of away with him, and they continued as an excellent client-agency team.

In the sixties, public relations began to grow significantly as a business. PR companies were relatively small with Hill and Knowlton and Carl Byoir, which is now defunct, being the largest. But more and more individuals were starting up small firms, just as Harold Burson had. While client PR budgets were edging their way up, they were still relatively small compared with today's. In fact these days PR budgets for some major corporations are larger than the total fees of many of the PR firms of the sixties.

During this period, account executives began to make greater attempts to get to personally know the journalists at publications that were most important to their clients. Journalistic luncheons became the norm. While some such luncheons still take place, they are far less common now because nearly all the media have fewer employees, who do not have much available free time.

Salaries in general were not taking you towards a financial nirvana. After I became engaged, Burson–Marsteller gave me a raise so that I would be earning five dollars more than my fiancée, Adele, who was then secretary to the head of marketing at General Electric. Today this might be considered sexist, but it wasn't then. Adele thought it was great.

Burson–Marsteller's growth and my own within the company were more rapid than I could have anticipated. I remained on the fast-track in spite of a difficult illness and an unanticipated inter-ruption in my career. Nearly a year after I joined Burson–Marsteller, Adele and I married, and we took off for a Bermuda honeymoon. On our second day on the island, I wasn't feeling well. When we went for breakfast, I dropped into the pharmacy for a thermometer. After breakfast I took my temperature and the thermometer registered 40°C (104°F). While my wife wanted to take credit for the heat, I explained that I thought it was more likely caused by an illness than by passion.

We sent for a doctor, who diagnosed me with German measles. I had to stay in bed and the doctor arranged to have a nurse sent to take care of me. So my wife was now spending her honeymoon with a newly-acquired husband – and a nurse. When I showed no improvement after four days, the doctor told me to return to the US to see a specialist. That ended our honeymoon.

My American doctor took the necessary tests and found that I had an extremely bad case of mononucleosis. He told me that it was highly contagious. I would have to stay at home for at least three months, probably longer. My wife and I would have to sleep in separate beds, and I was to be allowed no visitors. I figured if my wife was able to get through the start of married life with an ailing husband in a separate bed, the relationship would probably last a long time. After three months I was allowed to go to work. I had to leave for the office at 10 a.m. and come home at 4 p.m. so that I would not be on any crowded transportation. At Burson, everyone was highly sympathetic and acted as if I had never been away.

When I started out in the role of the in-house public relations executive it was not a very important one. In general, though not in every case, they were relatively poorly paid and had very little influence with the chief executive. It wouldn't be uncommon for the chief executive to say, 'Please get me our PR man, I don't remember his name. I want to dictate a release to him.'

The in-house people did, though, help make the PR consultancy more significant. Once, a client came to Harold Burson and told him he had an idea that he thought would be very beneficial for the company. He brought it up a few times with the chairman but not much attention was being paid to it. He asked Harold when he next was having lunch with the CEO so that he could bring it up.

Harold did and the CEO immediately put the idea into operation.

It was extremely rare that an executive from a consultancy left to join a client's organization. The money wasn't there. Today it is the exact opposite. Most PR firms lose some of their best people to corporations who want one or two very senior people for their PR department, and they are willing to pay whatever it takes to get them. That trend continues as good PR is now seen as a vital factor in a company's success. Corporations want the best people and will give them a senior role in the company and will pay accordingly.

Ironically, one thing that has not changed since I started is the negative view of PR itself. In the public mind, and especially with some of the press, the PR professional is looked upon as a spin doctor out to manipulate, obfuscate and turn the meaning of words and deeds to the benefit of their clients – often in spite of the 'truth'. Indeed, PR people are seen as manipulators, a term with very obvious negative overtones. But manipulation by itself is not evil and can in fact be used for good purposes, such as when you manipulate warring parties to find acceptable peace terms or get people to contribute to causes that will help eliminate poverty throughout the world.

Through the years I have seen public relations become more and more professional. Each year it continues to attract better and better people with greater and greater abilities. And with the growth of Corporate Social Responsibility and the opportunities provided by social networking, it can accomplish things that I would never have thought possible when I started.

But there is one area where all the PR associations will disagree with me: I maintain that what we are doing does not constitute a profession. It is an industry. It is a business. What's the difference? If I am a doctor and keep making mistakes to the misfortune of my patients, some of whose lives might have been taken away unnecessarily, I can be removed from the medical lists. If I am a lawyer and do something illegal, I can be struck off. The same is true of an accountant.

The PR executive, however, is not held accountable. He can never be struck off. As long as I have a phone and you want my help, nothing can stop me from plying my trade, whether my clients and peers consider me professional or not.

Burson–Marsteller continued to grow dramatically and so did my responsibilities. We were beginning to think that we could only reach our real potential if we became an international organization. And this was an area within which I could make a major contribution. Because of my studies of international history and my military service in Europe, I knew a great deal about the countries we would be looking to start in and their cultures. So I was made a vice president and soon the title was altered to 'vice president–international', before we were even truly international.

For a few years we had been placing stories for our industrial clients in magazines overseas that covered their industries, especially in Great Britain. I had gotten hold of the magazine directories from all major European countries and made a mailing list of all the major categories covering specific industries such as chemical, pharmaceutical, construction and financial. I also wrote to each publication for a copy and as they began to arrive we established an international trade magazine library in our office that was the most complete library of European industrial magazines in New York. We had people, many of whom were not even clients, come to study the magazines to see which ones their potential customers might be reading.

As we built up the list, and our contacts with editors abroad, we began to place a significant number of stories overseas. This success turned our belief into the conviction that we needed a presence in Europe. To kick off the effort I decided to visit the major editors of key trade magazines in England, France, Germany and Italy. To make this trip not only instructive but profitable I arranged to take a number of stories that clients wanted to appear overseas and offer them to editors. If I were able to place them, the clients would be more than happy to pay for my time.

I started in the UK – my first time since my army days – and organized a luncheon for fifteen editors. Just like Santa Claus, I had a bag full of technical articles for them and most of the editors with whom we had not been in contact before were amazed. They were not used to seeing the quality in both text and photographs that I could offer them. Many of the editors asked how much they would have to pay for the articles! When I said they were all free, there was no question that I was seen as Father Christmas. The same thing happened in France and Germany, and I placed so many stories that I was paid by clients more than four times what would have been my fees and expenses. . .

Only in Italy did I encounter any resistance. At lunch, an editor came over to look at a highly technical by-lined article on metering. The front page had the name of the author and his company, and the company was only mentioned once more in the article. The editor, who was surrounded by other editors, looked at me and said, 'Since you are mentioning the company in the article, this is advertising and you should pay me if you want me to use it.' Immediately, some of the other editors joined in the argument and told him he was completely wrong and that he should be happy to take it. He threw the article up in the air, the papers flew all over the place, and the argument became a screaming match. But we placed as many stories in Italy as elsewhere, and the incident added a little levity to what was becoming a tiring if successful trip. It was now obvious, by 1963, that we should be setting up both a public relations firm and an advertising agency in Europe. All we had to do was to figure out where to start and how.

When I returned to the United States, Harold Burson called me into his office and told me that at the next board meeting, he was recommending that I be put on the board of directors. He said it should be easily accomplished. This would mean not only more authority but a considerable increase in salary and, since I had just become a father, the future was looking rosier and rosier. The board meeting took place, and I heard nothing from Harold. A few days went by, and then a few more, and I finally went to see him and said, 'Harold, didn't you say something about my being on the board?'

Harold is not one who enjoys dealing with unpleasantries, but he had to tell me what happened. At Burson–Marsteller in those days you had to sign in every morning and sign out, no matter what your position was in the company. Nine o'clock was the sign-in time, and any time after that, even if you were one minute late, you had to sign in your time in red.

During the previous month I had been late twice: once, I believe, by four minutes, and another by six. Bill Marsteller, who believed in perfection in all things, especially by anyone he felt strongly about, and who believed that being on time was the closest thing to godliness, had vetoed my board membership. He said that I would be approved at the next board meeting if I arrived at work on time every day until that meeting. From then on, I made a concerted effort to arrive by nine, and I was able to join the board three months later. Bill is lucky he is not alive today, because punctuality is a lost art. It was easier to find Osama bin Laden than it is to get people to arrive at a meeting on time these days.

Once we had agreed to go overseas, the question became: where should we set up our office and who should run it? We decided first to send over an advertising executive and then a public relations man. We felt it would be best to start in Switzerland because at the time it was where most American companies operating in Europe were headquartered. It was also the country that handed out the best tax breaks. We decided it was most beneficial to set up in Geneva though most of our clients were in the Zurich area, mainly head-quartered in the city of Zug, because there you received by far the best tax advantages.

We selected an ad man from Marsteller's New York office who had been with us for many years and spoke French fluently. We also chose a PR man from outside the office who spoke French and German and had been in industrial public relations for many years and was presently at the Lead Institute. Both choices proved to be extremely wise ones as they were able to build up both busi-nesses dramatically from the start. They remained with us until they retired.

Within a year of setting up our first office we realized we had to be more local with the PR business so we established joint ventures in Belgium, France, Germany and Italy, and I went overseas to meet with our partners. I was quite impressed with what I saw – the opportunities for growth seemed limitless. Companies were becoming more interested in the benefits that professional PR programmes could provide them, budgets were being raised and excellent staff was available.

We also bought 10 per cent of an industrial ad agency in the UK that had a public relations arm. We began to get a great deal of coverage in the US press and new business leads proliferated both for advertising and public relations. Marsteller picked up IBM and DuPont, which gave them a really solid base.

On the PR side, things began to move even more quickly than we had ever anticipated. One day Harold came in to see me and said, 'Bob since you are running our international operation and it's starting to look like it could be the fastest-growing part of our business, Bill feels you should spend some time overseas getting to know the marketplace and the business even better. If you're over there, you could also be in a position to advise our partners.' I liked the idea.

By this time we had moved the Burson–Marsteller headquarters to Brussels because the Common Market had developed and nearly all the major companies were headquartering there. We had sent somebody from our New York office to run Brussels and were hiring locally as the business was pouring in. When I discussed the situation with Adele, I said that it would be a one-year assignment overseas and that the company would keep our New York apartment for us to move back in to when we returned. I would also receive all sorts of benefits, so it made sense financially. She too was very much in favour, and we started to make all the arrangements necessary to a move abroad. We decided that I would go over first and find suitable living quarters in Brussels, and she would follow about three months later with our son. I don't know what her reaction might have been if I had told her that we would still be in Europe forty-five years later.

Harold and I discussed my mission and decided we should look into eventually buying out our partners and setting up wholly-owned Burson–Marsteller offices. We also wanted to examine other areas such as Holland, Spain and Scandinavia where it might be smart for us to be operating. The plan was that after I had been in Europe for three to six months I was to prepare a basic overall strategy paper to be presented to the board. The decision to go overseas was the most significant that I have ever made and led to a lifetime of excitement and discovery, as I opened Burson–Marsteller offices all over the world.

3   Starting in Belgium

Even before I arrived in Belgium, I felt things were going to be very different for me there. Living in a foreign country and having to deal with other nationalities, languages, cultures and attitudes would be a major change, but one I looked forward to.

In 1965, I left New York for Brussels on a one-year assignment. I was to establish a basic plan for our European operations, deciding which countries we should operate in and how quickly we should establish offices there. I was to find people to join us who could fit in with us comfortably and who had the skills to ensure our growth. The fact that I am still overseas more than forty-five years later proves that you can't always trust American companies that send you on one-year assignments.

Brussels in the mid-sixties was an ideal place for any American going overseas – it was where the action and the opportunities were. US companies abroad used to establish their headquarters in Switzerland – not to gaze at Alpine views or picturesque lakes, but because that is where the lowest tax rates in Europe were. Then suddenly the Common Market came to life, with Brussels the head-quarters, and like lemmings heading to sea, the rush was on. At least 700 of the 1000 largest US companies had set up in Europe, and since Belgium was destined to become its political and economic centre, Belgium was where companies of all nations wanted to be, including Marsteller and Burson–Marsteller.

Belgium was a central location, had a great availability of both housing and office space, good transportation to other markets, and an educated workforce with the language skills that were important to any multinational corporation dealing throughout Europe. Soon after I arrived I learned that forty-five companies were planning to establish their headquarters there. At a newcomers' cocktail dance I attended, there were one hundred couples who had arrived in the previous three months.

For the British, raised in an imperial atmosphere, even one that was rapidly dwindling, overseas assignments were the norm and they felt comfortable no matter where they were sent. The situation was very different for the breed of Americans moving overseas for the first time. Americans who had worked abroad before usually worked for oil or construction companies or were entrepreneurs. But Americans now coming to Brussels included those from the American heartland, many of whom had never thought of living abroad and quite a few who had never been overseas before or even had a passport. Companies like Armco Steel from Middletown, Ohio, and Dow Corning from Midland, Michigan, were sending their people over and were among our first clients.

It was a great life for most Americans. The dollar was way overvalued, fixed at fifty Belgian francs. Equally important was the strong belief of many American companies that a man who was going overseas, especially if he was taking his family with him, was making a great sacrifice. That meant all sorts of allowances, such as housing, schooling, cost of living adjustments – for which one client was given a 13 per cent increase in his salary – numerous home leaves and an overseas bonus. In some cases, even a hardship increase. It is difficult to imagine living in Belgium during these times being considered a hardship. This is, of course, not the case today. Another added benefit was that at the time the US Internal Revenue Service was much more lenient about taxing perks as income than it is today.

As a result of all these perks, some employees decided to keep their life in the international arena and continued working abroad. Interestingly, many of the wives who had originally been very squeamish about living overseas when they were first informed that was where they were going found out that a life that included skiing in Switzerland in the winter, summer holidays in Spain or Italy and being able to travel throughout France was not all bad. And while some adjustments had to be made, the positives far outweighed the negatives.

After three months my wife and son arrived by boat. For Adele it was very exciting and she radiated joy. For Stuart it was more difficult. In Manhattan, we had lived one street away from both grandmothers. And the nanny who had helped raise my wife was my son's babysitter. All three believed when my son was born that a star had risen in the east, and they treated him accordingly. At the age of four, life was heavenly for him. Even on the boat trip over, the crew made a great fuss over him.

Things changed dramatically quickly. Nearly all Americans placed their children in the American School. We placed Stuart in a Belgian school, the École Nouvelle, believing that at his age picking up a second language would be easy. The drawback was that most of the students and some of the teachers spoke very little English, which put him at a disadvantage at the beginning, especially if he had a minor altercation – verbal or physical – with one of the other students.

When he tried to present his side of the case in English the teacher would nod sternly and three out of four times adjudged him guilty. For the first few weeks at the end of each day we would be regaled with tears. After a few weeks, however, he began to pick up some

French and some of his classmates began to understand a smattering of a 4-year-old's version of English. Camaraderie ran rampant. What looked like our first overseas error turned into an act of triumph, for which we each claimed sole credit. By the time he left his first school four years later he was first in the class and had a mastery of the French language that proved to be highly valuable during his business career.

Not too long after we arrived, ABC Television filmed a programme called *Power Of The Dollar – Destination Europe*, and their reporters interviewed a number of American businessmen from companies such as IBM, National Distillers, Honeywell and Minnesota Mining and Manufacturing. They also interviewed my wife and I about how families adjusted to life abroad. My wife told the programme: 'The major problem of any family coming over is that they normally have no home to come to. First they're in a hotel and then they have to find a place to live and the woman is very much occupied with the problem of setting up a home and having to deal in a language she probably doesn't know at the time of arrival. It can be very difficult at the beginning.

'Women find a great deal of fun in shopping and going to markets as this is a daily adventure,' she added. 'In the United States I believe that many housewives usually do the shopping once or twice a week in a very large supermarket. But here they go to smaller stores and buy products they never had before.' But it wasn't long before Belgium and the rest of Europe became supermarket conscious.

Many couples found themselves far higher up the social scale than they were in their home towns. This occurred because a limited number of executives came over from each company. So those who did were on the top of the social pecking order even if they were junior execs back home. They might, for example, in the US be invited to the chairman or president's home once a year, probably during the Christmas season for a major celebration. In Brussels there would be a number of grand events held by the American ambassador himself, or glamorous mixed company events that they would be invited to. Later, when the husband was sent home, perhaps with a promotion and a raise, it was the wife who was the most disappointed at leaving, knowing they would never experience that lifestyle again.

The only members of the family that had real adjustment problems moving overseas were some teenage daughters who came from communities and schools where they were the belles of the ball. Now they were no longer belles and were starting socially from scratch which many found very difficult to adjust to.

No matter where you came from, living in another country was an adjustment. This was especially true in the fifties, when American and European societies were more different than they are today, and when most Americans really didn't know much about these countries. The Belgians were not people in a rush. Many of the suppliers made snails look like four minute milers. It took a week to have a suit cleaned and that was that. If someone was coming to hang a cabinet, he came, studied the situation, meditated, returned a week later for a final perusal and two weeks later hung the cabinet. They didn't have to rush. The explosion of new companies and foreign personnel meant they had all the business they could handle. The mad rush to Brussels also caused salaries to go up for locals. Companies had to pay more for staff, especially bilingual secretaries. One client told me his secretary left for a 60 per cent increase in salary, a previously unheard of raise.

Not all Belgians were happy with this corporate invasion of their country. But among the happiest were the landlords. Apartment rental and purchase prices skyrocketed, making local property owners joyful. At the same time prices in general also rose rapidly, but this did not affect American expatriates so much as the country's citizens. For

Belgian companies, the cost of staff, especially the aforementioned bilingual secretaries, was dramatically increasing as American companies could more easily afford to pay much higher salaries.

I rented a relatively modest apartment as up-and-coming PR firms could not afford majestic houses. It was furnished, which should have been a good thing, but it signalled that we would have problems when we left. When you moved into a furnished apartment in Brussels, its contents were first examined by 'Monsieur l'Expert' before you were given the keys. He presented you with an 'état des lieux' – literally a 'state of the place'. This listed every fork, knife, cup, dish, towel, picture and chair in the apartment. If a seat cover was worn in a certain place this was duly noted in case you wore it elsewhere. Each nail hole where a picture was hung was also listed. This was because if you hung other pictures you were charged so many Belgian francs for each nail hole you added to the apartment. And I was told I could be sure that Monsieur l'Expert would be back when I was ready to leave, hunting for every hole.

After landlords, the next thing to be wary about was driving in Belgium – particularly taxi rides. Cab drivers back then were very creative in finding every way possible to get more money out of foreign passengers. Fortunately that has changed dramatically, as have driving conditions in general. When I first arrived in the country you didn't need to take a test to get a driver's licence. And Belgian drivers were legendary for their lack of driving skills. On highways, drivers from any other European country moved away quickly when they saw a car with a Belgian licence plate approaching. Belgium had the highest accident rate in Europe, though fortunately these rarely involved fatalities. Knowing what it was like on the Belgian roads most people did not drive too speedily. This also meant car insurance rates were the highest in Europe. Most accidents were a scratch on the side. One reason is that the law for driving included 'priorité à droite' – priority on the right. This meant you could come out of the smallest side street on to a major thoroughfare and you didn't have to stop as you automatically had the right of way. Many Belgian drivers didn't stop and many accidents resulted. Walking down just about any major street you would see numerous damaged cars parked – the results of the latest accidents.

In Brussels, though I can't claim this was true for all of Belgium, the hours between five and seven in the evening were notorious. For it was then that many (but not all) Belgian men would visit their mistresses. I always worked until seven but when I came home exhausted my wife was rightfully convinced that I was overworked rather than adhering to the local custom.

One Friday night we were at a lovely restaurant in Brussels' as main park and sitting near us was a gorgeous young girl with a much older man who was paying serious attention to her. The next night at the opera the same man was in the row in front of us with a woman his age. During the intermission, we talked with him and he introduced us to his wife.

One thing every American businessman learned very quickly in Belgium was that you had to be very careful when hiring staff. The cost of letting people go could be horrendous, even for a relatively small firm such as ours. When letting an employee go, no matter how generous a termination we initially offered, the employee could have it increased immediately by saying blithely, 'I'm off to court.' It made more economic sense to add another few months' severance than to foot legal fees for a case you were bound to lose. Belgian labour judges generally believed that no company should fire an employee regardless of cause – though rape or murder might have been an exception, but I stress the word 'might'.

We decided after five months to terminate an executive who was not performing well. We offered her six months' severance, congratulating ourselves on our generosity. She sued us for one year's pay.

This, despite the fact that she had already been hired for another job on a higher salary from the day she left us. The judge decided in our favour, probably making legal history and setting himself up as a pariah among other judges. A journalist in Antwerp writing for the *New York Times* noted that 'a severely disrupted civil service is the judiciary. For years, politics has been a factor in judicial appointments. For that reason the competence of the country's court system and its judges has been called into question.'

The Belgian situation forced me to establish a policy in that country that I did not institute anywhere else in the world. Harold Burson, chairman of the company, always cared very deeply about people. Any time he heard that an employee had done something special he would send them a letter of appreciation. But if we decided to fire that employee the Burson letter would sometimes appear as Exhibit A in a Belgian labour court and add another three months to whatever money the judge had been planning to award. So Harold agreed he would never send a letter of praise to any employee in Belgium without first sending it to me for clearance.

The Belgian economy suffered dramatically for this ill-conceived notion held by both government and unions that jobs are protected and that it should be nearly impossible to fire any employee. For despite its great location, many companies that opened in Belgium chafed at these restrictions and decided not to expand their Brussels offices. Instead, when adding new divisions, they located them in other countries and Belgium lost out on potentially thousands of jobs. But in the long term this might not have mattered to them because as headquarters of the Common Market they would continue to show growth.

Belgium was in reality two countries: one controlled by the French speakers, the other by the Flemish speakers. There was no great love between the two, and fifty years later there appears to be even less. There are still continuing calls for the country to be split into two. How serious this division was became painfully obvious during my first Christmas in Belgium. In a Flemish section, during a Christmas parade, the man dressed as Santa offered a holiday prayer to the crowd. The only problem was that he delivered it in the French language and was stoned as a result. The fact that the Flemish Belgians were willing to stone Santa created a crystal clear message in my mind that language was something that I would have to be carefully aware of, and act accordingly for myself and my clients. Having come from New York, which is a multiracial society and, even though aware that Belgium was a bilingual society, I did not expect the depth of animosity that existed between the two groups. In Brussels they tried to achieve some sort of kinship, but in other sections of the country the dislike was intense. This message was important to someone like myself in the communications business.

Everything that we sent out on behalf of a client company – a news release, a financial statement, a brochure – was done in at least two languages, and three if there was a reason to also have it in English. The difficulty was in personal invitations. In 75 per cent of the cases the name would reveal whether the person was French or Flemish. But what about the other 25 per cent? Sending it to someone in the wrong language was considered an insult and the invitation could find its way into the bin unopened. Sending it to everyone in two languages was unwieldy. We found a solution: when we handled the opening of Texaco's new technical centre, we sent all the invitations in English and everyone was happy.

Language was the basis of our business. Unlike today we didn't have offices in every major European country. So often we prepared the original release in English in our Brussels office and then had it translated into the other local languages. A number of our clients were industrial companies manufacturing highly technical products – a fact that made translation more difficult. One client was so concerned about possible errors that after anything was translated from English into another language, he would have it translated back from the foreign tongue into English by a different translator to make sure there were no errors. His wisdom became apparent when in the retranslating of a technical paper the words 'water goat' appeared, to everyone's surprise and consternation. When we compared it with the original paper, the term was supposed to be 'hydraulic ram', a kind of pump that was inadvertently turned into a new species of goat by the translator.

International communications was in its infancy, and not all of our American client companies accepted easily that things were different overseas. Why did it take so long to get a brochure produced, even if it was in seven languages? They often felt we were not tough enough on suppliers. As time went on though, the impatient clients began to understand and became realistic about how long things were going to take.

Some of our work was easier than the rest. Since most of our clients were new to the area, some jobs were as basic as preparing new releases, features, background sheets and editorial introductions. But, in a foreign country, some things take much more time than in the United States. A perfect example were plant openings, which we handled for many clients. I wrote an article for a leading business magazine entitled, 'There is no mystique to dedicating a plant abroad'. This included a ninety-three-step checklist for a plant inauguration abroad, all of which, fortunately, I will not list here. Great care had to be taken in dealing with the local police (for example making a donation to the local police and firemen associations in advance) and in finding out what guests the local burgomaster (or similar officials according to which country) would like to have accompany him. What gifts he and possibly they should receive, and the right mementos to be given to all guests. In some cases we had to prepare a wives tour. Even the routine things took a great deal of time and special care, such as the guest list selection, what written material would be necessary, what food and refreshments would be best, and how to best handle the print, radio, TV and newsreel media from various countries. I could go on and on. A plant opening can be very expensive. A classic reply made by one American executive to a competitor when told what their original budget was to be for opening a new plant was, 'What kind of plant are you opening – a tulip?'

While technical information flowed quickly from country to country, the same was not true of humour, which does not cross borders with the same ease. What is considered funny in the US or droll in the UK might not cause a chuckle on the continent. I often became embarrassed at client events aimed at local audiences when guest international client speakers would load their speeches with quips, asides or funny anecdotes that left the audience staring blankly into space. In certain countries, such as Japan, audiences will try to laugh or smile politely if that is what they feel is necessary to make the guest speaker comfortable – even if they don't have a clue what the joke is.

We had the same difficulties within our own company. One day I was sitting in my office with two other Americans. We were laughing and laughing. One of our Belgian executives walked in and asked what we had found so funny. I explained to him we had just lost a client, mentioning the name. He looked at me aghast. To him losing a client in more likelihood should have brought tears. But this client was by far our most difficult, and each of us was regaling the others with war stories that showed examples of exactly how impossible he was to deal with and how lucky we would now be not to be burdened with him anymore. With the Belgian executive still in the room, we continued to tell stories that proved, to us at least, that we were better off now that he was in our past, and we started laughing again. He nodded as if he understood why we were chuckling but I am sure that deep down he was thinking, 'While they have many positive qualities, Americans do have some very strange ways.'

Just as humour is different everywhere in the world, so is body language. We had to be aware of this fact and do some fast learning. An advertisement run by the British Airports Authority in the *Financial Times* once noted that making a circle of your thumb and second finger in America meant 'A-OK'. But in France it meant 'zero' and in Japan it meant 'money'. In Tunisia it meant, 'I'll kill you'. If you tugged your ear lobe you were telling a Spaniard, 'You are a rotten sponger', a Greek, 'You better watch it', and a Maltese, 'You are a sneaky so and so'. Touch your lower eyelid and a Saudi would think you are calling him stupid. And a South American woman would think you were making a pass at her. And should you give the British thumbs-up gesture to a Sardinian woman, her husband will be after you with a stiletto for making such an incredibly obscene gesture at his wife.

Once the Americans had settled into Brussels, they established an event that was to become legendary. Once a year the US expats held the annual American Men's Club Ball, a black-tie charitable event open to all nationalities. It had the highest attendance of Belgians of any event sponsored by Americans in Brussels. And there was a special reason. The money for charity was raised through raffles and the waitresses at the event were responsible for collecting the raffles. What made it unique was that all the waitresses had to be topless, not exactly the norm in the 1960s. Belgians you never ran into anywhere else attended this event. And clients who usually avoided meetings with you – even those promising information on how to double their sales – never failed to attend this gala yearly event. And in reality it raised a great deal of money for worthwhile charities. Different organizations were responsible for finding the waitresses each year and when it was Burson–Marsteller's turn, I had no problems finding volunteers among my staff willing to take the necessary time to find the proper candidates, which is easily understandable.

One thing that is not now the case but was frequent in the sixties when international business was relatively new, was that the domestic headquarters of many companies maintained almost absolute control over operations. American companies were among the most control-oriented then as they were among the newest to international marketing. The thrust for most Americans stationed overseas was to keep headquarters happy. Everything else was secondary.

Harold Geneen, head of IT&T, was probably the chief executive most feared by local staff. He was the darling of the business press at that time. He had taken a moribund company and built it into an international colossus by a series of acquisitions. Many of these were later disposed of by his successor when the philosophy 'Let us concentrate on core business' replaced 'Let us take over anything we can get our hands on'. When Geneen was expected in Brussels, 'terror' became the order of the day. Wives knew not to talk to their company-executive husbands for weeks in advance as the men prepared the voluminous sets of statistics they knew Geneen would demand to see. He was always well briefed in advance and likely to question any aspect of the numerous businesses that made up IT&T. One of the accountants who supplied background material for Geneen was later a client of mine in Hong Kong. His job was to go around ferreting out possible problems and to ask local management pertinent questions before each Geneen visit. He was always treated by the local company heads as a modern-day Judas Iscariot, one of the reasons he left IT&T. He told me Geneen's mind for detail was awesome, and he had very little patience for excuses. He expected the local managements to know every detail of their business. If they didn't he wasn't shy about making it clear to everyone present how he felt, and in individual cases how he felt would be the key to their future in the company.

Even some American companies that had been in the international market for a long time tended to kept tight control over their European operations. A running joke among the press in Belgium at the time was that if you called the local head of public relations for Texaco and asked, 'Is this the European Headquarters?' the reply would be, 'I'll call Houston and find out and let you know.'

We worked for General Motors and everything was always approved at headquarters, even the simplest news release. The belief was strong that the appendages could in no way have the knowledge base that was present in the home headquarters. One GM executive stationed in Brussels told me, 'Even if we want to order paper clips it has to be approved in Detroit.' And since GM was one of the most, if not *the* most, successful American company at that time, who was I to argue?

IBM, another client, was also inward-looking at that time. Most of the senior IBM people in Europe were far more interested in using us to help create presentations that they were readying for their bosses than ones they were preparing for customers. They felt, and they were probably right, that at that time most potential customers had nowhere else to go but IBM.

But times changed and competitors improved, and IBM's dominant position badly eroded over the years. Fortunately for IBM, Lou Gerstner, who was very customer-oriented took over. He pushed the company to start looking outwards and changed its focus to service rather than hardware sales. *Fortune Magazine* did a cover story reporting that he was now personally attending new business presentations. Under his leadership, IBM was soon on its way back up to where he felt it belonged.

But there was no one who kept headquarters control as firmly in hand as the Japanese. It was often silly to write a press release for a Japanese company because by the time it was approved – and in Tokyo this often meant group approval – it was no longer news.

A major concern to companies such as ours headquartering in Brussels was that we had to live with the Belgian legal system. The Americans and the British had happily grown up under English Common Law. Belgian Law was based on the Napoleonic Code and I felt that most of the codes were probably established when Napoleon was extremely mad at Josephine.

Under the Napoleonic Code, everything had to be exact and everything had to be in writing as we found out to our dismay in dealing with General Electric who were our landlord. We were growing and needed to expand at a time when they were cutting their staff, so I made an agreement verbally with their office manager to take over more space. Since our new lease was to begin a month later he suggested I take the space, start putting in phone systems, and the added accommodation would be incorporated into our new lease. What he didn't know was that his parent company had planned to use these offices for another division. After we had set up all the phone systems at considerable expense, I was informed by the office manager that they now planned to keep the space. When I pointed out that we had an agreement and what we had done was based on his approval, their lawyer pointed out in so many words that as far as Belgian law goes, Samuel Goldwyn was correct when he said a verbal agreement 'isn't worth the paper it's printed on'. I thought I would make one final try to get justice so I went to the General Electric European headquarters in Paris to ask them to reconsider. They were friendly and sympathetic but explained, 'The law is the law is the law.' So we removed the phones at our expense and moved out of the building.

For one client, Clark Equipment Company, then the largest manufacturer of forklift trucks in the world, we had calendars produced to send to distributors. These were printed in Brussels and shipped around the world. Within a month we were getting anguished cries that pages were falling out when some of the calendars were hung up because the binding was not properly done. We called in the printer, got no satisfaction, and went to court. The court selected an 'expert' who came to see us. He said he had to see each of the calendars that was considered faulty to make a judgement, including those that had fallen off the wall in such distant places as Pakistan and New Zealand. He told us that after studying each calendar he would take those he deemed faulty as a percentage of the total number printed and we would be recompensed by that percentage.

There was no such thing in Belgium as the industrial equivalent of pain and suffering, or acknowledgement that calendars only have a value in the year they were printed and thus could not be replaced. It also ignored the distinct possibility that some of the errant calendars might decide to dissolve in a later month. He wouldn't even authorize the payment for the cost of shipping them back. And what about the cost of preparing them? He had two deaf ears to all of these questions. We eventually decided that any chance of substantial damages were diminished, not only because of the legal system, but also because the court-appointed independent 'expert' and the printer turned out to be very close personal friends who often went out drinking together. Fortunately for us the client was, like us, headquartered in Brussels and appreciated the problems we were facing. We returned our profit on the job, and he called it even. He took calendars out of his merchandising plans for the following year.

One aspect of life in Brussels that made working there especially rewarding was the Belgian love of food. For the average Belgian housewife the main question on arising was whether she brushed her teeth first or started preparing soup. And the soup usually won. To this day, many consider Belgium the soup capital of the world. Not surprising when the choices include curried mussel and butternut squash soup, cream of Belgian endive soup, milk soup, fish and pumpkin soup, elderberry soup, broccoli and carrot soup, buttermilk soup and sweet ale soup.

In one of my first reports back to the US I wrote: 'This should definitely be the land of the fat man. The bread is magnificent and the butter would make Aunt Jemima run to make another batch of pancakes. *Pommes frites* (the ubiquitous French fried potato) are served in restaurants with every meal. The pastries are delicacies that would make Escoffier drool and there are pastry shops everywhere. And this helps to make the weak-willed (such as I) an addict. And in this country as far as addicts are concerned pep pills, goof-balls and sniffing glues are replaced by éclairs, cream tarts and sniffing fruit pies. And to make it worse for those who want to maintain a sylph-like figure is the potage. After twenty-seven tries I am yet to have a bad plate of soup.'

And that remained true for my whole stay except for one bad plate of soup that I had at a restaurant in the Ardennes. When I tasted it, I predicted to my wife, 'Since the soup is bad, good luck to us with the main course.' My prediction, unfortunately, proved to be true.

Back then, the quality of their meals was not a high priority for the average Englishman. In later years London was to become one of the great food capitals of the world, but this change was still far in the future. The difference in the two countries' outlooks became clear to me when, for some unknown reason, my family and I were selected as the stars of a British documentary about an average American businessman abroad. This was to run for several episodes. They filmed me at airports coming and going, meeting with various clients, meeting with my own staff, meeting with media, talking with my wife and son, and shopping at local markets.

In the final scene, I come home from a business trip and walk into my apartment to greet my wife and son. The director said it would be a nice touch to film the three of us as we sat down for dinner. This was a last-minute decision. Since we had planned to eat out at a local restaurant, the only food we had at home to eat was some Camembert cheese. After they set up the cameras, I walked in the door, kissed my wife, hugged my son, took off my coat, had a drink and discussed business developments from the trip. Then we sat down for dinner. The English production crew had put pieces of Camembert on every plate, and this was supposed to be our starter. I tried to explain that no continental watching the show would believe that we were having a piece of Camembert cheese as our first course. If any European who knew me saw this and thought it was one of my culinary habits, it would probably end our friendship. My English documentarians didn't really appreciate this breech of culinary etiquette, but we finally reached a compromise and the film was edited to make the cheese course a later part of the meal.

One thing that had become apparent to me was that public relations had a great future for growth and profitability. While it was relatively new and still lacking in sophistication in some areas, the interest and willingness to pay for it was increasing dramatically among clients and potential clients. Though in its infant stage, the infant could grow up rapidly if we had the right people and produced the right messages. At the moment the profits of the advertising business, still headquartered in Geneva and counting among its clients the likes of DuPont and IBM, were providing the money for us to expand our public relations business. I thought that could change.

We only had our own PR operations in Belgium and Switzerland but had established relations with small ad agencies in Germany, France and Italy that could be helpful and issue news releases or help stage client events. We had also bought 10 per cent of an ad agency in England that had a PR operation. It became more and more obvious to me that if we were really going to take advantage of all the opportunities available to a firm like ours, we would have to start to exercise control.

As I went around Europe looking for the right people to join us and deciding how much I should ask the board to invest, it became apparent to me that my army lectures on the differences among countries were correct and that one had to act accordingly. In each country the clients were different, the media was different and the attitude towards public relations was different.

There was no doubt that France would be the most difficult country for us to have a major impact in. General de Gaulle was still president and his dislike for the Americans and the British was not something he bothered to hide. He came out as being against the US role in the Vietnam War. He was against Israel and US support of Israel, saying in a 1967 televised interview that Israelis were 'this elite people sure of themselves and domineering'. He also called for American military forces to be out of his country within a year. This caused Dean Rusk, the then Secretary of State, to comment: 'Does this include all those who are buried here?'

My wife and I had a funny experience with General de Gaulle. We were driving from Brussels to Geneva and when we reached a French mining town called Champagnole, we were stopped by French security forces. General de Gaulle was scheduled to give a speech in the town and there had been reports that there would be attempts to assassinate him by a French group hostile to his policies. We were told we had to park our car and stay in town until the General's speech to the local public was over. So we settled into a local café that faced the main square where he would be talking and relaxed there for a while. Then all the local officials wearing sashes appeared and lined up to greet the General. This was obviously an extremely important event for the locals as the General had never visited there before.

De Gaulle arrived, welcoming addresses were given, and then he gave his talk. My very limited French did not allow me to comprehend what he was saying to any great degree. When the talk ended, as was his habit, he walked into the crowd to speak with the local citizenry. We were standing at the edge of the café and the first person he came over to greet was my wife. He said, 'Bonjour Madame.' My wife, whose French was far better than mine, replied to his greeting, but it was obvious that she was not a French woman. He spoke another sentence or two and then wandered off to converse with the electorate. Fortunately I had my camera ready and was able to photograph this historic moment in Burson–Marsteller-French relations.

The anti-American anti-British attitude we met with in those days in France was not restricted to the General and politicians. Many government bureaucrats and business leaders resented greatly that English had replaced French as the universal language – and French managers in general were not great believers in public relations at that time. Those who did occasionally practice PR believed they should be making all the decisions rather than allowing an outside agency to do so. The role of the agency, they felt, was merely to carry out management's decisions. So when we started in France we began relatively small. In all the years when I was in charge, I always thought it was best not to have a senior American or Englishman running the Paris office.

Germany was very different, of course. We started in Stuttgart because our German advertising partner was there. But it turned out not to be a key city for the growth we envisioned, so we soon set up in Frankfurt and later on in Berlin. In most cases the German companies entrusted their agencies to be deeply involved in the planning as well as the execution. The German press was also one of the best to deal with in Europe. They were willing to listen to story ideas as long as they felt they were good and even to work with us on the development of the story. And something that was not the case in some other European countries: if they accepted an invitation to a press conference they always showed up and always on time.

Italy also showed great early promise because Italian companies were starting to expand and had a great need for advertising and public relations. We had an Italian advertising partner, and we began to notice that whenever we had a meeting of all our offices he always arrived with a different, very attractive assistant. After the day's sessions were over, he was nearly always unavailable for dinner and evening discussions, for reasons I will only conjecture. We ended up having to part ways with him. If he is still alive, I am sure he is a great fan of Berlusconi.

My travels began to expand dramatically as we had decided we should be looking into setting up our own PR offices in Holland, Spain, Sweden, Denmark and Norway. In some of these countries PR was relatively new, so part of my assignment was to decide if and when we should start. In Sweden I was fortunate enough to have an appointment with one of the most senior members of the Wallenberg family – the leading political and economic family in Sweden. I asked him what he thought the potential was for PR in Sweden. There were small PR firms but as a business PR was in its infancy. He was highly optimistic about the potential so I arranged for Burson–Marsteller to give a major one-day conference on public relations, bringing very senior people over from the United States and inviting executives from all the key Swedish companies. There was a very high turnout and the questions and conversations with local businessmen made it quite clear this was a place we should be. I soon found the same to be true in Norway and Denmark, where PR had already started to grow.

Although the area is known collectively as Scandinavia, the people in the Nordic countries were very different in those days.

Nowhere did I find people more formal than in Sweden. I was invited by a publisher, whom I had met in New York, to give a speech in Stockholm. He also invited me to his home afterwards for what he said would be an informal dinner and that I should come at 6pm. Everyone else who had been invited showed up at exactly the allotted time. We went in and had drinks and when dinner started every male had to escort a woman to the table. The hostess could not drink until someone first had made a toast to her. When dinner was over, fortunately I was not on the right of the hostess, because that person by tradition had to get up and make a thank you speech before the dinner could end. Luckily, the gentleman from the British embassy was on her right, and he knew what to do. If it had been up to me, being so unknowledgeable in the ways of the Swedes, we would still be sitting there. When the dinner was over, everyone had to escort someone from the dining room. This formality was required even though, besides the British embassy official, myself and one or two others, all the guests were close friends of the host and hostess. Despite their formality, the Swedes were very warm, and my wife and I made some very close Swedish friends.

We decided against opening an office in Finland, but in the time I spent there I found some great differences between the Finns and the Swedes. At one point I was scheduled to give a speech in Helsinki, and it would be my first time in that country. On the way I stopped in Copenhagen to meet with a major distributor for Clark Equipment, one of our largest clients. We were having drinks at his local club, and when I told him I was going to Helsinki, he said, 'The Finns are very intelligent and they drink more and can hold their liquor better than any other nationality.' But, he warned me, 'While the limit of how much they can drink is greater, when they pass that limit they become more violent than anyone else I've ever known, and you must be aware of this.'

He told me a story to prove his point. He had once gone on a five-day fishing trip to Finland. For most of the trip he and his group stayed on the boat. There was a great deal of drinking. One evening two of the Finns got into an argument about a woman and their exchanges became more and more intense. Finally, one of the Finns pulled out a knife and stabbed the other. While obviously not meaning to, unfortunately, he killed him. The captain called the police and brought the boat to port. The attacker made no attempt whatsoever to get away. He was very upset and contrite about what he had done. There was no reason not to believe the story but I thought perhaps my friend was exaggerating a bit. Then he said, 'This will surprise you. The man who just walked into the club was the only other Dane on that boat with me.' He called the man over and asked him to tell me what happened on their fishing trip to Finland. The story he told me was identical. So I decided that I had learned something and would be on my guard in Finland.

A few days later I was in Helsinki giving my speech. I was put up at a beautiful luxury hotel and spa. After my speech, my hosts arranged for me to have my own sauna room. The sauna was next to a huge indoor pool, and when I went for a swim I found it was frequented mainly by members of the Finnish national circus, most of whom spoke good English, as many Finns did. At the end of the pool was an area where you could cook food and have your liquor. These people were very friendly, adopting me as the only non-Finn around. We got along really well. We would swim, eat, drink and then I would go back to the sauna. This routine went on uneventfully for a few hours. As my Danish friend had warned me, my new Finnish companions could really drink. They caroused a bit, had a lot of fun, but seemed relatively in control.

While I was back in my sauna there was a knock on the door. It was the manager of the hotel who told me that every sauna was occupied and would I mind sharing mine with another guest. 'Of course not,' I replied. The guest turned out to be a sales representative for BASF, a leading German chemical company. We had a relaxing sauna and were in the middle of a conversation when the door flew open. It was one of the largest of the Finnish circus performers. He said the group had sent him to bring me back to the pool to have more drinks with them. By now he was wobbly on his feet, his speech was slurred and he had clearly passed the limit the Dane had warned me about. When he saw the other guest, he rudely asked, 'Who are you?' The fellow answered, and his accent made it obvious that he was German. I could see the Finn's face contort with rage. The Finns at that time still had an incredibly strong dislike of the Germans and he started to rant, 'What are you doing here? You don't belong in Finland!' He raged on and on and became threatening. It was obvious that he was working himself into a frenzy that was going to end in violence.

Fortunately, the manager heard the commotion, came into the room and read the situation right away. She said firmly, 'This is the end of sauna time and we are closing the rooms.' She took the drunken Finn by the hand and led him out and back to the pool. The German and I decided it was now best to leave the premises. To this day I wonder what would have happened if the manager hadn't intervened. Would I have had the courage to step in between the Finn and the German? I just don't know and I am glad I didn't have to find out.

Three years had passed since my arrival in Brussels to establish a European presence for Burson–Marsteller and the growth and success of our operation was well beyond anything we had anticipated. One of the major reasons for our growth was the increased acceptance by clients of PR approaches that were then relatively new in Europe. These not only increased sales and profits, but in turn got many companies to increase their use of public relations to help improve sales even more. Sometimes the money came from the advertising budget, but more often it was new funding.

One of our earliest successes was on behalf of the US Industrial Chemical Company, a division of National Distillers. Every year there was a very important plastics exhibition that many of their key customers and prospects attended. One year it was being held in Düsseldorf, near the Rhine river. We persuaded the client to rent a cruise boat for the duration of the exhibition and use it as a hotel, something that had never been done before. They were not only able to provide their customers and prospects with free lodging for the period of the exhibition, but they also took only a very small booth at the plastics fair and held a major exhibition of their products on the boat. Many of their key executives attended, and it turned out to be one of the most successful fairs for new business they had ever participated in.

In addition, in order to get their name spread through the European media, we invented a game – Deck Chess – which was played on the boat. We set up a huge chessboard with chess pieces the size of young children. The players had to wrestle these huge pieces around the board whenever it was their turn to move. Hundreds of people, including some potential customers, came on board to watch the game being played and it received tremendous media coverage, even on TV, throughout Europe. This helped ensure a long and meaningful relation with the client.

With all our success, we now began to think seriously about offices in Asia, South America, and even possibly the Middle East and Australia. But running a worldwide operation of this scope would be difficult, and we thought it would be far better to be headquartered in London. While Belgium, with the advent of the Common Market, had become key to Europe, London was still the centre of the business world outside the US, with far greater resources, and a more entensive knowledge base and personnel base than anywhere on the continent.

Thus, I was asked if I would move to London for two years to set up our international headquarters. While my wife and I had thoroughly enjoyed our stay in Brussels, we were thrilled at the prospect of living in England. We had already partnered with a British ad agency but decided that we needed a partner more focused on PR than advertising, so we offered to sell back to them our 10 per cent ownership of their company. Our soon to be ex-partners were very amiable about the transaction. They felt that we were becoming too competitive on the advertising side, which was their primary business. They were also happy to have a PR subsidiary that they could control completely, even though it would be smaller after our departure.

We decided to buy a local PR firm as our new base. PR was growing rapidly in England and there were some good companies operating there. So I started looking for acquisitions. We also decided we would open a Marsteller office with a completely separate staff to handle our advertising business. While both businesses were growing dramatically, it was apparent that as we grew the advertising segment we would have to start competing with bigger agencies that were already well entrenched. As far as PR was concerned – the sky was the limit.

Europe was becoming the place to be. Business growth and personal promotion opportunities were abundant. At Marsteller and Burson–Marsteller, a growing number of senior people who were doing very well in the US put in requests for an overseas assignment. Their contribution would be a factor in our increasingly rapid international growth. Companies – potential clients – were busy expanding into more and more geographic markets, fuelling our own expansion. At the same time the quality of local people in different countries was getting better and better as public relations became a business that more people wanted to enter.

During my time in Belgium, one thing that refused to change

was the Belgian civil service, which was stifling the country's economy. Its biggest employer was the government, with 800,000 civil servants: 19.8 per cent of the working population. The *New York Times* noted at the time that 'their operating infrastructure is outdated and their working conditions are poor'. Further, the *Times* reported that the Belgian civil service was highly politicized – supporting the right political party was far more important for advancement than competence.

When we were ready to leave, as I had been warned, Monsieur l'Expert came to review our apartment. We had kept the apartment in excellent condition, but still I was presented with an eleven-page report listing every transgression and a sum to be paid for these heinous acts of destruction, including, of course, each and every nail hole. I was really upset, but my Belgian assistant explained this was the norm and merely an opening salvo towards a final settlement. Following her advice, I wrote a letter at how surprised and hurt I was especially after I had enjoyed my stay in Brussels so much. After a series of negotiations the fee was reduced considerably and I was able to leave the country smiling.

When I left Belgium for London in 1968, I could look back with great satisfaction. I had helped build an office that was thriving and growing and we now had wonderful staff from different nations that would be a major factor in our success going forward. But I was also ready for London, a city that I had visited many times and looked forward to living and working in. I knew many things would be different there – laws, culture, business environment. But I also knew that, as on the continent, the opportunities for PR there would be limitless. There was no reason to believe that Burson–Marsteller's expansion would not continue dramatically.

4   Moving to London

At my farewell party in Brussels, the Belgian staff made only one suggestion, not completely in jest: 'Bob, we hope you will fly back from England for lunch and dinner each day, won't you?' They knew how much good food meant to me, and London was not the place for a would-be gourmet. In those days, the average Englishman had comparatively little interest in food and most of the restaurants operated accordingly. No one could drown vegetables like the British. You had to wring out your beans and your Brussels sprouts so they would not float away. But now, more than forty years later, the food scene in England has come into its own. In fact, I would say that the greatest change in England has not been economic, nor has it been political – it has been culinary. Food is extremely important for business, tourism and for a nation's image, and the English have met the challenge. London, incredibly, has become one of the gourmet capitals of the world. According to some guide books, it is number one, and the quality and variety of restaurants has even brought plaudits from leading French chefs.

One public relations company, C. S. Services, was a favourite from the start in Burson–Marsteller's search for a local partner. It was run by two very dissimilar people, John Addey and Claude Simmonds. John was larger than life, a man of many faults and virtue. He was extremely intelligent and was the ultimate charmer. At his best, he was one of the outstanding PR men in London. He was gay, which in those days was of greater significance than it is today, but his sexual orientation did not have an impact on us in any way. He knew our company, very much wanted to join us, and when he attended a party at Harold Burson's home in the US, his charm ran rampant. Everyone was impressed by John, including me.

The problem was Claude Simmonds. There was no one more British in his attitudes and prejudices than Claude. Compared to him, Winston Churchill might have seemed continental. To Claude the very thought of working for a company owned by Americans was anathema. Once we had decided they were the firm for us, John went to work on Claude, convincing him that the future of their business called for a larger operation, one with worldwide capacities. Since Claude was approaching sixty, John emphasized the importance of increasing profits dramatically as his retirement approached, and that argument won the day.

We appointed a law firm, Baker McKenzie and Hightower, to draw up a purchase document and they did so based on the financial information C. S. Services provided them with, which they had prepared with the greatest attention to detail. Both sides agreed to the documented terms. Thus Burson–Marsteller, C.S Services was born and given a name much too long and not ideal for people in a business that teaches people how to communicate simply.

And then the bombshell dropped: C.S. Services's accountant, a very timid and completely honest man, came to Claude Simmonds and reported that the numbers that had been provided to us as a basis for the purchase were completely wrong, due to bookkeeping mistakes. The multiple we were using for payment to them was thus incorrect, meaning that we were overpaying by a significant amount. Claude was not only concerned that the sale price would be lower but even more significantly that we might think a British company had tried to cheat an American firm. When I came to see him after he called to describe the error, he was distraught. I explained to him that we realized errors could be made and we appreciated his complete honesty in letting us know so quickly. When I called Harold Burson and told him about the meeting, he said, 'Bob, the board has approved the amount, and London will in all probability grow to become our most profitable international office. So let them keep the original amount.'

When I told Claude about Harold's reaction, he couldn't believe it and said that very few British firms would have acted with such generosity and understanding. From that day forward, he was one of our most loyal and devoted employees, and a vital factor in our initial growth as he actively went out to seek new business. We also became very close personal friends.

While Britain was at the forefront of European PR, it was still far behind the US. Soon after I moved there the leading advertising publication, *Campaign*, gave me a three-page centre-spread inter-view, probably the first they had ever run on public relations. They headlined it: 'Why Britain still has to be sold the PR idea.'

I was quite open and honest with their writer. England had a lot to learn from the US, and this was not said as bravado by a dyed-in-the-wool American. English companies did not have the same belief in public relations that existed in the US, and its use had not yet developed to any significant degree.

As we started building up our business and signing up clients, we were shocked to realize that many British companies knew very little about themselves. We started most accounts with an internal audit: this is the norm today but seemed very novel back then. We investigated all aspects of the company: its staff, its products, its distribution, its competition, and what management felt the company's image was in the marketplace. Then we did external audits with the company's customers, clients, suppliers, and far too often found that their views of the company varied greatly from how management perceived it.

The biggest problem we faced in the US market was competition from other good, highly-qualified PR firms. In England, we competed against the concept of public relations itself. Many companies just did not rate it very highly. The PR role internally at that time was minor and in most cases those involved in it on the corporate side were very poorly paid and poorly regarded. The average internal public relations executive usually saw outside consultancies such as ourselves as a competitor and often worried that his position would be endangered if we were too effective.

In the US, I told *Campaign*, the chairman of Armco Steel, the fourth largest steel maker, once served as its public relations officer – a case of upward mobility that would never happen in England. But it wasn't only England – it was all over Europe. I told the journalist, for example, that at the time, 'a PR man [was] considered a step below a horse thief' in Germany.

As a result there was very little money in PR. Ad agencies had PR divisions, but what they were earning for the agency was so far below what the ad business provided that not much attention was paid to those departments. Some ad agencies did, however, have effective PR departments. PR salaries in-house or at consultancies were extremely low, something I knew would have to change and change quickly.

The British press in general were not too favourably disposed to public relations as a profession, and I noted in the article that 'any business needed to promote itself through its public relations'. But surprisingly, in the UK, PR people were far closer to their journalistic contacts than in the US, because they were all headquartered in one city – a situation that did not exist in America.

I did want to end the interview with the *Campaign* reporter on a positive note, telling him: 'The literacy of the average young man coming up in public relations in England is far beyond what I could have ever envisioned when I first moved to Europe. They're very well read. They understand public relations and this is why I am so excited about England. There's all this potential here.' And while I truly believed what I said, even I greatly underestimated what the potential would turn out to be.

Our own public relations took a huge boost when John Addey brought in Australian media mogul Rupert Murdoch as one of our initial clients. Murdoch was interested in making his first London acquisition, the *News of the World*, and his opponent in the battle for the paper was a significant one – Robert Maxwell. Our main role was to present Murdoch to the shareholders as a far better choice than Maxwell to take over the paper. The *News of the World* was first published in 1843 and was the cheapest newspaper of its time, aimed at the newly-literate working classes. It has a fascinating history. By 1950, individual editions were selling over nine million copies, making it the biggest selling newspaper in the world.

The Murdoch-Maxwell competition for the newspaper was a cut-throat contest, with no love lost between the opponents. Murdoch, at this early stage of his career, was not very well known outside of Australia. Maxwell, on the other hand, was an imposing celebrity business tycoon. He had escaped from Hungary during the war and most of his relatives died at Auschwitz. He joined the British Army, rose to the rank of captain and was awarded the Military Cross. He already had a reputation as someone you didn't want to cross. At a shareholder's meeting in January 1969, Maxwell's bid for the *News of the World* was refused by the shareholders, and the paper went to Murdoch. Maxwell accused Murdoch of abiding by 'the laws of the jungle' and did not take this defeat kindly.

Burson–Marsteller received an unwelcome mention in an article about the meeting in the *Wall Street Journal*, where it accused John

Addey of Burson–Marsteller of unprofessional behaviour. After this accusation appeared in print I waited a day before I called Harold Burson, knowing he must have seen it. I was expecting a pretty strong reaction from him about an article in the *Wall Street Journal* criticizing his firm. But Harold surprised me. 'Bob,' he said. 'I've gotten call after call congratulating us on our role. Most of the callers commented that they didn't know how strong an operation we had in the UK. I'm sure this will result in a number of new business leads.' Which it did.

Rupert Murdoch, I must say, was extremely pleasant to work with at this time and he was very appreciative of our efforts before, during and immediately after the takeover – and he told us so. He was always willing to listen to suggestions though that didn't mean he accepted them all. It was obvious to me then that I was dealing with someone who was going to go places. And I must admit that I did feel sad when I watched him questioned by the Commons Culture, Media and Sport Select Committee on phone-hacking after the demise of the *News of the World* – particularly when he said: 'This has been the humblest moment of my life.' You could tell that he meant it. I do believe, however, that he and his organization could have handled their overall public relations concerning the whole issue much more effectively and created a far better perception than they achieved if they had followed certain rules on how best to answer questions.

Fortunately, Robert Maxwell forgot our role in his defeat because he hired Burson–Marsteller some years later and I personally worked on the account for many years. Knowing Maxwell, I can be certain that he would never have let me in the door if he had had any idea of my previous association with Murdoch.

Meanwhile, it was becoming more and more obvious that the name Burson–Marsteller, C. S. Services was far too unwieldy and had to go, particularly as in every other market we were known as

Burson–Marsteller. John Addey came to see me and said he agreed with our discomfort about the name, as did Claude Simmonds. He said that he and Claude would like to see the name changed to Burson–Marsteller, Simmonds and Addey. Since we appreciated the efforts both Claude and John were making to help us become successful, the US board had no problem with changing our name as John suggested, but not for long.

After a spell of travel around Europe, I returned to London and lunched with Claude. During the lunch, he said, 'You know, Bob, we continue to do better than we had ever envisioned, and I have had no reason to question any of your decisions. But there is one thing I will never understand. Why did you change the name of the company to include my name? I'm retiring soon and I have no family in the business, so what is the sense of using the Simmonds name as part of the company?' I was more than surprised by his comments and replied, 'Because John Addey told me that is what you wanted.' After that conversation Claude could never feel comfortable with John again and tried to have as little contact with him as possible. It was obvious that John's future as part of Burson–Marsteller was limited.

In 1968 we acquired an account in London that grew to become our largest in Europe and the key to our success in London: Unilever's Flora margarine. We retained this account for twenty-four years without having to pitch for it again. Our relationship began when I received a call that someone from Unilever would like to meet me for lunch to discuss a possible account, as someone had recommended that he talk to me.

At lunch the executive explained that Unilever was going to launch a new product – Flora margarine – which was very high in polyunsaturated fats, a key factor in lowering cholesterol levels in the body. The company wanted to promote Flora as a health product rather than as a tasty butter substitute, but under British advertising regulations fats manufacturers could not advertise any health claims for their product. PR would have to carry the message and would be a vital factor to the product's success.

I then met with the ad manager for the product, a man who had never used PR previously. He was very interested in what we could do for him so we had a team present for the account which we were awarded for £1,500 a month. We were very fortunate that the head of Unilever's 'yellow fats' business unit was Paul Clark, a firm believer in public relations, and also a visionary. If he liked an idea, the necessary budget was never in question. From the beginning of our campaign it was agreed that the key was to bring our message to the medical profession. The idea was to present Flora as one worthwhile part in a heart disease prevention programme.

At this time, the US was ahead of the UK in research and awareness of coronary disease, so we flew the leading English medical journalists to Chicago on behalf of Flora to meet with medical experts in this field. In the UK we held a major conference for doctors on the subject of heart disease at the Churchill Hotel in London. To enter the conference they had to walk through a huge beating heart that we had constructed. I came with a doctor and as we walked through the heart he told me we had made a mistake. The heart was beating perfectly, and we would have made our point better if it were beating irregularly. He was right.

Much to our surprise, we found that Finland was the European country known for being the best at heart disease prevention so we flew a group of medical journalists to that country to meet with doctors to discuss their approach. This trip received a lot of coverage and brought us closer to the medical press. The sales of Flora began to mushroom, and it became one of Unilever's most profitable products, as well as one of Burson–Marsteller's most profitable accounts. It was possibly the highest budgeted product PR account in the UK.

Jill Phillipson, who ran the account, was sent throughout Europe and also to Japan and Brazil to train the local Unilever people, as well as the local Burson–Marsteller offices, in how to present Flora. We wanted it positioned in the most positive way to the medical profession and the public, not as a product alone, but as part of a total picture. In addition to Jill's travels, we gave courses to many Unilever people from around the world in our London office.

Clive Butler, who headed Flora's marketing in the UK, was another devout believer in public relations. His contribution to the marketing of Flora in the UK was a major factor in his promotion to the top of Unilever's 'Yellow Fats Division' in the US – where he hired Burson–Marsteller to handle the company's public relations.

As Flora grew and grew, we expanded key audiences. Instead of only aiming information at general practitioners, we ended up sending over six million information packs a year to 18,000 nurse practitioners who were beginning to focus on counselling and preventative health care in general medical practices.

After many years of primarily targeting the medical profession, we began to broaden our focus to the general consumer. For one major Flora event, we sponsored the making of a 700-foot sandwich with fillings devised by celebrities. Two of the celebrities, Glenda Jackson MP and Lord Archer, attended the photo call along with the boy scouts who made the sandwich. This generated significant TV and national newspaper coverage. There is no doubt that these PR activities helped boost Flora's sales far beyond what had originally been anticipated. For many years Flora was the bestselling yellow fat, ahead of any butter product. Unilever did tracking research that found consumers of both sexes and all ages related to Flora as good for health and relevant to their lives. Awareness of the role of poly-unsaturated fats in a healthy diet reached over 80 per cent of the respondents. Formal tracking research among influencers and target media showed they believed the scientific claims made by the Flora

Project more than those made by the government through its Health Education Authority. There is no doubt that the work on Flora boosted Burson–Marsteller dramatically and was a major factor in our becoming one of the largest PR firms in the UK at that time.

The quality of our work in London was getting better and better. But difficulties still existed. One was salary inequities. In a report to the board I wrote:

> No company has solved this and we never will completely. You have to relate to local market conditions rather than abilities. Many of our London staff are under-paid compared to their skills, but so is everyone else in England. Regardless of ability, the European salaries will not reach the level of Americans. What this means is that we must be very careful to employ Americans only where necessary and to make sure we reward the Europeans in comparison to other companies. We have got to constantly increase our benefit package. We are about to install an insurance and pension scheme in England. We have got be flexible in our methods of remuneration. This is especially the case in England where prohibitive taxation exists. Management personnel do not want raises. They want 'perks'. And since we live with the local system of low wages we must also live with the system of non-salary rewards.

I also noted that we would have to increase our personnel training and upgrade our minimum fees. I was extremely bullish about the London bosses being aware that in the previous year we had gotten better clients, better budgets, had hired very good young people, and that morale was excellent.

While I was continuing to travel throughout Europe, London was still my home – my new home. As a family we had looked forward to moving there from Brussels, and the city more than surpassed our expectations. My wife became secretary of the Multiple Sclerosis Society, a relatively unknown organization when she joined. Through some sad and unfortunate circumstances, it soon became one of the country's most recognized charities. One of the leading musicians in England was a wonderfully talented cellist named Jacqueline du Pré. She was a leading light in the classical music world, played on two Stradivarius cellos, and moved in circles that included such legendary figures as Zubin Mehta, Yehudi Menuhin, Itzak Perlman – and her husband, the pianist Daniel Barenboim. She played with, among others, the London Philharmonic, the New York Philharmonic, the Los Angeles Philharmonic and the Berlin Philharmonic. Then at the peak of her career, she developed a severe case of multiple sclerosis, and her health and her playing deteriorated dramatically. Her last performance was with the New York Philharmonic in a concert conducted by Leonard Bernstein. She died in 1987 at the age of forty-two. Throughout her illness, multiple sclerosis received reams of publicity, far more than a public relations campaign on its behalf could have ever accomplished, and thousands of people started to contribute to charities supporting a cure for it.

In the UK business world, public relations continued to grow in acceptance. The Institute of Public Relations, later to become chartered, had begun in 1948 and was growing rapidly. In 1955, the International Public Relations Society was founded. Then, in 1969, the Public Relations Consultants Association, of which I was one of the founders, came to life. All these organizations worked actively to improve the capabilities of those individuals now calling public relations a career. In 1986, *PR Week* was born, increasing the reputation of public relations and providing a media outlet that could publicize some of the successes that effective public relations had achieved.

In 1979, Marsteller and Burson–Marsteller was sold to Young & Rubicam. Discussion of a possible sale had been going on at board meetings for years. While we realized we could become a dominant force in public relations – and in fact that was already happening – the same would never be true in advertising. We were far too low in the pecking order and needed to align ourselves with a real heavyweight in the industry, so the motivation to sell was not to cash in or to enrich the shareholders. We were a privately held company and did not have to try and please either Wall Street or the investment community. And although we wanted to get a good price for the firm, the main focus was on finding a buyer we would be comfortable working with. We wanted someone who would provide backing and support and help us grow, but who would not try to run our business, leaving that to us. There was general agreement among the board members that there were only two advertising agencies who met our specifications: Ogilvy and Mather, and Young & Rubicam. They were both known as not only being very creative but very staff-oriented. So we started discussions with both.

We ultimately selected Young & Rubicam, whose chairman Ed Ney was the best leader anyone could ask for. He was smart, likeable, and he listened. As the years went by, it was obvious that much of Marsteller Advertising would perform best by being absorbed by Young & Rubicam and the rest would function best as a division of Burson–Marsteller, providing products such as literature and corporate ads which could help to make the PR programme for clients more effective. On the PR side of our business, Young & Rubicam provided financial support and new business leads but never interfered with the management of the company. In all the time I was international chairman, they never once overruled a decision we made.

That year, Bill Marsteller turned sixty-five and retired. He had not been well for quite a few years, but his mind remained as sharp as ever. Although he was an ad man and saw the PR side of the business dramatically overtake the ad side, he never in any way tried to interfere – except perhaps once.

As I previously mentioned, if he really liked someone, he demanded perfection. A few years before he retired, we had one major clash. He decided that I should return to the US because he believed some time in the future I should probably become the chief operating officer under Harold, and possibly further on in the future, go on to replace him. But I sincerely believed Jim Dowling was a far better choice for this role than I.

He was far more knowledgeable than I was about the domestic business, which still remained the largest segment, and had been a major factor in our becoming the largest PR agency at that time. I sent a letter to Harold spelling out my feelings. I felt my contribution to the company would be far better if I remained abroad. (Clearly I was no longer looking at my overseas assignment as short-term.) Bill did not agree. He wanted me back and said that if I stayed abroad, all my benefits would be cut and I would report to someone else internationally, which would have been a demotion. Fortunately members of the board convinced Bill that I was firm about staying overseas, and with our PR growing so strongly internationally, my experience on a Europe-wide basis would make me highly marketable to other companies, should I decide to leave. Such a drastic move on my part had not ever entered my mind, but I thank the directors for bringing it up. Bill relented and I stayed put.

In the meantime, we were continuing to grow rapidly, and not only in the UK. We had opened up offices in Sweden, Denmark, Holland, Spain and Italy in addition to the continental offices we were already operating in Belgium, France, Germany and Switzerland. While the clients were different in most countries, both in their attitude towards PR and how they saw their needs, one commonality was the growing quality of the local staff throughout

Europe as PR became more of an 'in' thing. With proper training of staff we could create a homogeneity regardless of the country we were setting up, as the new local teams would be taking the same approach we did on a company-wide basis – and thus implementing what we felt was the best way to fulfil the clients' needs.

The philosophy that Harold Burson instituted at the time he started the company – namely that everyone regardless of position or size of office was important – was followed rigorously. I established a European Management Committee consisting of the heads of each office, and camaraderie resulted to the degree that we very rarely lost any of our managers to a competitive company in those early years.

Despite our successes, it became clear to me that one cannot run an international business without facing some rough moments from time to time. In one of the early years in London, and for the first and only time in my career, a client asked to have me taken off his account. It was Beefeaters Gin, and I had been part of the pitch that won the account. I was not the major account handler but acted as an advisor. Then, one day, the executive running the account said he would like to talk to me privately. He explained that the client's ad and PR manager had told him he would rather I no longer work on the account. He explained why: I had written the Beefeater ad manager a letter and, as was policy, had copied in their chief executive. But while on the copy going to him I had signed my full name, instead of signing my full name on the copy to the chief executive, I had merely signed my initials. He felt that this was such a display of disrespect to his most senior executive that he preferred that I take my skills elsewhere. I had no choice but to accept that request, and we kept the account for many years after without my involvement.

In all the years that I have lived in London, one event in particular has had a great emotional impact on me: the violent death of

Giving a talk at the American Chamber of Commerce in Brazil about the impact that PR is making in South America.

At the opening of new Burson-Marsteller offices in Hong Kong. It was customary to have a suckling pig that was to be shared by the whole staff to ensure good fortune.

Signing the agreement to set up the first international PR firm in the Middle East with Ramzi Raad, a leading advertising executive in the region.

Arriving in Warsaw with British publishers during the Cold War as guests of the government to give a speech on communications. I gave similar speeches in Budapest, Bucharest, Prague and Moscow.

With Japanese staff celebrating the company's tenth anniversary.

With my wife Adele on one of many foreign trips we enjoyed together.

a man who had run the London office, whom, for reasons of privacy, I shall call Bill. He had been recently promoted to a position as head of Europe. He was very close to me as I had hired him, worked with him in Brussels, and subsequently made him head of our Argentine office. Later, he ran our operations in Canada, and then had returned to London to become head of the office.

We were holding the year's major international Burson–Marsteller executive meeting in the UK for all top executives, including Harold Burson and Jim Dowling. Bill was responsible for putting the programme together for the event, which was taking place in the Portman Hotel – where most of the overseas staff were staying. After a full day of meetings, a dinner was scheduled and some of the senior executives' wives were invited. Bill and I walked out of the hotel together to go home to get our wives. That would be the last time I would see him alive.

When I came back to the Portman with my wife, we waited patiently for Bill and his spouse to arrive. Bill was late, which was very surprising as he was always punctual, and time was dragging on. Then we received a call from a hospital that Bill was there and was seriously injured. We imagined he must have been in a car crash. We sent two people to the hospital, and they returned to tell us Bill was dead! Eventually, the story unfolded.

When Bill left me and went across the street, I thought he was going to get his car. But in reality he was going to the Churchill Hotel to meet the Canadian husband of one of our Toronto employees, who was staying there. The Canadian had demanded to see him as he had learned that Bill had been having an affair with his wife; Bill had agreed to meet him. From the trial, we learned that the conversation got more and more heated. At one point Bill said he had to leave to pick up his wife and get back to the Portman. This so angered the other man that in a fit of anger he broke a bottle that was in the room and stabbed Bill with it. While he absolutely did not intend whatsoever to kill Bill, the puncture proved fatal. The Canadian waited at the hotel for the police to arrive. At the subsequent trial, testimony showed that the Canadian was considered by those who knew him to be a very mild, non-emotional type, and his reaction to be completely out of character. The result was that he was sentenced to three years and released a year and a half later.

As a sidebar to this unfortunate happening Bill, in his position at Burson–Marsteller, had a special insurance policy worth $100,000 if he died during working hours. Whether he had was open to question since he was killed after the day's meetings had taken place, when it might no longer be considered working hours. I got involved and was able to document that the dinner Bill was to return to was a business dinner, so technically he was still at work. The insurance company paid the full benefit to his widow. Bill was universally liked throughout the firm, and it took quite a long time for us to cope and get back to normal. Unfortunately this was not the last time our company experienced a killing in its ranks, a story I will tell later on.

Meanwhile, PR kept growing and growing, especially in England. The competition became far more intense as large PR firms came into existence. At the same time, more and more specialist firms aimed at specific audiences – such as financial, governmental or health care – opened up, and more and more companies began to divide their accounts among a number of different agencies rather than working solely through one.

In spite of our growing presence, public relations people were still not able to shed the reputation of primarily being spin doctors. As late as 1990, *International Management* wrote: 'Europe's public relations industry is booming but the PR agencies need to polish their own image before they can cash in. Some candid PR industry

experts concede that public relations agencies have a poor reputation and scant credibility. And that business journalists have this
terrible image of those engaged in PR as the gin and tonic brigade.'

But I found PR becoming more accepted and increasingly
attracting better and better people. We were fortunate in that we
continued to employ bright young people. Headhunters would direct
them to Burson, telling them, 'Go to Burson. They do the best
training. They treat young people very well. Then after three years
or so leave if you think there are better opportunities elsewhere.'

Though business continued to be exceptionally good, 1978 became
a year of great personal tragedy for me. I came from a small family.
My father had died at the age of fifty when I was nineteen, and I
only had one brother. I learned that my mother, to whom I was
very close, was terminally ill and it was just a question of time – in
all likelihood a relatively short time – before she passed on. At the
same time, my brother, who was fifty-two, was diagnosed with a
brain tumour. At first, we were told by doctors that it was benign,
but later tests showed it was malignant and not operable. This was
something my brother was unaware of as we did not inform him
of the later opinions. I met with the doctors who told me that he
would feel fine for a time but that the tumour would continue to
grow and eventually destroy all of his brain functions. The doctors
felt that he had a few months of normal life left, aside from the
possibility of an occasional seizure, before deterioration began in
earnest.

My sister-in-law wanted the four of us to have one last memorable trip together and asked me to select a destination that would
provide the greatest pleasure. The dilemma I faced, however, was
the need to stay in New York with my mother, because while she
was deathly ill she remained coherent, and there was no way my
brother and I could leave her. It was a terrible situation. If my mother
lasted a very long time, then my brother's condition might not

permit him to travel. As it turned out, when she did pass away, the doctors agreed that my brother could go abroad for a period of three weeks or so. We held a very brief remembrance period for my mother, and then struck out for Ireland with my brother and his wife.

My brother and sister-in-law had never been to Ireland, the country my wife and I had carefully chosen for this trip. We had always found the Irish warm and friendly, and in those days the Emerald Isle was still relatively untouched. I knew that my brother, who was very personable by nature, would love the country, and all of us would have a great and, unfortunately, really memorable time. I say unfortunately as we knew this would be my brother's last trip.

We started in Dublin and had a magnificent time. There was much to see. We then went to Bunratty Castle, where they specialize in medieval dinners and entertainment. There was an adjourning folk park with replicas of all the kinds of homes that existed throughout Ireland in the nineteenth century. An excellent guide showing us one of the homes first took us through the kitchen, which was the only warm room in the house. All the whiskey was kept there along with drinking glasses for each of the friends who would congregate on the weekends for a few glasses. She then showed us the coldest room in the house, which was where the local priest would be received – in the hope that he would not stay too long.

Our next stop was Dromoland Castle which had been turned into Ireland's most luxurious hotel and had been recently bought by an American. When we were sitting in one of the downstairs rooms we started talking to an American man sitting nearby, and asked him what he did. He replied, quietly: 'The bank and I own this place.' He was charming and I'm happy to say Dromoland went from strength to strength in later years. We travelled all over Ireland and visited the Ring of Kerry, Dingle Bay, Waterford, Cork and then back to Dublin. My brother had only one minor seizure. In most places we spent a good deal of our time in pubs and the people, as I had hoped, could not have been nicer or friendlier. Both my brother and sister-in-law who had travelled quite a bit, agreed that this was one of the nicest holidays they had ever had. When the trip ended, my wife and I stayed in Europe, and my brother went back to the US. I saw him once more before, as the doctors predicted, he had a seizure that completely incapacitated him. He died soon after that.

In 1984, one of the real high points of my career took place when we became the largest public relations firm in the world, surpassing Hill and Knowlton. The public relations business in general was booming and according to O'Dwyer's Directory of Public Relations Firms, the fifty largest PR firms grew by almost 20 per cent each in 1983. Reaching this peak was something none of us would have thought possible in the early days. When I joined Burson–Marsteller with its six executives I am sure that Harold would have signed a pact with the devil if he had guaranteed that the company would reach the top five before he retired. We did have certain advantages, so the devil's assistance was not necessary. Back then, we had far less competition than there is today. We had gotten into the international PR business early, as all over the world companies were beginning to appreciate how PR could benefit them. And our international presence gave us the ability to be able to promote American companies in nearly all the major markets, giving us a huge edge.

But I always felt that the primary reason for our success was the attitude of the management, starting with Bill Marsteller and Harold Burson, towards their staff. In those years we had far less turnover of senior executives than our competitors. From the founding of the company, Bill Marsteller instituted a programme whereby all employees, from mail room clerks up, were given 15 per cent of their salary a year tax-free to put into a retirement trust. Some years later we had the leading benefits company look into the firm in great depth. This was the recommendation: cut the 15 per cent to 10 per cent. They reported that the way we were going, junior employees with many years of service would end up with more money than senior people at other companies. And 10 per cent was still very generous. The other 5 per cent should be given in bonuses to the top fifteen employees, thus helping us to ensure the retention of our key executives. And their final suggestion was: 'Please give Harold Burson a raise.' As he underpaid himself, it could lead to the people under him not earning enough.

When Harold was interviewed for a major piece in the *New York Times* entitled 'New No.1 in Public Relations', he attributed the growth 'to a core of seasoned top executives, many with over twenty years at Burson and a strong marketing orientation that moves the products off the shelves'. The second part was especially true, because starting as a PR firm with only industrial clients, most of the assignment was to move products and this philosophy remained strong even as the client base dramatically changed.

Becoming number one also gave us the opportunity for major coverage throughout the world, and I was interviewed in many countries that I visited. For example the *Business Times* in Malaysia published an article noting that we had grown 33 per cent from the previous years and that interest in Malaysia by multinational companies had grown dramatically. This led to more leads.

One of our earliest UK clients who helped fuel our growth was Forte Hotels, a company I stayed involved with for more than twenty-five years. Lord Forte, whom the press was to call, rightfully so, Britain's greatest hotelier, was born in Italy in 1908 in the small hillside village of Mortale, later renamed Monforte, near Rome. He moved to Scotland aged four. At eighteen he worked in a family restaurant and then struck out on his own, purchasing a milk bar in London. He grew to be London's largest milk bar proprietor. He then moved into restaurants. His first major purchase was the

Criterion Brasserie in Piccadilly Circus, then the Café Royal restaurant and banqueting rooms, and then later the Waldorf Hotel. He continued purchasing more hotels, starting the roadside service areas Little Chef and acquiring his one and only property outside of the hotel and catering business – Lillywhites, the UK's largest sporting goods store. By 1970 Forte's Holdings had forty-three hotels with 12,500 beds and was also the largest caterer in England. That year Charles Forte became Lord Charles Forte of Ripley when Queen Elizabeth II knighted him for contributions to charitable and cultural events. At his seventieth birthday, Margaret Thatcher was the guest speaker and was extremely complimentary, saying Charles Forte epitomized what a person with his beliefs could accomplish on behalf of the country.

While he radiated authority, Forte was kind and cared for all his staff. I was at the Café Royal having lunch with him one day when he called over his manager and said, 'I heard your mother is ill. I hope she gets better quickly.' He was not one who constantly sought personal publicity, but he was willing to give interviews when I suggested it. Early in our relationship I suggested to the editor of *Management Today*, a relatively new publication then, that he interview Charles Forte. He said he would do it but would not guarantee any coverage as he wasn't really sure there was a story there. The three of us had lunch and he became enamoured with Charles Forte and how straightforward he was. The editor asked, 'What is the biggest mistake you've made?' Forte answered, 'Buying a company called Mr Whippy.' His whole demeanour so impressed the editor that the result was a four-page cover story that was highly favourable and established Burson–Marsteller's reputation within Forte's company.

While the initial budgets were not huge, I developed such a liking for the company that I spent more time on this account than any other. One highlight was when Forte bought the George V and the

Plaza Athénée, two of Paris's most famous hotels, along with a third French hotel, La Trémoille. The furore that resulted in France was unbelievable. The unions, the press and even the general public could not believe that a British ex-milk bar owner could acquire two such significant French landmarks. I went to Paris with Lord Forte to talk to people working at the hotels and some of the press, and slowly the uproar simmered down. Lord Forte ran the hotels far better than his predecessors, and made them even more successful, as they are to this day, and the French later gave him a medal for what he had accomplished.

One day, Charles Forte asked to see me. He said his son Rocco was joining the company's executive ranks, and he was afraid that the press and others might think it was just because he was Forte's only son. Forte said his abilities were of the highest calibre. Rocco had graduated from Oxford and had been working for an accounting firm. He was very familiar with the Forte organization having started at thirteen working in the wine cellar at the Café Royal and then moving to other jobs throughout the company. Charles Forte rang his son and asked him to come up and meet me. We had a pleasant conversation and Lord Forte suggested that we could work well together. Rocco said, 'Mr Leaf, a problem sometimes with service businesses such as PR firms is that you meet the CEO at the beginning, but once they start working with you on the account you see very little of them after.' I told him that this was not the case with Forte and that I continued and would continue to put a lot of my own time into the account. He agreed to have lunch the following week. He took me to the Connaught and a strong personal connection developed: I continued to work with Rocco even after he set up his own company many years later.

In 1992, Rocco took over as the CEO of Forte, by which time it had merged with Trust Houses to become a billion-dollar empire. In 1996, he faced a hostile takeover bid, and while he could not thwart it, his defence was credited with increasing the purchase price, which was initially planned to be £2.30 a share before the bid, but ended at £4 a share. The family was left with £350m.

Rocco, however, was not one to retire to a life of luxury. He quickly built up Rocco Forte Hotels and I continued providing PR advice. He had a name that was bankable, considerable funds and soon he had twenty hotels in cities including London, Brussels, St Petersburg, Rome and Florence. Under his guidance, the business kept growing. In an interview with the *Daily Telegraph*, he said it was not like when he ran an empire of 100,000 employees, but that he liked this better because he could be more hands-on and visit all his properties on a continuing basis.

In the meantime, Burson–Marsteller had developed all over the world. Initial successes had allowed us to build a very strong management team in Europe. By 1968, the business had expanded and continued to do so, beyond expectations. In light of this, the board agreed that now the time was ripe for us to expand into Asia – the key to our future growth.

5   Starting in Asia

When I started our operations in Asia, I realized that that part of the world was different from the West, especially from a cultural point of view, but I had no concept of how truly different it would turn out to be in just about every imaginable way. Attitudes towards business, of course, differ greatly from the West, as well as from country to country. How was I to cater to these differences?

Nothing made the challenge clearer to me than the time Burson–Marsteller pitched to Air Vietnam, the official airline of South Vietnam, for their public relations account. This was during the Vietnam War! Considering the political make-up of Vietnam, I appreciated that we would have to present our credentials and ideas mainly to the military, as they ran the airline. I never anticipated, though, that our contract would be with Maury the Caterer. Maury was a food specialist and handled dinners and banquets for the government. For reasons I will never understand, the Vietnamese had placed PR under the control of catering in their scheme of things. We really never learned much about Maury and his background, and in reality we did not end up having many dealings with him. But what turned out to be a fantastic break for us was that our contract was with Maury and not with the Vietnamese government.

When the war ended, with the Vietcong the winners, we anticipated that they would not be particularly interested in paying Burson–Marsteller for outstanding bills that the South Vietnamese government had accumulated for public relations. But our contract was with Maury the Caterer. . . In order to collect his own unpaid fees, he had arranged for an Air Vietnam plane that was in Hong Kong when the war ended to be impounded and sold. He collected what he was owed and, since our contract was with him, and since Maury was an honourable man, he paid us what we were owed. We were one of the few companies with debts outstanding from the government to be paid nearly in full at the war's end.

Our successes in Europe had gone well beyond our expectations. The board now felt that it was the right time to expand elsewhere, but primarily as a public relations firm, rather than PR *and* advertising. Harold Burson and I agreed that Asia offered the most opportunities because, next to Europe, the Asian region was where most of our clients were expanding. In all probability, the most likely place to establish our initial office would be Hong Kong because it was the communications centre of Asia. We began to look into possibilities of either starting Burson–Marsteller from scratch or purchasing an existing company over there and renaming it. Then came an unexpected break.

In 1982, Harold and I were attending an International Public Relations Association Conference on a boat plying the fjords of Norway. Also on the boat were an Englishman, Peter Bostock, and an Australian, David Mitchell, who were in charge of PR offices in Hong Kong and Singapore for an international advertising agency. They both had become dissatisfied with their relationship with their present employers. Both felt completely unappreciated for what they had accomplished and the way they had managed and grown their business. They had recently decided to leave and set up their own company. Nearly all of their present staff had agreed to join them. In addition, they had a strong client base, so the future looked rosy for them.

As the boat went from fjord to fjord, the four of us got on extremely well. Harold and I broached the idea of opening Burson–Marstaller in Hong Kong and Singapore with Peter and David as part-owners. They were interested, but their less than positive experience with the international agency they had just left had soured them to the notion of being tied up with another big firm. They weren't sure they wanted to go through that again. After further discussions in London and New York and a subsequent visit I made to Hong Kong, they decided we would make good partners, and we reached a satisfactory agreement. We would own 60 per cent of the company and they would each own 20 per cent. The arrangements also included generous terms by which they could sell back their shares if they decided to leave at any time. Moreover, they would be running the operation without anyone looking over their shoulders.

David Mitchell had been in Hong Kong for six years after managing a PR firm in Australia, and he had experience in all areas of counselling on the use of public relations and handling promotion. Peter Bostock had been political, defence and aviation correspondent for the *Daily Sketch*, public relations officer for the *Daily Mail*, information officer for the UK Ministry of Defence and information officer for the Treasury. They both had built up strong staff of local and English executives. We started with clients such as Bank of America, Hapag Lloyd, BOAC, Lockheed, Volvo and SAS, in addition to some well-known local companies.

Our company had agreed from the beginning that we would make Burson–Marsteller in Asia a truly local company, not merely a branch of an American company. This commitment meant understanding the local culture and becoming a part of it. We followed this rule very closely as we expanded throughout the area, and it was a major factor in our growth. There was no question that the Chinese were different from the Japanese who were different from the Thais who were different from the Indians who were different from the Indonesians. It soon became apparent that Hong Kong, too, was unique – a fact we had to pay attention to from the very beginning.

At that time, before it became part of China, most of the Hong Kong Chinese felt that their earthly raison d'être was to make money. And they usually succeeded in doing so. This spirit permeated the whole society. Even those selling goods from carts would remain on a street corner well past two in the morning if they believed that a customer might wander by – which they sometimes did. It was a city where things got done. Suits were made quicker than anywhere else. House painters arrived on short notice. If you wanted your office completely repartitioned, it could be completed within a week.

It was also a city steeped in superstition. The rules of feng shui were not to be disregarded even by westerners. Feng shui, literally 'Wind and Water', dictated how your office or building must be designed. It is an ancient Chinese practice that uses astrology and geography to improve well-being by controlling the flow of energy. Even the leading banks in Hong Kong had their own feng shui experts. For example, it was sincerely believed that if a door or room was incorrectly positioned, bad luck would follow and profits would flow out of the business.

Sometime simple remedies were employed. The placement of plants in a certain manner could reverse unfavourable influences. Properly stationed tanks of goldfish could ward off possible disasters. In those days, among westerners working in Hong Kong, there were many converts alongside the many sceptics. When the Western editor of a very influential magazine, the *Far Eastern Economic Review*, found that a great number of his staff were falling ill, he agreed to call in the feng shui man. Desks were moved and an entrance which apparently looked too much like a coffin was redesigned. Various other architectural changes were made, and the illnesses among both westerners and Chinese employees dropped dramatically. The editor was quoted as saying: 'Once everything was finished people stopped getting sick. You can say this was psychosomatic. I suppose it was, but if people believe in it, it's a reality, and all this certainly seemed to have worked.'

Feng shui played a significant role in our office design, as I found when I moved with my wife to Hong Kong for two years. Our local staff, many of whom were highly educated, believed in it. One Chinese woman on our staff told me that 'it is better to believe in something than not believe'. I wanted to respect these local beliefs, so when we expanded and moved to new offices we consulted a feng shui master. He insisted that the managing director change the proposed placement of his desk to repel demons – even though our MD believed the new design was less convenient. On the actual moving day, the MD's most precious possessions were brought in between 10 and 11 a.m., this being the most auspicious time. This became doubly important because the director was out of the office making a new business presentation at the time and his personal items represented him and his spirit. My office was put in the dragon's corner, which was highly favourable, but this location was less important to the staff as far as feng shui was concerned, for in reality it was the MD who would be guiding their destinies.

We held the requisite celebration for the official opening of the new office: blessings were given at all four corners of the space, and incense was burned. A very large pig had been roasted as a good luck omen and placed outside my door. I had the pig brought inside, cut up, and served to all the staff. It was just about the most delicious pork I have ever tasted. I've come to believe that it was possible that this and other ceremonies contributed to how well we did the following year. At one point, I asked each of our Chinese staff, primarily young people, if they believed in feng shui. They all said yes without hesitation.

One of our brightest female employees told me that feng shui had become bad in the previous Burson–Marsteller office because an overhead roadway had been put up close to the office building, providing the demons with direct access to us. She even believed that this close proximity may possibly have had some responsibility for the recent deaths of her mother and co-workers.

The Hong Kong Chinese also placed a great deal of significance on numbers and dates. Most women planning a wedding consult the Chinese calendar book to choose the most fortuitous dates. Some numbers were considered particularly lucky. Three was the number that ensured good living, and eight prosperity. These beliefs could vary among communities. One young executive in Taipei maintained that terrible misfortune would befall the union of a man whose bride was exactly six years his junior. He said his mother could never attend such a wedding, and if he fell in love with a girl that age, they would have to change the bride's birth certificate so that she would appear five or seven years younger. In Mandarin, the number four sounds like the word death and as a consequence in Hong Kong some companies have buildings where there is no fourth floor.

Some beliefs engendered strict rules of communication, especially within the family. A young woman explained to me that she could never call her grandparents by their first names since this would show tremendous disrespect. Also, she could never give her children the same names as the grandparents because she might have to call her children by that name in the presence of the grandparents, thus insulting them. After living in London the previous twenty years, where the only demons were the tax inspectors, life and work took some adjustment. Of course I was well aware that staff attitudes and beliefs differed in the offices that we had already opened throughout Europe. But, interestingly, I also found that training programmes for local staff on the best uses of public relations for the greatest benefit of the clients did not have to differ from country to country or culture to culture. In each office we opened, there was an extreme eagerness to learn our way of PR and to use that knowledge successfully. I believe that common, universal attitude was a key to our becoming the biggest PR firm in Asia. Another reason for our success was the fact that populations were willing to accept foreign companies and products, and these companies could be helped by our Western promotional approaches.

One of our great early successes in Hong Kong was McDonald's. Kentucky Fried Chicken had opened the year before and had failed because they tried to localize the product. We embarked on a programme that stressed that the McDonald's hamburger you ate in Hong Kong would be the same as in Chicago or New York. After a four month 'no change' campaign in the English and Chinese media, we floated a giant Big Mac across Victoria Harbour with the press following in a boat. The official opening was extraordinary, and thousands of people descended on the store to get a taste of the real McDonald's. Hong Kong's Causeway Bay was brought to a standstill even though the police had been pre-briefed. In its first year, the Hong Kong store was the most profitable of any of their company stores.

To follow-up the opening and establish McDonald's as a company with community spirit, we invited the local populace to take part in the Hong Kong Community Chest Walk. Everyone who participated got a free McDonald's meal and tee shirt. In return, participants were asked to raise money for the Community Chests to be distributed to good causes. That year, over two million people walked for the Community Chest in McDonald's tee-shirts. As a sign of appreciation of the company's success, we presented the millionth customer, a young boy, with a solid gold Big Mac.

Nearly all the expatriates who lived in Hong Kong before it became part of China liked it enormously. Britain had ruled Hong Kong since 1842 when it was ceded to them by the Chinese under the Treaty of Nanking, after the First Opium War. It was returned to China in 1997. Even after this, westerners didn't want to leave and most tried to extend their stay if they were on term contracts. Not one Western employee of Burson–Marsteller stationed in Hong Kong requested a return home after the Chinese takeover.

The only cost problem we had there was housing, the demand for which grew so fast that prices began to equal those in Tokyo. On the other hand, Hong Kong had one of the lowest income tax rates in the world at that time – the maximum being 16 per cent – which more than compensated for the high housing costs. This low tax rate unfortunately had less meaning to Americans since the US did, and still does, charge its citizens based on their nationality rather than location. But Americans are allowed to deduct any taxes they have to pay locally. Citizens of all other major Western countries paid no income taxes to their home country when living abroad for more than a year. For many foreigners, a return to their home country, some of which had extremely high tax rates, could turn out to be financially traumatic.

When one Swedish airline executive learned of his transfer back to Sweden, a country whose tax rates are among the highest, it almost occasioned thoughts of hara-kiri. He softened the blow by having the company throw a farewell party for him that I attended, and which is still memorable. He took over the Hilton ballroom and had food stalls offering the cuisines of all the different countries of Asia served by his airline. Alcohols of all type flowed freely and a band serenaded him. His co-workers did not consider this celebration excessive and sympathized with him: not for tax reasons, but because he was returning to a city in the north of Sweden where the main activity seems to me to be trying to avoid the cold and searching for sunlight.

Hong Kong was the gateway to business with mainland China. As a result, companies from every country headquartered there. The various nationalities representing these companies got along very well. I worked with Swedes, Germans, French, Italians, Australians and many others. There was a real feeling of camaraderie among almost all of us. Surprisingly, the indigenous British were the one group many expatriates found it difficult to relate to. This was especially true of the British who were sent to Hong Kong on term assignments similar to those given to Americans. Usually it was not the top executives of local British companies but those of the middle level who proved difficult to work with.

Let me put this into perspective as I am a confirmed Anglophile – having spent most of my working life in England – and have dealt closely with British executives in Malaysia, Singapore, India and Australia. Hong Kong was the last remnant of the British Empire. Many (and I stress *many*, not all) who lived in Hong Kong for years considered themselves the social elite of this last colony. They believed that they held a unique position as the movers and shakers. Most of the people were not wealthy but they enjoyed a unique, rich lifestyle through the perks offered by their employers – including housing and in some cases house staff, cars, drivers and club memberships. With such benefits coming free with the job, they did not have to earn the amount of money normally necessary to finance such a good life back home. And they were well aware that they were living far above the standards they could have normally afforded. Many projected an image and attitude of privilege and considered others, including the other British stationed in Hong Kong, as coming from the wrong side of the tracks. We were tolerated, especially for fund-raising events, but we were expected to know our place even if we occasionally slipped out if it.

Justice did prevail in the long run, though. The large British companies headquartered there began to cut staff and lower the retirement age as 1997, the year slated for the return of Hong Kong to China, drew nearer. Many of the expatriate 'royalty' had to decide whether or not to stay in Hong Kong when their jobs ended. Everything was becoming increasingly expensive and a retirement income was not usually sufficient enough to sustain the lifestyle they had become accustomed to. Many of these long-term British expats began to consider a return to the UK. Those who had not maintained residences in their home country or elsewhere were stunned at the cost of buying property there. Most of these people were not affluent, in spite of having enjoyed cars and servants and big houses during their years of service. You can't bank such perks: you can only enjoy them while you have them. Some solved the problem by purchasing property in places like the Algarve or Portugal where the cost of living at that time was considerably lower than in the UK. Others, however, had no choice but to return home to a poorer reality that they hoped they would never have to face.

As both the Hong Kong and Singapore offices began to grow we started to look for new markets, and in 1974, Malaysia seemed like the next place to go. Peter Bostock, the head of our Singapore office, was able to quickly find office space and staff and even some initial clients. We were confident that we could duplicate our success, as we had always been able to find the right approach to a new market. In Malaysia, with a growing number of companies entering the country with the desire to expand their public relations activities, we could provide what they needed.

One success in Malaysia was the launch of the Guinness Stout Effort Award scheme – a campaign to foster, recognize and reward civic consciousness and national pride among Malaysians. Journalists from various papers formed a panel of adjudicators and met monthly to select a person whose efforts had had a significant impact on the community. We arranged to have a recognized national or local leader hand over an award to a recipient in a ceremony which was covered in depth by the media. Our programme received Malaysian government praise for its contributions to building national pride and civic consciousness.

It soon became clear to me that individual countries have their own unique sensibilities. I was once asked in Malaysia to take part in giving prayers with a local religious leader to help drive away an evil spirit that some believed was frequenting the ladies' room in our office. The belief was so strong that some mothers did not want their daughters to come to work. While I in no way claimed any expertise in dealing with evil spirits or with ladies' rooms, I did what I was told, and fortunately the spirit was exorcised. Malaysia did turn out to be a very successful office for us and we grew to be the largest PR firm in the country, growing at a rate of 33 per cent in one year.

When we opened in Thailand we were lucky to find an American living there to run our office who was an expert in local customs. When I officially opened the office, he arranged for me to meet with Buddhist monks, and we exchanged gifts and prayers. It became apparent to our local staff that we believed in their culture and planned to honour it and work within it. This office also flourished.

The one thing that really surprised me as I worked throughout Asia, though, was the degree of corruption that we had to deal with. It still exists today but to a lesser degree than previously. Having been raised in New York, whose history includes Tammany Hall and Boss Tweed, both synonymous with corruption and greed, I always took it for granted that corruption existed everywhere. Of course, it still does, as was underlined when the *Daily Telegraph* detailed how many members of Parliament had illegally fiddled expense accounts to make claims on housing and other expenses that were unjustified. But in Asia it was much more a part of the local fabric, involving all levels of business and government.

India, which we opened a little later than our other Asian offices and which grew to be one of our biggest and most successful, had the dubious distinction of being a leader in corruption. There, for many companies, it was not a question of whether you had paid anyone off but rather how much and to how many people. I was working directly with the president of a small energy company head-quartered in Houston. He had opened offices in one section of India with an Indian minority partner and was quite optimistic about what the future held. That is until he found out the number of pay-offs he would have to make just to operate, let alone to secure any degree of success. I met with him and his partner in London and they named all the different people that would have to be paid and the amounts each would be expecting.

A few days later my client told me that he would be pulling out of India altogether. The US government had recently passed the US Foreign Corrupt Practices Act, after 400 companies had admitted to making questionable payments totalling more than $300 m to government officials. This amount was what was admitted so imagine what the real figure was. . . The new law made it illegal to make payments to a foreign official for the purpose of obtaining or retaining business, or directing business to a specific person. My client was an extremely strong believer in the reputation of his company and the need to be 100 per cent honest, so he pulled his entire operation out of India, never to return.

In certain Indian states, pay-offs are still the way of life. To make things happen, money has to change through many hands. I had a telling experience at an airport. I had gone through duty-free without purchasing anything when the official who was to stamp my passport to let me go through to my plane suggested that I go back and buy a bottle of liquor. I explained that I didn't want any liquor. He replied that I could give it to him, and he then began talking about some possible problems with my passport that he might have to investigate – problems that could force me to miss my flight. Of course he'd do his best to avoid delaying me and again suggested that I needed to buy some alcohol. I completely missed his point. I looked at him blankly and thanked him for wanting to help me. I told him it was very kind of him, I really didn't need the spirits but I appreciated his efforts. Again he intimated what he wanted, which I again completely misunderstood, and he then passed me through, shaking his head at my apparent stupidity.

In 1989, the *Wall Street Journal* wrote a major piece, 'Hard Going: India Beckons and Frustrates the Foreign Investors That it Sorely Needs'. India had thrown out the Coca-Cola Company because it had refused to surrender its secret formula, which it had done for nobody. There were also rules then that no outsider could purchase more than 40 per cent of an Indian company, and approval could take years according to government regulations. Of course, now things are much different as the country grows into a commercial giant, but no one I know who works there would say that corruption has disappeared. And in some of the smaller districts, it might even be growing.

But while corruption in India is rife, it doesn't mean that there aren't Indians who stand for the exact opposite. I was fortunate to work with one of the most important of these, S. P. Hinduja – head of one of India's and the world's wealthiest families, with a business empire comprised of oil, gas, power generation, heavy goods, truck manufacturing and banking. S. P. and G. P., the next oldest brother, live in London. One brother, Prakash, lives in Geneva, and the fourth brother, Ashok, lives in Mumbai. Twenty-five per cent of their enormous worldwide empire remains in India, and it is growing.

S. P., who is incredibly religious and family conscious, once said in a newspaper interview: 'Our concern as a group has always been how to do away with corruption. There is no point pointing fingers at others. We must demonstrate by example. These principles also keep the family together. We believe in complete transparency. The minute you let corruption in, you encourage them to manipulate, hide, lie; you're asking for trouble. That's how splits occur in family businesses. That's the price you pay.'

The Hinduja family founded a non-profit national hospital and research centre in Mumbai which now has 381 beds and is being expanded to 600. It is one of the country's most advanced hospitals and, among other firsts in Mumbai, it was the first to introduce MR angiography, high-resolution lung scanning, the first to perform laparoscopic gall bladder surgery, and the first to perform awake craniotomy for epilepsy. They have the latest equipment, and when I was interviewing a number of the doctors at the hospital who had all been practicing in the US, they all said they would not have returned to India to practice their profession if it had not been for a hospital of this quality.

It was through the Hindujas that Adele and I attended one of the greatest events we have ever witnessed: the wedding of S. P.'s daughter Shanu, which took place over the course of a ten-day ceremony in Mumbai in December 1987. The Hindujas are fervent Hindus and different days featured different rites with different people attending. We were present for four days, including for the official wedding itself. On one day we were sent the most beautiful Indian outfits to be worn and at that day's ceremony Adele's hands and feet were painted with special designs.

For the Hindujas, the ceremonies began on 9 December with the completion of twenty-four hours of continuous recitation of the Guru Granth Sahib, one of the Sikh holy scriptures. A few days later, after a series of family-hosted events, there was the invocation of Lord Ganesha, son of Shiva, who is considered by Hindus as the giver of success in any ventures. The wedding day itself was on 17 December and started with a private religious ceremony performed by a priest, followed by the tradition of the ladies of the family applying oil to the bride's hair, and the consecration of the platform where the wedding ceremony was to be held. Then, as part of the final procession, the groom mounted a *ghodi* (white mare) to take him to Param Jamuna, the Hinduja estate, where the wedding ceremony was to take place before 12,000 guests.

The ceremony started with priests invoking eight blessings, which included ones to the universe, the goddess of wealth, the god of the sea, and Brahma, the creator. The bride's father washed the bridegroom's feet, and the bridegroom prayed to the sun to give him strength. The bride's mother removed hair from the bridegroom's head and made a tuft of it with red thread. At five minutes past six, the sacred fire was lit, and the couple's hands were joined. Then the bride's parents gave away the bride to the bridegroom. A cow was then offered in a further ceremony before the bridegroom pronounced the new name of his bride. At this juncture, the bridal couple set eyes on each other for the first time.

Then, the ritual of the sacred fire began. First the bride led the groom around the fire, then the groom led the bride around. The brothers and maternal and paternal uncles of the bride then offered puffed rice to the sacred fire as a token of their having witnessed the wedding ceremony. Seven lots of rice were placed in front of the fire, only to be later brushed aside by the bride with her big right toe while she recited each of her vows. Then, the bride and bridegroom gave a series of promises to each other concerning what they would be responsible for. The groom sought Lord Vishnu's blessings and the bride said: 'You are my Guru, you are my everything. We shall always live in peace and tranquillity.'

Then, after being blessed with holy water, the bridegroom placed his arm on the right shoulder of the bride and said: 'We are now one on body, mind and soul.' Offerings were then made by the bridegroom and priests to Lord Brahma and, as a mark of respect, the bride's father offered a bowl of coins to the bridegroom's father before they embraced each other. To add to the festivities, the bride's parents offered sweets to all present at the wedding. But it didn't end there: the Hindujas, who are vegetarians, served a vegetarian feast made up of the most amazing dishes I have ever seen. Then there was a laser and fireworks display that I have rarely seen equalled.

For me, the highlight came soon after the ceremony. When Adele and I reached the bride and groom to pay our respects, S. P. stopped the line and said: 'This is the only person who lectures me', before taking Adele and I to be photographed with the newlyweds and their families. He later sent us a personal album of pictures of us at the various ceremonies. These were moments not to be easily forgotten.

While corruption ran rampant in India, Indonesians at that time were probably even more skilled at soliciting bribes. For example, the officials in charge of letting in exhibitions for local trade shows were always taken good care of or you could be waiting a long time for your exhibit materials to be unloaded from the boat and delivered to the show. The amount of bribery going on should have been apparent to the government, as many very low-level officials lived in homes they couldn't possibly afford on their salaries. Their bosses were well aware of the situation but left it alone.

Foreigners learned to accept bribery as a way of life and the accepted way of doing business in Indonesia. You often gave a tip at the airport to the person labelling your luggage or else there would be a possibility you would go to Singapore and your suitcase might go to Australia. There existed a set of informal rules governing bribery ensuring things didn't get out of hand, as exemplified by the story a client told me.

He was driving with a chauffeur in a small town in Indonesia when a policeman pulled him over and asked for his passport. The officer took a look at it and kept shaking his head. My client asked his driver what was wrong. The driver said, 'He would like a little something. Or else he can order you to the police station where he could keep you for a couple of hours and then let you go. But by then you could miss your meeting.' My client told the driver to ask the policeman what he wanted and give it to him. When he named his amount the driver became very angry and said, 'You know this offence is only worth half that, and that's what you're going to get.' The policeman accepted the lower amount and allowed them to drive away.

There were variations on this kind of policing in other countries. One of my staff in Malaysia was pulled over for a supposed driving offence by a policeman and was told he could pay the fine directly to him. When he asked how much he was told the amount but that it would be cut in half if he didn't ask for a receipt.

An Asian Intelligence report by the Hong Kong-based Political and Economic Risk Consultancy included a survey of expatriate business executives in the region asking them to rate the countries on corruption. Indonesia was voted the most corrupt, with India coming in second. Regarding Indonesia, the report said: 'A series of high-profile cases highlighted the extent to which politically influential individuals were able to arrange matters to their own financial benefit.' A fascinating editorial in the *International Herald Tribune* noted that corruption in Asia is often a companion or stimulant for economic expansion. For sometimes pay-offs allowed companies to enter a region or expand, which they might not have been allowed to do without the payments.

In explaining in this editorial piece how corruption can differ, and how it is largely endemic in Asia, Robert Elegant wrote:

Malaysia, Thailand, the Philippines and Indonesia were not primarily shaped by the teachings of the ancient Chinese political philosopher Confucius. In those non-Confucion countries the ruler had the aura of semi-divinity that clothes the ruler – whether raja or king, as in the past, or president or prime minister today – has sanctioned corrupt practices. Because they are so far above the people, the rulers and ministers are virtually required to take whatever they want. They often do so.

In Confucian Asia – Korea, Japan, China, Vietnam and Taiwan – another imperative operates. Since his primary Confucian duty is to his family, every official is expected to take graft so that he can support his kinfolk lavishly.

While I might not agree completely with all of the above there was no doubt in my mind that many Western businesses in Asia considered pay-offs to those in authority as business as usual. Fortunately, we did not have to get involved in pay-offs either for the firm or on behalf of our clients, but there is no way for me to know what our clients did or didn't do.

We once did become embroiled, to our detriment, in the US Foreign Corrupt Practices Act. Before we had our own Indonesian office, we had a local partner who handled activities for us. He put out releases, set up interviews and handled press conferences. He was organizing a press conference for a client we handled out of Singapore, Chemical Bank. When it was over, he sent the bill directly to the client – mistakenly – rather than sending it to us first for review and editing before it went to the client.

On the itemized bill he had written 'Payment to the Press' for a relatively small expense. The reason for this is that the press in those days had limited funds, and in Indonesia you often paid travel expenses for journalists who travelled to press conferences from different parts of the country. The client, upon receiving this bill, thought that such a payment to the press could possibly violate the Foreign Corrupt Practices Act. They cancelled all work by

Burson–Marsteller on their behalf throughout Asia. . . It took a few months before we were able to convince them that this was not a bribe. Eventually they gave the account back to us.

Corruption has certainly not gone away. In Africa, it is probably getting worse. The US government has decided to try and fight it more strongly, and, in 2011, 150 companies were being investigated for violations of the Foreign Corrupt Practices Act. During the last three years, the US government has collected $3bn in fines for violations of the act. Other countries too are taking a greater look at corruption and in July 2011 the UK Bribery Act came into force.

As we continued to expand throughout Asia and other parts of the world, it became obvious that our overseas activities were fuelling our growth in the US. More and more companies were facing public relations issues that were worldwide in nature. One of the single best examples of this globalization was the Dalkon Shield case. You wouldn't think that a company would hire a public relations firm to let women throughout the world know that they had the right to sue them and should by a certain date. . . And then be pleased that the campaign was so successful that claims were being filed from as far away as Bangladesh and Botswana. Or that the person the PR firm had to satisfy with the results was not a corporate executive but a United States federal judge. But that is what happened.

The Dalkon Shield was an intrauterine birth control device. Made of plastic, it was oval in shape with small fins extending from its right and left sides and a tail string to facilitate its proper placement and removal. It was developed in the late sixties in the United States and marketed by the Dalkon Corporation, which sold about 27,000 of them. In June 1970, the A. H. Robins Company of Richmond, Virginia, acquired the product and began to market it vigorously both in the United States and abroad. By 1974, it was estimated that 2.2 million Dalkon Shields were implanted in American women and

1.4 million in women outside the US. Half of those used outside the US had been distributed through the Agency for International Development (AID), which was actively promoting birth control.

But by 1973, problems had begun to arise. The company started receiving reports that the product had been linked with certain medical complications and it notified the US Food and Drug Administration (FDA). After discussions with the FDA, Robins decided to withdraw the Dalkon Shield from the market pending further study. The FDA conducted its own study and decided that the company could resume marketing the shield with certain modifications and a special system in place for registering patients. Until 1983 the position of the FDA was that women who were using it without complication had no need to have it removed. But the company was getting concerned and decided to remove the product from the market, and by March 1985 sales were discontinued.

However, this did not end the story. Many women still had Dalkon Shields implanted in them. Articles in medical journals were suggesting a possible relationship between the duration of use of intrauterine devices and pelvic infections. So, in 1980, Robins advised doctors and clinics to remove the Dalkon Shield from women using it even if the device was causing no complications. In 1984, by which time they had begun to face litigation by women claiming injury, they again urged all women using a Dalkon Shield to remove it. By August 1985, as a result of the growing number of lawsuits, the company felt it had no alternative but to file for reorganization under the US bankruptcy code before a federal judge in Virginia. The judge, however, could not authorize the reorganization until he knew what the outstanding liabilities of the company were and this included the possible damages that could result from future lawsuits. To quantify these. the judge established a cut-off date of 30 April 1986, after which the company would no longer have liability. But to protect women who had legitimate claims, he told the company that they must make every effort to notify all users of their legal rights no matter where they resided. This was not difficult in the US, but Dalkon Shields were being worn in eighty other countries, and every user had the same rights in US federal courts.

In the US, the company embarked on a public relations programme and advertising campaign costing $2.5m to reach potential claimants. It was estimated that a similar advertising campaign to reach all the other countries, even at its most basic, would cost $50m. There was no way the judge would authorize that expenditure, as this would dramatically cut the amount left available for claimants whose lawsuits were successful. I met in Washington with our health care experts who were representing A. H. Robins and arranged for our offices and affiliates round the world to provide input on how to publicize the claims procedure in a way that would meet the judge's demands. In the judge's official words, 'Burson–Marsteller designed a public relations programme whose general purpose was to disseminate the foreign notice as widely as possible without direct payment of advertising.'

For such a programme to be effective, especially in the time frame the judge had established, there was a need to harness all those organizations that would spread the message. The media, I believed, would be very supportive because this was a public service campaign and not an attempt to sell a product. But equally important were medical organizations, health officials and government agencies that had their own channels of communication to their publics. Because the 'client' was in effect a federal judge, the controls had to be tight. All initial news releases and accompanying background material were to be approved by the court. Twenty-nine languages were involved and each of the translators had to swear before notaries that the translations were true and accurate.

We sent press releases and detailed background papers to more than 4,800 media outlets. All the major international wire services carried the story, as did the BBC and the Voice of America. Sixteen press conferences were organized at which client spokesmen provided the complete background to the story. Letters were sent to medical associations, health ministers and the US Embassy in every country where the shield had been distributed. AID sent background material to all its missions. About 770 personal contacts were made with organizations such as the World Health Organization in Geneva and UNESCO in Paris. Information went to 567 medical organizations, 447 Planned Parenthood units and 5,760 other organizations. Expenses for every single activity in each country had to be itemized and documented.

When the drive was over and the results were presented to the judge, he declared, 'The court finds the results of the foreign notice not only staggering but comprehensive. The notice reached women in eighty-one foreign countries.' What really swayed him was the fact that before the PR campaign became active there had been 16,000 claims – a figure dwarfed by the 300,000 women who went to file claims before the 30 April deadline. Some consumer rights organizations wanted to move the deadline back to allow for more complaints to register. They appealed the district court's decision. But after listening to the appeal, the judge's decision was upheld unanimously by the three-man appeal court. The court said, 'It appears to this court the extensive notification was a success. Women from such unlikely locations as Kenya, Botswana, Pakistan and Bangladesh ultimately filed claims.'

Thanks to a campaign that cost less than $1 m, women from all over the world learned about the situation and were compensated for personal damage caused by the use of a faulty product. Moreover, we gained great respect for both the American legal system and for the good that public relations can accomplish when aimed in the right direction. This gave me the opportunity to merchandise how effective our worldwide capabilities had become. While this project was particularly unique, we were finding that more and more news releases increasingly had to cover greater parts of the globe. Hong Kong had become the PR hub for Asia, in addition to being its news centre.

I saw how important it was to have a presence there and had to spend more and more time there. I didn't mind at all: the city had many appealing attributes and a major one was food. Hong Kong was then the Mecca of Chinese cuisine. You could have Peking duck served to you as it was to the emperor when his capital was Peking. The food was far better than in the Republic of China and probably still is today. In China, each region had its own specialities, but Hong Kong had restaurants that featured the main five schools of Chinese cooking: Pekingese, Cantonese, Shanghainese, Sichuan and Chiu Chow, along with some offshoots such as Hunamese and Hakka.

Since Chinese people from all walks of life ate out more frequently than any other people I had encountered, the number of restaurants in Hong Kong was awesome. So were the portion sizes. Sunday lunch, a timeless tradition, included every member of the family, from the youngest infant to the eldest of the family elders – all of them gathered around a large round table. The noise level in large dining rooms was ear-splitting. A lot of the dishes offered in these restaurants would surprise the Western gourmet: with a constantly rising population, the Chinese learned not to discard but to cut and cook to advantage every part of just about every animal imaginable. High on the list of frequently consumed delicacies were chicken feet, fish lips and snake soup – which were not to the taste of most westerners.

In my career, I was most fortunate in two very important ways. I had a job that increasingly took me to new and exciting parts of the world, and I had a wife who loved to visit and explore with me. She was equally happy whether visiting the Black Hole of

Calcutta, the jungles of South Africa or the museums of Florence. And though the number of hours at work I put in, which could include fourteen-hour days, never concerned me, I strongly believe that holidays away from work are an important part of anyone's lifestyle. It certainly became central to ours.

Highlights of our travels, excluding Europe which we grew to know intimately, included Petra in Jordan, Jerusalem, Baalbek in Lebanon, the Valley of the Kings in Egypt, Iguaçu Falls in Argentina, Rio de Janeiro during Carnival, the Inca ruins of Machu Picchu in Peru – which maintained their uniqueness because the Spanish never found them when they conquered the area – and the ruins of Chichén Itzá and Teotihuacán in Mexico.

Asia provided us with the greatest number of special memories. These included Agra and the Taj Mahal in India, the ruins of Pagan in Burma, ruins in Thailand at Sukhothai, the Buddhist monument in Borobudur in Indonesia, Bali in Indonesia before it became overrun by tourists (the one Hindu-dominated island in an otherwise totally Muslim country) and cities in Malaysia where festivals were the norm. I'm not even including Japan and China in this list – they will come later.

The two places we remember most fondly and still constantly think about – for extremely different reasons – are Fiji and Tibet. After a period that had been extremely hectic, I needed a few weeks off. I wasn't interested in seeing another of the world's unique sites. I just wanted to rest. Someone suggested we go to Turtle Island in the Fijis. Very few people knew this island, even though it had been featured in a movie with Brooke Shields called *The Blue Lagoon*.

At this time there was only one hotel on the island, which was owned by a rich American. The hotel only had fourteen habitable cabins so there were usually no more than twenty-eight guests and no children. One flew in on a small aircraft from Suva in Fiji to be greeted by musicians at the dock near the landing strip. The large staff were extremely friendly and accommodating. Breakfast and lunch were served individually and at whatever time a guest requested it but dinner was a group event with everyone gathering in the hotel dining room. There were as many beaches on the island as there were couples visiting. The staff really catered to the guests. One day a young Australian couple on their honeymoon were taken to a beach accompanied by a number of staffers and were treated to a magnificent private wedding dinner on the beach.

The highlight of our stay came with the appearance of Ringo Starr of the Beatles and his wife Barbara Bach, who had become famous as the lead girl in the James Bond movie, *The Spy Who Loved Me*. Their cabin was far up into the hills where they enjoyed complete privacy. But nearly every evening, they joined the group for dinner. Ringo couldn't have been nicer. He sometimes would play during the day with the hotel musical staff, and he became friendly with the young honeymoon couple, giving them a number of his records. Barbara Bach told us that it was one of the few holiday spots that Ringo really wanted to return to, and we could appreciate why he felt that way.

The weather was ideal, the beaches magnificent, the food and drinks superb. No one could ask for more. On some days we were taken by boat to other Fijian islands to meet and have lunch with local tribal chiefs who were fascinating to talk to, telling us about the history of Fiji and their current way of life. Unlike Ringo, my wife and I had no desire to return to this paradise. We felt this was a once in a lifetime holiday and that our wonderful experience could never be equalled on another visit.

Despite enjoying Fiji tremendously, the most memorable time we ever had abroad was in Tibet in 1986. While living in Hong Kong, a friend introduced me to a guide for a travel company who specialized in tours of Tibet. He was a Scot and had studied the Tibetan language and culture at university in Scotland. He was married to a Tibetan woman and spoke fluent Tibetan. I decided Tibet was a must and convinced two other American couples – one living in the US and one in the UK – to join us for the trip the following autumn. I made all the necessary arrangements for two weeks in Tibet and then a few days in Kathmandu in Nepal.

Shortly before we were scheduled to go, the storm hit. The Chinese decided to take greater control of Tibet, arresting many Tibetans and shooting those who resisted. They closed the border with Nepal and refused to allow any visitors into the country, except tour groups that had already registered for a tour previously. We decided we would take the risk of trying to get in and so flew to Chengdu so that we could fly directly into Tibet from China – our thinking was that that would increase our chances of being let in.

The tour guide had arranged for a Tibetan lama to be our driver and to meet us at the airport. When we arrived in Lhasa, I was able to convince the Chinese authorities that we were an official tour group and had booked this trip months in advance, which was true. After a period of uncertainty, they allowed us in. From the very beginning, starting with the drive from the airport, Tibet was an amazing place to see. View after view was unimaginable.

However, another major problem disrupted our trip soon enough, after the initial Chinese interference. The weather – incessant snow – was the worst it had been for decades at this time of year. Many climbers were being brought down from the mountains, some injured. Six tourists were found frozen to death.

The tour guide was proving to be unbelievably resourceful. Everywhere he took us he was well-known, and in most places we were the only tourists. We heard fascinating lectures and singing performances by monks and their students in their monasteries. The tour started with the Potala Palace, the most famous of all palaces in Tibet, which had been the home of the Dalai Lama before he fled the Chinese and set up camp in India. This had happened shortly before our arrival. We were taken to the White Palace where the Dalai Lama lived, the Red Palace devoted to religious studies and Buddhist prayers and the Saint's Chapel, the holiest shrine. We were even shown the private apartments of the Dalai Lama and his mother, which included, much to my surprise, a relatively modern bathroom with American appliances. Many years later I had the opportunity to meet with the Dalai Lama himself when he gave a talk at the Foreign Press Association in London. I'm sorry that I never told him about my visit to his home.

Never in all my travels had I taken such a fascinating 'insider' tour of an important place. But it turns out that there was a reason why our guide was so good. We later found out that he was an agent for the supporters of the Dalai Lama and that his job was to visit key locations and find out which Tibetans had been killed or arrested by the Chinese. If the Chinese had discovered his role while we were with him, I am sure we would have needed legal assistance or perhaps divine intervention to stay out of jail.

The weather, meanwhile, continued to be miserable, causing landslides that made the road between Tibet and Nepal, where we were heading next, impassable by bus. We were told that the bus could take us as far as our next hotel, but no further. Then, if we were prepared to take a thirty-kilometre walk across the mountains, we could get to our final destination in Tibet, a village on the border with Nepal.

Our last stop before reaching the hotel was Tingri, where, to our surprise, we were put up in a Chinese army barracks. The Chinese had confiscated half of the village and razed it to the ground, and then put up their camp. Surprisingly, we were given a hearty welcome by the Chinese soldiers and received as their guests. They served us a meal which consisted mainly of cabbage prepared in different ways. Our Tibetan driver could not join us, since the Chinese always served foreigners separately from themselves and the Tibetans. The rooms were filthy and each had three beds. We pushed two beds together and got under all the bedding and kept our clothes on, including woollen hats and scarves, as the temperature had reached -29 °C (-20 °F) during the night. Candles were lit only for a short time. We received two thermoses of hot water for washing up. Unfortunately the loo was outside, far away across an icy, snow-covered field. It turned out to be a filthy slit in the ground, so we only used it out of extreme necessity.

The next day we began the last leg of our bus ride. We finally arrived at our hotel, a place you would only stay in by choice if you were there to receive last rites. If cleanliness was next to godliness, the hotel was run by a band of heathens. It was incredibly crowded due to unfortunate circumstances: members of an Australian climbing team who were unable to complete their climb because of the weather were staying there, along with men from a failed British Everest expedition. Unfortunately the British climbers had lost one of their Sherpas to an avalanche, and the victim's brother had stood nearby helplessly watching him go under. Another injured Sherpa was waiting at the hotel for a ride to Lhasa, where he was to have his leg amputated.

Now we were faced with a final question: should we walk along one of the highest mountains in the world for thirty kilometres to get to a hotel bordering Nepal? Or should we take the bus back to Lhasa and fly home? All three middle-aged couples voted: 'Onwards!' Our Tibetan guide rounded up a group of local guides and donkeys for us, because all our belongings would have to be carried by them.

We soon realized that each of the couples walked at a different pace. One couple, the man and woman both being fitness freaks and in great shape, were to start first. We were next, and the other couple who made us look like Olympians in comparison, were last. So off we went with some candy bars to eat and plastic cups – because we could drink the snow off the mountains. And so started one of the most exhilarating journeys of our married life, a scene my son still finds difficult to imagine: his parents walking across the mountains of Tibet in freezing weather.

We reached a place on the path with two choices: one a downhill rock climb, the other one longer but safer. We chose the more dangerous route, and some porters stayed with us to provide a helping hand when necessary. We found our guide and the rest of the porters with the luggage resting at the bottom. He told us the rest of trip was relatively straightforward, so they went ahead to the hotel, planning to get us registered, change money and make further arrangements concerning our stay in Nepal. Off they went, and we were left with no maps, no food, no torches, no liquid containers, no survival kits. I was a bit worse for wear having fallen in the final rock descent. I'd had my breath knocked out of me and had hyperventilated.

Not too far from where we were heading, we came across another Chinese army camp. Again, this was fortunate. Some of the soldiers decided to accompany us. A good portion of the mountain overlooking Tramo, where we were going, had collapsed, and we would need to scramble over three very steep and slippery rock falls to reach the village. Falling could be very dangerous, and the soldiers insisted on carrying my wife over the third rock fall, which was the most dangerous. We reached a series of tent villages where we could see a fire in the middle of each tent, with lots of faces sitting around it lit up by firelight. Since we would have to descend a good 1,000 feet in the dark to reach the hotel, one of the boys led us through a longer but safer route. We reached the border village and were shown the way to our hotel. It was satisfactory but far from memorable and we were up early so we could be at the Chinese Custom House for clearance by 9 a.m. when it opened.

The Chinese customs people were somewhat rude. They were mainly looking to confiscate any writings relating to the Dalai Lama.

Our guide, who was smart enough to know this, had no such material. We crossed the border into Nepal and found a truck driver offering to take us to Kathmandu for an outrageous sum. We had no choice and started on what was an incredibly scary ride with numerous hairpin turns on small roads looking down thousands of feet. But the driver knew his business and got us to the Oberoi, Kathmandu's luxury hotel, where the staff were especially glad to see us arrive. They had just hosted a major conference of heads of states from surrounding countries, including Indira Gandhi, and a number of the staff mentioned that government officials never tip.

I will save Kathmandu for you to read about in guide books but will end by saying that the beauty of the mountains of Tibet would be tough to emulate.

Holidays aside, from the time I started our Asian operations to the present day, public relations has grown dramatically and continues to do so. But certain things have remained the same. It is extremely rare to have a pan-Asian PR campaign. The countries, the clients, the staff and the key audiences are very different, all unique, and you have to understand each country individually if you are going to operate effectively. The only thing that is the same throughout Asia is that personal relationships are far more important for business than in any other part of the world.

6   Japan

In Japan, saving face means everything. I found that out the first time I tried to find our office in Tokyo. Finding my way in that great city was not easy, especially in certain quarters where buildings used to be numbered according to when they were built rather than their position on the street. Number one could be next to number five and number two could be on the other side, two streets down from number one. This is no longer the case, but back then the phenomenon even caught the attention of the *Washington Post*, which published an article about a woman living in Tokyo on a street with no name off another street with no name where her house and five others were numbered twenty-two. Getting around was a challenge in those days.

When going to my Tokyo office for the first time, I entered a taxi and told the driver the address I wanted. He wasn't sure exactly where that was but drove off in what he thought was the right direction. Then he suddenly pulled over in front of the Israel Embassy and asked a guard who appeared to know and seemed to be sending us in the right direction. Even with the guard's advice, the taxi driver still couldn't find the office. He drove to a few places around where he thought the office might be, but he still wasn't getting it right. I suggested he call my office for assistance, and I gave him the business card with the telephone number. When he called, he found that we had pulled over just opposite the office. Some of the staff went to the window and waved to him. This gesture made him lose face to such a degree that he refused to take any fare from me and drove off apparently chastened.

Now that we were well established in Hong Kong and Singapore, it was very important that we set up in Japan, as this was a key country for many of our clients. Harold Burson and I had a series of meetings with representatives of Fuji Ad Systems Corporation (Fasco), a subsidiary of Fuji Bank and a member of the Fuyo Group – a number of companies that when combined were then responsible for nearly 10 per cent of the country's gross national product (GNP).

There was no way that we could afford to start an ad agency of our own from scratch in Tokyo. Instead, we came to an agreement with Fasco that our ad agency, Marsteller, would become part of Marsteller/Fuji and be under their control. Burson–Marsteller/Fuji, part of the overall group, on the other hand, would be under our control, and we would run it in the same way as we ran other Burson–Marsteller offices.

After I helped set up the Japan office, I visited Tokyo at least once a year for the next fifteen years. My experiences in the country taught me to appreciate the words of a Jesuit priest who once said, 'Now that I have lived in Japan for twenty-five years, I am beginning to partially understand the Japanese.' It amazes me that the priest was able to attain even that degree of knowledge in such a relatively short time. In those days, there was no other country where the need was greater for Western businessmen to truly understand the local culture and the perceptions of the native people. This was not always easy and many Western businesses suffered accordingly. While some things have changed from the time when I first launched our Tokyo office, many things have remained exactly the same.

Let's start with business cards. Nowhere else is the business card treated with such respect. After the Second World War, General MacArthur encouraged the Japanese to become less formal. At that time, when two Japanese people met, they automatically exchanged cards before even speaking. The card would not only provide information about the person's name, but it would announce his position, indicating which of the two had to bow lower.

When we started doing business in Japan, business cards still had to be treated with great respect. Every person you met had to be handed a card. To leave anyone out was to diminish his status, so it was advisable to always have many, many business cards on you. But it was important always to greet the most senior executive first and then go down the line in order of rank. Presenting a card first to someone more junior was an insult to those higher up. I was warned always to present my card with two hands, to never fumble with it, or hand it out casually. The business card was, in effect, an extension of the person giving it, and immediately set a tone of respect – or lack of it.

When receiving a card, you had to give it obvious attention and inspect it with care. If you just dropped it into your pocket or shoved it into your wallet, you were disrespecting your opposite number. While this form of etiquette seems trivial to many in the West, it could set the tone of personal and business relationships. A senior Japanese executive with our firm once called me in London and asked me to tell one of our senior people visiting Tokyo to stop his habit of taking out his business card and playing with it before giving it out. 'To the Japanese' he said, 'this is the equivalent of masturbation.'

Strict formality was a must in all interactions in this country. This high standard remained the same whether one was dealing with friends, foes, strangers or colleagues. Our senior Japanese partners never once called me by my first name. To do so, they felt, would be an insult, as I was senior to them. In turn, they did not want me to use their first names. If I did, others might follow suit, even their own employees, and this would be alien to their culture.

Small talk had a large meaning in Japan and was always a prelude to business. They wanted to know about you – your likes, dislikes, where you had just come from, when you will leave and where you were going. Then they were ready to discuss more serious matters.

It took quite a while for many American companies to get a grip on these problems when negotiating in Japan. Even simple words would cause a problem. For example, when you asked a Japanese executive if he wanted to make a deal with your company, and he answered, 'Hai', you might think you had a deal, pack your bags and head home with a smile on your face, congratulating yourself for a job well done. Imagine the surprise later to find that the company you thought you had an agreement with had turned around and made a deal with a competitor. You were not being lied to, because in reality 'Hai' does not mean, 'Yes, we have a deal', but rather, 'Yes, I have heard you ask me if I want a joint venture with you.'

One great difference between our cultures is patience. Many Western executives want things to happen quickly. They need to sign an agreement before they fly home. The Japanese are in no such hurry. They feel that they could finalize a deal on the negotiator's next trip. Or the one after that. There were times, though, when they might use this sense of hurry to their advantage and ask for something a little extra just as the visiting executive's departure time approached.

This lack of understanding between the cultures often created an unfortunate effect on many westerners. They ascribed motives to the Japanese that were often untrue. Many felt they could not penetrate the Japanese psyche and that something devious was lurking there. I am not intimating that some Japanese do not sometimes use their inscrutability and westerners' impatience to their own advantage. The key, however, is the difference in our cultures, not in our ethics. The lesson is that if one is operating in an alien culture, one must try to understand it in order to succeed.

I found the Japanese to be incredibly polite, and this has not changed over the years. This is not a ploy. They are extremely serious about politeness and in no way ever want to insult you. One evening I was giving a speech in Tokyo before a section of the Keidanren, the Japanese equivalent of the Confederation of British Industries or the American National Association of Manufacturers. The audience was sizeable. The turnout was not so much a tribute to my reputation as a modern-day Demosthenes as to the Japanese sense of politeness. It would have been too great an insult for a guest to speak at an important organization in front of a sparse audience. The host made sure people turned out and that I would see a full room as I rose to the podium, even if he had to go and rent a crowd.

An evening lecture provided problems of its own. Work for the Japanese usually started quite early. Many of the audience arrived very tired. Even an honest desire to learn something new could not overcome fatigue. So many in the audience did fall asleep, but they politely attempted to nap surreptitiously by resting their head on their hands. Thus, they would appear to be in deep thought, contemplating how to take advantage of the deep wisdom I was imparting. Since the translation was not simultaneous and the translator would speak only when I paused, I could stand there waiting for the translator to catch up while watching quite a number of my audience pass blissfully from contemplation to slumber.

My translator was as interesting to me as my audience. Sometimes, after I had spoken a few sentences or so, he would translate for what appeared to be five minutes. Other times I would hold forth for quite a while, before turning over to him. He then uttered a few sentences, convinced he had transmitted all of my meanings to his satisfaction. Those awake in the audience really seemed to enjoy what I supposedly had said. I have always believed that his speech must have been much better than mine.

Back then, but possibly not to the same degree now, Japanese companies followed a policy of gift-giving that we decided to emulate. There were then customary payments of congratulatory money, condolence money and compensation for injuries. This provided an insight into the then prevalent Japanese thinking; that employees were there forever and in reality were part of the family. Each new child was provided with 10,000 yen – a substantial sum at the time. The same was given to families with stillborn babies or whose babies had died before the birth notice was sent. But in the latter case it was paid as a compensation for injury, and no condolence money was given.

Upon marriage, an employee could count on a congratulatory gift of 20,000 yen (£160). There was no congratulatory gift for a second marriage, though. If both employees to be married were members of the company, each received congratulatory money. When an employee died while still working for a firm, his chief mourner received 100,000 yen. If an employee's spouse died, the survivor received 50,000 yen. If he is chief mourner he received 20,000 yen for the death of father, mother or child. If he was not the chief mourner, he collected 10,000 yen.

Companies also helped out employees if they experienced a property disaster. If an employee's house burned down or was lost in a flood, he received 100,000 yen. If only half burnt, or was damaged rather than totally lost, he received 60,000 yen. Many companies also contributed to an employee's funeral and some even to ex-employees', since in those days most employees worked for one company for life. It was rare to change jobs as there was a built-in loyalty within both the employee and the employer.

If an employee looked like he might cause a problem, he was moved somewhere else in the organization where he could be neutralized. If he remained a serious problem, little by little his status was diminished to such a degree that the only honourable thing left for him was to take early retirement.

The paternalistic stance of Japanese companies made it difficult for militant unions to make any headway in Japan. Very few workers wanted to make waves. Very few workers needed to make waves. That is why when Japanese companies went abroad they were often uncomfortable with the local unions who played by different ground rules. Even more difficult for them to cope with, for example, was the concept of a plant having many different unions as in Britain, with each fighting its own turf war.

When Nissan was looking throughout Europe for a place to establish its major manufacturing facility, it decided on England only after the trade unions agreed there would be only one union. They did make one compromise in return. The workers did not have to sing the company song, which was then the practice in Japan. And Nissan allowed us to give media training to their personnel director and other members of staff – something that would not take place in Japan.

One thing that made me appreciative of the Japanese was that I always found them to be very hard-working and loyal employees. They would never be critical of the company, of other employees, or of the client and their employees. It was often very difficult however, to know what they were really thinking. And sometimes when you did find out, the answer was quite unexpected.

One young Japanese executive had really impressed me. I was surprised when I received a telex in London informing me that he had handed in an official letter of resignation. As I've noted, it was quite rare for a Japanese employee to change companies, even if unhappy. Since I was coming to Tokyo the following week, I telexed back to the general manager asking him to ask the employee to reconsider until I arrived and had a chance to meet with him. The employee was extremely surprised that I wanted to meet with him, because rarely in Japan would an international chairman meet with a young executive.

When I asked him why he wanted to leave, his answer was quite direct. He did not believe he was good enough to work for us. He was not going to another company. In fact he had no offers and had, as of yet, approached no one. He sincerely believed he was not of our calibre and so would eventually be letting us down. Our general manager had talked to clients and senior executives, and they all thought highly of him. I told him this and also that I felt he had an excellent future if he stayed. I asked him to please go home, to reconsider his resignation, and to come back to see me the next day. He was unquestionably stunned.

We met again the next day. He said that if he had had any idea of how we felt about him, he would never have resigned. But he had no alternative but to leave because his wife and mother had seen the letter of resignation (and thus he would lose face), and so he did leave. When I next heard of him, he was a clerk in a store.

I came across 'face' again when during a later trip to Tokyo I learned that one of the executive secretaries, whom I thought highly of, was getting married. I asked the senior Japanese staff if it would be acceptable for me to send a telegram of congratulations to the wedding ceremony. They said the bride and groom would be extremely honoured by this coming from the international chairman and the letter itself would receive a place of honour in their home. I sent the telegram and was surprised that I never received an acknowledgement. After the wedding took place I spoke to an executive who attended the ceremony, and he said my telegram had never arrived and never been read. My secretary checked and confirmed it had been sent.

Months later when the British chief executive of the Tokyo office was having dinner at my home in London, he told me of the upcoming wedding of someone else whom I was fond of and I asked him if I should try again. He said, 'Bob send it to me at the office. I will make sure she gets it. We found out what happened to your last telegram. At that wedding, there was someone assigned to read greetings. The person given this task could not read English. As this would have caused him a great loss of face, your telegram had to disappear.'

Entertainment has always been looked at differently in Japan than in the West, where expense accounts are scrutinized to make sure executives, especially those at a lower level, are not living off the company. In Japan, management demanded that employees entertain key customers, no matter what their level, and this did not mean at McDonald's. In fact, many Japanese executives were forced to entertain more than they would have liked to. It was extremely rare for a wife to be included, for home life and business life were completely separate.

The Japanese are a generous people. One evening, I was the guest of honour at the home of the director of one of our Japanese partners. He had a mixed-style apartment, part-Japanese with tatami mats and part-Western. He hired a sushi chef to prepare dinner. The chef brought out types of fish that I didn't know even existed, all flavoursome. I was told by one of our Japanese staff who was in attendance that the dinner would have cost at least $4,000.

Another director took me to a very old Japanese restaurant that had once been a farmhouse for a veritable feast. The third course was sashimi. The host was surprised and amazed when I told him sashimi was a favourite dish of mine. We talked and drank sake for what seemed a very long time without the arrival of the next course. The waiter then arrived and placed before me a very large, beautiful rose. I looked at it for a while before realizing that this rose had been made from red tuna. This was sashimi in its most pleasing form. I can't imagine what my host's gesture cost him.

Since wives are usually not part of the company social mix, family relationships differ widely from their Western counterparts. A senior Japanese employee told me about life in his suburb. One husband usually arrived at home at a reasonable time, between 8.30 and 9.00 p.m. His wife told him the other wives in the neighbourhood were convinced he could not have a very important job. All of *their* husbands came home later or often stayed in town. She told her husband it would be best if he began arriving home later since she was losing face.

Giving gifts in foreign countries can be fraught with danger. Lyndon Johnson, when he was president of the United States, alienated the Dutch while visiting their country because he handed out ballpoint pens. They thought he was equating them with a third world country. I was told gift-giving took place mainly over two periods in Japan. One was in summer and one around Christmas. Important customers or clients must be given important gifts. At that time food such as steaks, which were then very expensive in Japan, were popular gifts, as were food hampers. Presentation was important. Much attention must be given to the gift paper and the ribbon, along with the calligraphy which made up the accompanying note. Should a gift of money be given to a major customer's son or daughter upon their marriage, the banknotes had to be new.

The Japanese are able to maintain a very strong, indigenous culture, partly because they are the most homogeneous society of any major industrial country. Except for a small percentage of resident Koreans, there is very little other ethnic influence. Foreigners are welcomed, or at least accepted, but they seldom become a real part of Japanese society, and thus do not create subcultures as immigrant groups do in other countries. By contrast, in the US, Chicago has the second largest number of Poles living in a city after Warsaw, while London is increasingly cosmopolitan.

This strong traditional culture meant that Burson–Marsteller

Japan would be much different from any other Burson–Marsteller office. We would certainly have far fewer indigenous clients than elsewhere. Japanese companies were far more comfortable with Japanese PR firms, such as Dentsu. And they did not believe in public relations as we knew it and were far more comfortable with advertising. Many companies were far happier working with their inside PR staff than with outside consultants. And this was, and still is, a reason that far more college graduates who have studied communications prefer an in-house job when joining the PR industry.

The Japanese have always lived in a world of consensus. Finding a company spokesman was sometimes very difficult. Very few Japanese employees want to be pushed to the forefront. And it is very rare to suggest anything that in any way questions some decision made by a superior. These accepted practices make it difficult whether you are in-house or an outside consultant looking in to solve a problem.

While American companies have changed dramatically in giving authority to overseas divisions, the Japanese in most cases haven't. Control comes from the top and stays at the top. Recently, in the case of Toyota, this tendency came home to roost. Toyota employees in the US were aware of possible safety problems with Toyota's vehicles, and some were even brave enough to inform their immediate supervisors. But these warnings were not heeded by headquarters. Toyota suffered accordingly. Nothing made this fact clearer than when James Lentz, the company's president of US sales, admitted to the US House Committee on Energy and Commerce that all safety decisions were made in Tokyo.

Toyota's US business is the third largest automobile company in the US and provides an estimated two thirds of the company's profits. Yet, rather than have a single headquarters for the US they kept the operation broken into various functions, with each reporting back to Japan. Thus, Toyota was slow to respond and unclear in their initial explanation of the problems. One American executive noted that 'Toyota's internal distrust and flawed communications are the root causes of its current crisis.'

Crisis management planning or crisis training is not inherent in most Japanese management thinking. Nor do they usually train spokesmen on the messages that should be aimed at key audiences because, as noted, they like to act in unison rather than individually.

Even in Japan itself there is much too much central control. An American ambassador said that 'Japanese companies are incredibly innovative but they find it much harder to turn their ideas into products.' He noted that innovations in a large company that do not fit into its strategic plans are much more likely to go to waste than in the US. He also explained that Japanese universities generate tremendous amounts of research and patents but are less likely to lead to the creation of new companies.

Time Magazine ran a major story arguing that Japan was in decline, while India and China were on the rise – even before the tsunami and subsequent nuclear disaster. 'Japan is an island of inertia in an Asia that is in a state of constant flux,' wrote *Time*'s reporter. 'Japan once shared Asia's dynamism and mission. But not anymore. While Asia lurches forward, Japan inches backward.' And this attack went on and on mentioning that Japan had gone 'from a dynamo to a dinosaur'.

There is no greater example of the need for a country to have a programme to manage press and public perceptions of itself. Unfortunately, perception management has historically not been developed as a skill in government or business circles. But the resources are there, and the talent is there, and I hope this might change. Fortunately for Burson–Marsteller, Japan was an important international market and remains that way. It was our work for Western clients operating in Japan that helped accelerate our growth and make Tokyo a great success for us.

One of our most successful activities was on behalf of Avon. The company wanted to extend its sponsorship of women's distance running events to Japan to help the company be identified as a supporter of total well-being and health, not just beauty. The sponsorship would help it establish the legitimacy of the 'Avon Lady who would knock on doors', a concept alien to Japanese women who tended to be basically shy and not desirous of standing out from the crowd.

As a perfect start, the company hired a Japanese-American marathon runner for us to use as a spokesperson. We helped establish the Avon's Women's Cultural Centre that would in turn sponsor the running events. This helped greatly with the resulting publicity as TV stations would not otherwise have used the Avon name in their coverage, thus crediting a commercial company.

Getting agreement from the authorities, mainly the Japanese Athletics Federation, was not easy. They did not believe that Japanese women would ever run a marathon or even a half-marathon, so in the end we had to settle for a five-kilometre 'fun run'. We also had to agree to have medical attendants every 500 metres or so to tend to women runners who they were sure would be collapsing.

We were able to get the National Stadium (site of the 1964 Olympics) as the start and finishing point, to draw in police cooperation and tremendous media coverage and – of great importance – nearly all the runners wore a bright orange Avon tee shirt (adding to the success of the TV coverage). Over the years, Avon's run grew to 7,000 participants and became an important part of the company's overall marketing programme. To the benefit of the Japanese, the importance of Japanese women runners grew to a point where they dominated the 2000 Sydney Olympics, for which Avon can take a lot of credit.

We also found out, in contrast to what we did with Avon, that we could create very limited programmes that were still very important to the client. In the early nineties, United Distillers (now Diageo) wanted to build brand engagement and loyalty for Old Parr Superior, one of the many whisky brands in the Johnnie Walker family. Old Parr Superior, at that time, was very popular with the upper echelon of Japanese business leaders and a huge hit with Japanese business people travelling abroad. It was an *omiyage* (souvenir) which conveyed tremendous prestige and respect.

When we studied the demographics and psychographics of the Old Parr Superior drinker, we saw that they were usually over fifty and, quite often, were CEOs or in other top leadership positions. We found that in general they were too busy with their work commitments to engage in many other activities. We put that finding together with the fact that Japanese society ran on relationships, and networking for business purposes was essential. Thus, we created the Old Parr Superior Society. It was established as a truly exclusive, invitation-only group of top CEOs who would meet periodically, in very exclusive restaurants or clubs, to enjoy delicious meals and first-rate service, sip Old Parr, and listen to one of their favourite authors speak about his or her latest book. The gatherings were intimate – usually twenty to twenty-five people – and the authors were some of the best and most respected at that time. The guests were able to relax, network and socialize with a literary celebrity whom they ordinarily would not meet. The different guests were invited back once or twice a year. There was no attempt to promote or sell the product and the feedback from the participants was excellent. The programme went on for a number of years.

Japan was a country I loved to visit not only for business reasons, but equally for pleasure. Tokyo was exciting, but so were Hiroshima, Nagasaki or Kyoto. I saw the splendid temples at Nara, the temples, shrines and monuments at Kamakura and the UN World Heritage Site at Nikko. But the place my wife and I enjoyed the most was the Hakone area, less than one hundred kilometres from Tokyo. It faces

Mount Fuji and includes forests, mountains and volcanoes. We stayed at a Japanese *ryokan* (traditional inn) which claimed to be the oldest hotel in the world. It was a delight. The breakfast served each morning in our room was a real feast, as were the thermal baths for which the *ryokan* was well known. They were a bit different from what a westerner was used to in that boys, girls, men and women all bathed together – completely naked. It took this shy westerner and his wife a little time to get used to bathing with all this company. But we did.

7   China

China has passed Japan to become the number two economic power in the world, and a number of leading economists have said that in all likelihood it will pass the United States sometime in the twenty-first century. I have dealt with the Chinese for more than forty years, beginning when I signed an agreement in the Great Hall of the People in Beijing – the first time the Chinese government had gotten into the PR business. Over this time, I got to know and understand the Chinese people very well. Nothing that they ever accomplish will be a surprise to me.

On 31 August 1984, on behalf of Burson–Marsteller, I signed an agreement with the New China News Agency, a government body, establishing a joint affiliate: China Global Public Relations – the first Chinese organization to operate a public relations business in the People's Republic of China.

The agreement was for eight years. Hong Kong's leading paper, the *South China Morning Post*, called the agreement 'a major coup' and quoted me as saying, 'We could not have hoped for a better partner for our China activities.'

One thing that fascinated me was the difference between signing an agreement with the Chinese government and signing one with the Russian government. The Russians in that period feared that they might be taken advantage of in some way and reviewed every full stop and comma in legal documents in great detail. The Chinese, on the other hand, had a great confidence in themselves and their history and clearly felt they had nothing to fear from their new American business partners. The agreement went through without a change to the draft presented to them.

The New China News Agency engaged over 6,000 people and had twenty-nine branch offices in China, which gave us excellent positioning. To maximize our expanded China capabilities to present and potential clients in the US, we appointed Scott Seligman, who was based in Washington, as co-ordinator for Chinese affairs. Scott was fluent in Mandarin and had previously acted as director for development and government relations in the National Council for US-China Trade.

We knew that China would be a significant factor in Burson–Marsteller's future growth. Considering its geographic position, size and population base, it was becoming an increasingly important market for our clients, and it was obvious that its importance would continue to expand in the future. It was also a two-way street. China not only wanted to become better known as a country to do business in, but their business and government leaders were seeking more and more knowledge about the West, from a political, social and economic point of view.

To build our relationship quickly, we started by immediately training three members of China Global in our Hong Kong office. They were quickly followed by five others. We also sent staff from our Hong Kong office to work on behalf of clients in Beijing. Within three years, China Global had grown to sixteen people.

The fast growing interest in public relations in China was exemplified by the fact that Burson–Marsteller and China Global were able to hold a two-day public relations seminar in Beijing. Two hundred leading executives and government officials attended. We brought in seminar speakers from the US, UK, Japan, Hong Kong, Thailand, Singapore, Malaysia and New Zealand. Yu Xiaohuai, chairman of China Global, noted: 'Although public relations is a relatively new discipline here, it can be of tremendous assistance to Chinese enterprises in marketing products abroad and in developing foreign investment at home.' The speakers gave examples of every type of public relations activity the Chinese audience should be aware of. I gave examples of what we had done for clients in China. By then, we had already worked on behalf of thirty-five multinationals.

The Chinese are a confident people. This became obvious to me during our earliest negotiations with them and later as we worked in China on behalf of clients. In fact, I would say they are extremely confident. They are the product of one of the oldest civilizations in the world, and they have a strong belief in themselves, their history and their ability to take on whatever is sent their way. And there is no doubt that today, even more than back when I first started doing business with them, they believe the future belongs to them.

Reputation and status are more important in China than anywhere else in the world. One reason that PR was so important for companies wanting to enter the Chinese market was that the reputation of the company, and the individuals representing it, was extremely significant and a vital factor in developing relationships. The Chinese only want to deal with the best. One of the reasons they were willing to team up with us was that we were going through an extremely successful period, and they were well aware of this.

In general, the Chinese like foreigners. Surprisingly, they are far more comfortable with westerners than they are with the Japanese. Study the history of their relationship and the reasons become clear. The Chinese appreciate westerners who make an effort to learn and understand their culture. In fact, they will make judgements about outsiders based on their openness to Chinese ways. This came home to me when I concluded our deal in the Great Hall of the People. After the official signing, the Chinese hosts threw a banquet. A real Chinese banquet is something to behold. There was table after table filled with delicious-looking food, and you would have thought they were going to feed the entire Burson–Marsteller organization.

The waiters served dish after dish of beautifully prepared delicacies. When they approached me with some new dishes, one of my hosts said, 'Not for Mr Leaf.'

'Why?' I asked.

'Because those plates contain chicken's feet and duck's lips which obviously you would not care for,' my host replied.

I then explained that not only did I really care for chicken feet and duck's lips, but that in London I was a member of a Chinese gourmet club. We often dined at restaurants featuring all the five major schools of Chinese cooking. This really impressed my hosts. Most Chinese, even though they might know key dishes from all over China, would usually be most familiar with food from just two areas – the one where they were raised, and the other where they presently worked and lived. My in-depth knowledge of their different schools of food meant more to my hosts than my position as international chairman of the then largest PR firm in the world. From then on, my relationship with China Global really flourished.

How you relate to the Chinese when you initially meet them is extremely important. For a company entering a market, the key is to meet with the right people as soon as possible. The Chinese are extremely polite and will arrange for you to meet with a large number of officials. It is important to find out in advance who are the key decision-makers and to arrange to see them as quickly as possible. It is also vitally important to get the proper information about one's company and its products to the key people in advance of meeting them.

When you meet the Chinese, as the Japanese, they like to learn a little about you, where you've been, what you know about China, and whether you have visited before. They are willing to answer questions about themselves as long as they are not too personal. And it is certainly advisable to avoid discussing politics.

Because the last thing they want is to embarrass you, the Chinese will very rarely say no to anything. Do not work yourself into a position where yes or no are the only possible answers they can provide. They will always prefer to answer in a way indicating the subject still calls for further thought before they come to a decision, though in their minds they might already have reached a conclusion. When communicating in China, never underestimate the significance the Chinese attach to the name of a company or product. A Chinese proverb says, 'Once a man is given an ill sounding name he will never be able to wash it off.'

My colleague Scott Seligman, who knows China very well, once wrote:

Translating company names and trademarks into Chinese is a complicated problem that requires a number of decisions. There is no one way to translate a given name into Chinese. Unlike English to French where James becomes Jacques and Peter, Pierre, there are few generally accepted translations of foreign names. If you used a dozen translators, they could come up with a dozen versions.

A pharmaceutical company hired us to study their trademark, as it had been put into Chinese for a specific product. Our staff was well aware that Chinese doctors and consumers prefer a trademark with some indication of the function and use of the product. Here is where the problem lies. A trademark can be made up of three Chinese characters, each with a specific meaning. And it is possible that while each of these individually are positive, together they could have a negative connotation.

In our review, we found that the first character meant stomach; the second meant obtain, gain or result; the third stood for effective or quick. To the client's happiness, the three put together stood for an effective medicine for the stomach, which was what the product was for.

All written material must be checked carefully. One firm wanting to describe itself as an old friend of China unwittingly used a character meaning 'old' in the sense of 'former' rather than 'longstanding'.

The interest in public relations in China began to grow to a greater degree than I had anticipated. The Third World Advertising Congress was held in Beijing in 1987, three years after we established our business there. I was asked to deliver a major talk, appropriately enough, on 'The Expanding Role of Public Relations'. I went into detail about what public relations entailed and its growth throughout the region. I stressed that companies eager to sell in China should see it as a long-term proposition. This would be true whether the economy improved or got worse in future years. Because of the 'reputation' factor, it was desirable to keep a continuing – if modest – press relations programme aimed at their important audiences.

One of the outstanding public relations successes at this time was on behalf of a client, Arthur Andersen, then a leading accounting and management consulting firm. They already had a significant operation in China and foresaw great growth opportunities. To show its appreciation of the Chinese government, in partnership with China International Trust and Investment Corporation, they co-sponsored a concert to raise funds for the disabled.

This was not just a normal concert. The Queen Mother agreed to be a patron, along with Chinese Vice President Ulanhu, marking the first joint patronage by a member of the British Royal Family and a Chinese state leader. The concert was held in the Great Hall of the People. Former British Prime Minister Edward Heath conducted China's Central Philharmonic Symphony Orchestra in works by Elgar and Tchaikovsky. In addition he conducted a disabled Chinese orchestra, playing music on Chinese instruments. Heath had previously conducted the London Symphony Orchestra at Royal Festival Hall and also had conducted the Royal Liverpool Philharmonic and English Chamber Orchestras and told me afterwards that he felt this was one of the finest events he had been personally involved in.

Arthur Andersen also hosted a buffet at the Great Hall before the concert and gave a banquet the following day for major contributors. Around $1m was raised for the first phase of the rehabilitation and recreation centre for disabled people at Horse Island in Yantai, Shandong Province. The event gave Arthur Andersen a chance to work closely with a number of important clients and prospects as well as Chinese Government leaders. They also showed their willingness to help humanitarian causes within the Chinese republic, an important factor in developing an overall excellent reputation within the country.

The company that showed the greatest understanding of the Chinese from the very beginning of their relationship was Coca-Cola. They quickly learned how to work in close harmony. The executive in charge of China for Coca-Cola was an Australian, Douglas Daft, who had previously been an academic. We became good friends and later, partially because of his outstanding performance in China, he became chairman of the parent company in Atlanta.

From the onset, the company's policy was to work closely with local officials on events that would help establish their image as a good corporate citizen, and at the same time help familiarize the public with their brand. They sponsored the Coke Cup, organized by the Chinese Football Association. It was an under-sixteen football tournament featuring teams from China, Hong Kong, Singapore, Malaysia, Japan and Indonesia.

At the signing of the contract Yang Xiuwu, the director of the football office of the State Physical Culture and Sports Commission, said: 'This was the first international youth event of its kind to be held in China.' Coca-Cola subsequently sponsored an extensive range of events including football, table tennis, gymnastics, chess and athletics.

Sporting events were not the only area where Coca-Cola used public relations techniques. In order to reach across generations, they co-organized the Guangzhou Family Talent Quest with the Guangzhou branch of the All-China Women's Federation and Guangdong TV. They worked with the Chinese authorities to develop a theme and format, secured local celebrity support and worked closely with all media. The contest was to find the most talented family in the region and the rules specified there had to be at last two members from each family involved. The contest was presented on live TV and received great acceptance throughout the area.

Other corporations soon followed suit. AT&T sponsored a Chinese little league team to play in the United States. This too was a huge success. The Chinese team succeeded in winning all four games they played and met a number of American dignitaries, including Vice President Bush.

Nike entered the Chinese market in 1980 with four factories and wanted to get known quickly but had limited funds. We helped them establish an Asian Gold Medal Quiz in which the participants had to guess how many gold medals would win the Asian games. China Global arranged for a leading sports newspaper with a circulation of more than a million to be a co-organizer. It was cleared with necessary government officials and we set up a system for collecting and sorting entries and arranged for announcing the results and prizes. The Nike Asian Gold Medal Quiz drew 1.3 million entries and was widely reported through all media. In fact, it was so successful that we had to hire people to help the post office in collecting the entries and sending them to the sorting places.

Another client, General Motors, had received permission to produce engines in the People's Republic and wanted to get its relationship with Chinese officialdom off on the right foot. We worked for months with General Motors to prepare four key elements: an official contract signing, a buffet reception, an office opening and a gift-giving ceremony. The contract was signed at the Great Hall of the People. A real General Motors engine was exhibited in the Great Hall. A ribbon cutting ceremony took place outside the General Motors office. A large banner flew outside, and a banner and a rhyming couplet that linked General Motors to China's four modernizations – then the key to the government's economic policy – was situated at the office door.

Inside their offices we set up a photo exhibition and a giant board with a brief description of General Motors and video monitors playing tapes about the company. Fireworks and a lion dance heightened the festivities. Guests were transported to the banquet by a fleet of ten Cadillac limousines – a General Motors car, of course. A key element was the presentation of the official gifts. Selection of the right gifts has always been important in China. They must have meaning but not be too ostentatious. The gift that was given to each government official consisted of a General Motors Chevrolet steering wheel mounted on a wooden plaque. The GM corporate logo and the GM car division logos were inset in the plaque. In addition, a traditional Chinese idiom different for each plaque expressed belief that the official receiving the plaque was steering China in the right direction. What was most important was that the event provided a clear indication that General Motors understood its hosts and would thus be an excellent partner.

When dealing with the Chinese, especially your own staff there, it is wise to remember that, despite the Cultural Revolution, the philosophy of Confucianism remains dominant. One of its main dictates, social harmony, is the pronounced philosophy of the government and even became an official doctrine in 2006. One key aspect of Confucianism is obedience to all aspects of authority, whether government officials, company executives, ancestors, elders or parents. Obedience leads to acceptance. You do not question. You do not second guess. When I recently spoke to Burson–Marsteller's top Chinese management, they said that, while such behaviour has changed to some degree in today's world, it is still implanted in the average Chinese person's philosophy.

There is no doubt that many Chinese companies see themselves as riding the wave of the future and that they know that public relations can be helpful in sustaining that wave. There are now more than 2,000 PR firms in China and the number of young people interested in becoming part of the PR industry has increased dramatically. Because Chinese consumers have become far more affluent in recent years there is a greater need for product information and brand awareness. Thus, companies have increased their expenditures on publicity, advertising, sponsorship, promotional give-aways and public open days. In fitting with the Chinese thinking, brand reputation is the key. Even people in low- to middle-income brackets spend relatively large amounts on luxury goods if they perceive them to be good value for money.

A number of years ago, as affluence was growing, Hennessy, whose prestigious XO Cognac category had dominated the Asian market, saw competition increasing. So Burson–Marsteller was asked to develop an Asian-wide campaign to promote the product, with the emphasis on China, where the potential for growth was the greatest. The strategy centred on 'Project Shanghai', a celebration of the 120th anniversary of Hennessy XO's presence in Asia. A 44-metre schooner, rechristened the *Spirit of Hennessy*, was chartered for a nine-month journey from France to its ultimate destination, Shanghai, stopping en route in Malaysia, Singapore, Thailand, Hong Kong and Vietnam. Media and trade events were held at each port of call. The grand finale was a three-day event in Shanghai, highlighted by an arrival ceremony for the *Spirit of Hennessy*. More than 300 guests, government representatives and journalists from all over the world attended.

The results in China were impressive. Some sixty lifestyle publications carried heavily branded coverage and four separate television shows devoted time to the voyage. The reputation of Hennessy XO mushroomed in China.

Relations with the Chinese government can be confusing for businesses. Although its absolute authority is still unquestioned, the leaders' grip has eased somewhat. The government still has the final say. It is still centrally controlled, forcing decision-making to take quite a long time. There is a little more autonomy in regions and even in cities than had been the case, but even in these situations you can be dealing with a number of people, and most things do not move quickly.

The critical challenge is figuring out exactly who can approve what. And it does not always have to be the man at the top. But whoever is the decider, there is no doubt that personal connections are usually the key to getting the approval you are seeking, probably more in China than any other country.

You should never send an executive to negotiate or work in China who doesn't have patience. The Chinese have the advantage of being the host in negotiations, and they can spread them out as long as they like. It's often difficult to understand what's happening, what's been agreed to, and what has not. Sometimes you think they have given in on a specific issue and they really haven't. And just when you think the negotiations have reached the final point, they will start asking for just a little bit more. Often generalities take the priority over specifics. Henry Kissinger knew that when he reopened diplomatic relations with China in 1972 by not demanding decisions on specifics, but coming away with a general agreement to cooperate.

The Chinese have great respect for expertise and have always known that the Americans were best in class in the field of economics. They wanted to learn from them. But that changed when the economic meltdown started in the US. Kissinger, in an interview with *Business Week* in 2011, stated that the crisis had created a great deal of disillusion in China and a feeling that maybe the Americans were no longer the guiding light.

Chinese education is improving and many of the brighter young people are deciding to study in their homeland rather than go abroad. And many who have gone to study in the UK or the US are returning earlier rather than staying to gain some years of work experience abroad first. Among China's other improvements since we entered the market are its restaurants. As I mentioned, food at Chinese banquets or at major events such as wedding receptions was tough to equal. But the level of quality was nowhere near as high at many of their public restaurants, and they were nowhere near as good as equivalent places in Hong Kong. The worst Peking duck I have ever eaten was in Beijing itself (formerly Peking). And when I went to Xian, where the graves of the now famous warriors had just been found, after eating there for three days I began to wonder whether many of them had not perished from the food – so bad was what I had eaten there for three days.

But fortunately, that is not the case today, and China will continue to grow as a major tourist attraction and the tourists will have great meals.

The growth of Burson–Marsteller in China has been exciting. Twenty-five years after I began our venture there, we now have five offices in China with a staff of 200. Clients include a growing number of Western nationals selling in China as well as Chinese companies selling abroad.

Digital and social media have become vitally important in the practice of PR in China: 477 million people (35.6 per cent of the population) use the Internet – the highest number of Internet users in the world. Consumers are now spending $77bn online, roughly 3 per cent of total retail sales. A study showed that 94 per cent of Chinese consumers trusted companies that used social media more than those that do not. That is why Starbucks, Coca-Cola and PG have become very active in this area.

As far as the attitude towards public relations is concerned, there has been a vast improvement among the highly educated. However, there still remains only a small group that truly understands what it does and what it can accomplish. A wider group still connects the term in general with dining, drinking, entertaining, flirting and manipulating. But this too will change.

From its very early days Burson–Marsteller has always conducted a training programme called Burson–Marsteller University, which has been held in different parts of the world. They recently held the first one in China by the Great Wall. This was in addition to conducting a digital training week for Chinese employees. I asked some of the Western attendees what their impressions were of the young Chinese staff. They were unanimous in the feeling that they were eager – especially for advancement – enthusiastic and diversified, very hard-working and had great hopes for both their future and that of their country. I feel the exact same way. There will be ups and downs for China but I am sure the ups are going to predominate.

8 Opening in Australia and South America

Public relations was becoming a truly international business. As I travelled around the world opening offices, it became clearer and clearer that in each country the level of professionalism differed, as did the level of acceptance by potential clients, the availability and quality of local staff, and the make-up of the media. To be successful, we had to take these differences into account, but regardless of region, I still kept the opinion that perception management was the key.

In spite of the regional differences, the methods used to help a client build his organization or solve some local problem could be quite similar. Many of the messages necessary to accomplish the desired objective would be the same. So with the proper training, staff could easily be interchangeable from country to country and be effective in each of the different markets. Thus, it was highly advisable to have many of our executives spend time in more than one country. The same is true today and is perhaps even more important.

With all the commonalities, we could still make mistakes. And I personally made a major blooper – and I mean major. I opened five offices in Australia. The one thing that I have expressly noted that

I do *not* want to be put on my tombstone is: 'Bob Leaf opened FIVE offices in Australia', because you need five PR offices in Australia as much as you need five wives.

As Burson–Marsteller continued to grow and be successful throughout Asia, it became apparent that the next area for us to move into was Australia. Our parent company, Young & Rubicam, had its headquarters in Adelaide, so we started Burson–Marsteller in their offices, where we would already have support staff. Adelaide was a very pleasant city and had excellent Greek restaurants.

Public relations was already well accepted in Australia. The company that really gave it a boost, Eric White, had started in 1947. Eric White was also one of the first PR companies to see the great potential in international public relations.

Where public relations really shone in Australia, from the very beginning, was in the area of public affairs. There was a good reason: because of the very political nature of the Australian people, and the importance of individual states, local government lobbying was vital, and companies and consultancies responded by developing the skills necessary for this sort of activity. For some smaller consultancies the political side was their primary activity.

In those days, unlike today, personal security was not a problem. Casual one-on-one meetings with high government people were not uncommon. Nowadays, by contrast, one cannot meet government officials without advance planning, detailed security checks and other formalities. Australia, in any case, was then a very laid-back society. Government officials in the various districts were always open to meeting with public relations executives or their clients on a regular basis. There was no concern that they would be open to criticism just for meeting with lobbyists. I visited Australia ten years in a row and I never had a problem having the local office set up a meeting for me with someone in local government, if I was so inclined.

Government officials, for their own political reasons, kept up with the PR industry to a greater degree than in most countries. Once in Melbourne, the local PR association was having a one-day lecture session and a dinner afterwards to which all PR firms were invited. After the formal meeting took place, during the cocktail hour before dinner, Bob Hawke, then the Prime Minister of Australia, came by to visit with some of his associates. By chance, soon after he arrived, he walked over to me and started a conversation. Once he heard my accent, he became very interested in discussing my opinions about Ronald Reagan, then the US President, whom he was scheduled to meet in the near future. We talked for a while, and the front page of the local paper featured a picture of us deep in our tête-à-tête.

The main cities in Australia were all very different from each other. Melbourne had many of the characteristics of London, and Sydney could have been a twin of San Francisco. Brisbane and Adelaide, the next two important cities, did not have international significance, and Perth, which was on the west coast, a world away from any of those cities, developed a personality and lifestyle that was unique and relaxed.

Having been convinced by some of our local Australian management that to become a dominant force in Australian PR we had to operate from all five major cities, I agreed to open an office in each of them. Perth was the last city in Australia where I opened an office. That is a story of its own. When I planned to set up there, I had decided to put an English woman, who had greatly impressed me, in charge of the office. I had one serious concern though, which had absolutely nothing to do with her competence. Australia at that time had the most macho society I had ever encountered. The women, though very bright and stimulating, were content to let the men be dominant in most cases. Employing the first woman in Perth to head a PR office might have created a problem. Before finalizing the appointment, I decided to seek some advice from possibly the most famous man then living in Perth, Alan Bond, and arranged to have lunch with him.

Born in Hammersmith, in London, Bond moved to Australia and became one of the wealthiest men in the country. He achieved international recognition when he purchased a Vincent Van Gogh painting, *Irises*, for $53.9m. At that time it was the single highest price ever paid for a painting anywhere in the world. He also paid $1bn to buy Australia's nationwide TV channel, Channel 9, from Kerry Packer. In addition, he helped finance Australia's yacht team in the America's Cup. When they won the cup, he became extremely popular throughout the country. Unfortunately he ended up spending four years in prison for activities that were not of an equally charitable nature.

When we met, he was the essence of charm and asked me how he could be helpful. I told him I was planning to put a woman in charge of our new Perth office and wanted to know whether he felt this was a mistake in judgement. 'Bob,' he said, 'I ran an advertisement looking for someone to work for me and handle our company's PR. I got more than eighty responses. The best one by far was from a woman, and I hired her.' His answer made it quite clear I should go ahead as planned.

The woman I hired was extremely competent. But we didn't really need an office in Perth: the business was just not there. Our miscalculation became apparent after a short time, and we decided to turn the office over to the staff. We later disposed of Brisbane and Adelaide in similar fashion.

With just Melbourne and Sydney left standing, we became and still remain one of the leading PR firms in Australia. These were the cities we needed to be in. Sydney was the nation's international gateway city and Melbourne the nation's corporate power base with influential company players located there. At that time Melbourne's listed entities comprised the largest asset block on the Australian Stock Exchange (ASX).

Within a short time we became a major player and had a list of top companies as clients. The Melbourne office was working for Colonial Mutual (insurance), John Holland (heavy construction), Potter Partners (a leading stock broking and investment house), Elders IXL (marketers of Fosters beer), PA Consulting and Bankers Trust, and BHP, the world's largest mining company, for whom we held a three-issues management exercise for their global executive team.

In the Sydney office, a 23-year-old young lady proved that great ideas do not only come from the longest serving. She devised the idea of 'Breakfast for Sydney' for Du Pont to promote its non-sticking Silverstone. The idea was to be listed in the *Guinness World Records* for the most eggs cooked in a day. This great feat was accomplished by frying more than 6,000 eggs for a multitude of happy Sydney diners, resulting in a great deal of publicity. The power of PR was proven when Du Pont did conducted surveys before and after the event on consumers' 'intent to purchase' a Silverstone-coated frying pan. Eleven per cent more said they would buy it after the stunt, while the 'would not buy' responses went down 7 per cent.

While I was in charge of our offices in Australia, our biggest problem was retaining staff. I explained this in detail when I was the guest speaker in 1986 at the Noel Griffiths Lecture, sponsored by the Public Relations Institute of Australia. I said:

This is the most difficult country in the world to keep staff. Marco Polo was born in the wrong country. He belonged here. Every young Australian's secret ambition is to backpack in Laos. And Australians more than anyone else constantly question: are we in the right job, are we doing the right thing,

wouldn't we be happier somewhere else, or shouldn't we open
a bar or restaurant?

The problem this creates is that there are constant staff changes
on accounts, and clients begin to question the stability of working
with outside public relations consultancies. You don't find as big a
turnover with doctors, lawyers, accountants or priests.

In another act which I also constantly try to erase from my
memory, I decided to add New Zealand to our growing chain of
countries. New Zealand had quite a number of PR professionals,
surprising for a country of its size. The only other area where it was
so numerically buoyant was with sheep, though this is not to indicate any similarity between these two groups.

New Zealand is one of the most beautiful countries in the world.
The New Zealanders are extremely nice but the need at that time
for a Burson–Marsteller office was negligible at best, and the
office was eventually disbanded. One fortunate aspect of our over-
expansion was that I was not purchasing existing firms but starting
our own offices from scratch. Opening costs were minimal, as were
our losses. With fewer offices, we still became a major factor in
Australia, and I learned never to open an office anywhere else in
the world just to mark our presence.

At the same time that we were expanding throughout Asia, I began
to consider opening offices in South America. There were primarily
two countries at that time that appeared to have great promise: Brazil
and Argentina. These countries were very different in size, ethnic
orientation and the kinds of clients who would offer the greatest
potential.

Brazil proved to be a very interesting possibility for our first
South American office because there were already a number of small
PR firms and a PR association operating there. I made some initial

contacts with PR people in São Paulo, who in turn made every effort to convince us that we should expand into Brazil, believing our arrival into the country would most likely open up and expand the PR business dramatically – from which we would all benefit. That proved exactly to be the case.

We opened in São Paulo, the largest city in Brazil and the country's commercial and financial centre. We soon decided that this was the only city in Brazil we needed to be in (I had learned my lesson in Australia). This might appear surprising with Brazil being the largest country in South America, but it worked out nicely for us.

Brazil is a country whose regions differ in types of population, culture, and basic beliefs and values. Because of its variety, Brazil was a wonderful country to travel in because you felt you were visiting more than one country. For example, I took a thrilling boat trip from Manaus in northern Brazil down the Amazon and into the rainforest where you could easily believe you had travelled to a different world and a different time.

One of my most interesting travel experiences concerned flying to Salvador, the capital of the state of Bahia. Bahia, in 1532, was the region where the Portuguese first landed in South America. Until 1763, it was the capital of Brazil. The city, famous for its cuisine, music and architecture, remains today the centre of Catholicism in the country, and, unlike the rest of the country, 80 per cent of its population is of black African heritage.

Flying to Bahia from Rio, I had the worst flight experience I've encountered in my many, many years of air travel. When we arrived at the airport there had been a series of extremely violent storms, and flight departures had been postponed for hours. Then airport control finally allowed our flight to leave. Besides the crew, there were only seven of us aboard. Soon after we took off, the storm returned with an even greater ferocity. The high winds smashed us up and down and back and forth like a ping-pong ball. Suddenly, every one of the stewardesses went into the aisles, holding rosaries and reciting prayers, apparently feeling this would improve our chances of survival. Their efforts were of no particular comfort to me. I didn't join them in prayer but stayed glued to my seat, holding my wife Adele's hand. Fortunately, after about half an hour of this terror, the storm began to dissipate, and we arrived in Bahia where perfect weather awaited us.

All the wonderful things we had heard about Bahia turned out to be true, and we had a great visit. There was only one exception. One evening I heard that in a certain part of town candomblé voodoo rituals were to be performed. I decided that watching these would be the high point of my visit, so I ordered a hotel car. When the car arrived and the driver told the hotel manager where I wanted to go, he would not let him take me. He explained that what was taking place that evening was the most fanatical of the rituals this particular group held, and they sometimes made onlookers participate. And while the manager did not explain exactly what this meant, I bowed to his judgement and decided to do any incantations I cared to back in the hotel.

One event I did attend was Carnival at Rio. I discovered that its worldwide reputation was well deserved. Nothing I've seen before or since could equal the experience, and that includes Mardi Gras in New Orleans and the Oktoberfest in Germany. Both of those were exciting and very enjoyable, but they were minor league compared to Rio. The parades and the crowd responses were really something to behold, as was a stretch of beach that allowed topless sunbathing, something relatively new in those days.

Brazil, like our other offices, began to grow faster than we had anticipated, but we believed Argentina could be our focal country in South America. It was the most Western of the South American countries and was of greatest interest among many of our clients.

I sent Bill, who was later killed in London, to head the office, and we signed up a major client very quickly – the Argentine Minister of Economics. Our main objective for his Ministry was to work with our US and European offices to help bring about greater investment in Argentina by Western companies. The Minister was extremely articulate, and we set up an excellent interview with the BBC on the advantages of Argentine investment.

At this time the country was ruled by a military triumvirate, who were later to be imprisoned for atrocities. They did not trust the Minister of Economics or anyone on his payroll, and that included us. Bill told me he had reasons to believe that our phones were being tapped. During one visit I was to get to meet with the leaders personally under an extraordinary set of circumstances.

In our London office, one of our senior executives was Tony Iveson. Tony was a famous pilot during the Second World War. He was one of the Dambusters, aka 617 Squadron, probably the best known of all UK Bomber Command Squadrons. They carried out a daring bombing raid in Germany destroying the dams in the Ruhr Valley with a revolutionary bouncing bomb invented by Barnes Wallis. They were immortalized in *The Dam Busters*, a film which co-starred Richard Todd and Sir Michael Redgrave. Tony was also a pilot of one of the bombers that attacked and sunk the German battleship *Tirpitz*, the largest battleship ever built in Europe. Its destruction removed the last surface threat to Allied control of the North Atlantic.

After the war, when Argentina and the UK were close friends, the Argentineans purchased some bombers from the UK. Tony flew one of these down to Buenos Aires. I realized that he would be the ideal person to accompany me to Argentina when I went there for a business review. Little did I realize the wisdom of my decision. It turned out that the bomber Tony had piloted to Argentina was now on display and the major feature in an outdoor museum. When it became known that it was Tony who had flown it over to Argentina and that he was in Buenos Aires, he became an instant media hero and was interviewed by the press and appeared on television. In addition, we were taken to meet the heads of the military and photographed with them.

Tony and I also met with the Minister of Tourism. He told us we should pick any place in the country we'd like to visit, and he would arrange for a plane to take us there and back, and provide accommodation for our visit. We selected Iguaçu Falls, one of the world's most beautiful waterfalls, situated on the border with Brazil.

After a lovely stay there, we got on the plane to return to Buenos Aires. Soon after take-off the pilot came back to see us, and knowing Tony's reputation, invited him to the cockpit to fly the plane for a while. Tony accepted the offer and the pilot settled himself back in the cabin opposite me with a bottle of Scotch and a deck of cards for playing solitaire to keep him company. I doubt Tony had ever flown a Piper Navajo before, but I wasn't particularly nervous. When we were close enough to the airport to talk to the control tower, Tony gave up the controls and joined me as he doubted the controllers would be interested in hearing from him.

From this initial start, Burson–Marsteller currently has ten wholly-owned offices with a staff of 300 employees and three affiliates in Latin America. It is the largest international PR firm operating there.

9   The Middle East

From the time I moved to England in 1968 and had become firmly established on the European continent, we began to think that it was time to look into the Middle East as the next significant area we should expand into. However, we were also well aware that this region had a variety of internal problems that we would have to be aware of and prepare for. This situation has never changed.

The Middle East has too often been thought of as a homogeneous bloc. The Arab World is made up of twenty-two countries and is incredibly diverse. There are regions of great wealth and extreme poverty. Some parts of the same country have very little in common with other parts, with hostility existing between them – Shiites ruled by Sunnis; Sunnis ruled by Shiites. Alongside these potentially volatile situations we were also witnessing the emergence and growth of some far-right religious organizations with agendas of their own. And let's not forget the conflict with two other great religions, Christianity and Judaism, both of which were born in the Middle East.

Just as we were wary, many of our clients, who at that time realized there was a growing potential for their business in the area, were also concerned about how best to enter some of these markets without taking unnecessary risks. For our own business, the first thing we had to consider was which country to start in – and how to begin. Should we risk going in on our own, or should we look for a local partner right from the start? We quickly came to the conclusion that a local partner would be the most reasonable approach. There would be so many opportunities and problems that were different to anything we had yet faced. We did our research and came to the conclusion that Lebanon would be the very best country to dip our toe in first. The decision made sense for a variety of reasons.

Lebanon was then by far the most Western-oriented of all the Middle Eastern countries in terms of values and business activities. From a business point of view, the Lebanese were the most similar to the Israelis, and their relations with Israel the best of any Arab country. While there was an undercurrent of dissatisfaction among the populace that seemed to be growing, as an outsider I had no concept of what was about to happen there – and happen quickly.

Beirut was then known as the Paris of the Middle East. It was the country that most well-off Arabs living in more restrictive lands came to for relaxation (and even for the occasional drink). In Lebanon you could swim, ski, sightsee and eat some of the best food the Middle East had to offer. I decided this was the best country with which to begin our Middle Eastern adventure.

Public relations as we knew it did not in reality exist in that part of the world. So it made the most sense for us to team up with a local advertising agency that would be interested in expanding into public relations and welcoming us as a partner. Most of the ad agency clients were multinational companies who were seeking ways to get greater coverage in the regional media. The practice of public relations in that region was, as I found out, inextricably linked to the advertising sector. After checking around, I decided that the advertising agency Intermarkets would be the right company with which to hold some initial discussions.

In 1975, I was given a letter of introduction to Erwin Guerrovich, the chief executive of Intermarkets, headquartered in Beirut. When I wrote telling him exactly what our interests were, he replied saying he would be very much interested in holding serious discussions with me and would like to be my host during my proposed stay in Beirut. When I met him, we were joined by his number two man, Ramzi Raad, who was in later years to become one of the leading advertising executives in the Middle East.

Both from a business and a social point of view, it was a match made in heaven. Our personalities meshed in a way that made our relationship a lasting one. Both men thought, as I did, that great opportunities existed for public relations to play a more significant part in communications in the Middle East. There was so much that could be done for all types of potential clients that was not now being done, as PR was truly in its infancy there. While a significant job of educating potential clients would be necessary, at this stage we would not be facing much, if any, major local competition. We immediately agreed to set up a joint venture that would launch Burson–Marsteller in the Middle East.

The plan was for me to return to London after a brief holiday and prepare a draft document outlining our arrangement. My wife joined me for a day of relaxation in Beirut and then we headed to Egypt for a short stop in Cairo before visiting Edfu, Karnak and Luxor in the Valley of the Kings, where we saw the tombs and monuments of the ancient pharaohs. When we then returned to Cairo for a final day's stay before heading home to London, I noticed a paper at the news stand with the headline 'Hundreds killed in Beirut'. I took it for granted that it was a plane crash or some similar disaster. I bought the paper and started reading only to find out that a civil war had started just shortly after our departure. Our flight had been one of the last to leave the country as some of the fiercest fighting took place near the airport. And while I had been aware of some dissension within the country, the degree of violence that took place took me and most of the West completely by surprise.

This was, of course, before the days of mobile phones or laptops. I had not been in contact with the office which had been trying to track me down to see if I was safe. I called and informed them that I was fine. But it was clear that our chance to open an office in Lebanon was now dead for the present. Guerrovich and Raad, well aware that the situation in Lebanon was not going to improve quickly, soon arranged to move their headquarters to Dubai. We were still eager to work together, and in 1976, we jointly launched Burson–Marsteller Middle East in the Dubai World Trade Centre, the first international PR consultancy to operate in the region.

At that time, Middle Eastern companies had a completely different idea about public relations. They established internal PR departments which were manned by 'meet and assist' junior executives whose main role was to look after what was becoming a rapidly increasing stream of foreign visitors. They felt that the main role of a PR man was getting on with potential customers. With their limited view of the PR function, very few locals had the experience or training to carry out the kind of PR that was being practiced in the West.

Most of these companies did not believe that PR was something they should pay for. For them, it was considered primarily a component of advertising, and many ad agencies felt the same way. The common practice when you placed ads was to negotiate with most of the local publications for some free editorial space as part of the deal. So getting coverage was not difficult, and companies didn't see the need to go beyond that.

Even after local firms developed a better understanding of the benefits of public relations, and the quality of PR executives had grown dramatically, working out terms and budgets with local clients in the region was not always easy. It seemed like different mind-sets were at work. I explained the problem when I gave a speech at the Corporate Communications and Public Relations Conference for local companies in Dubai in 1994. I presented ten basic rules for setting up a public relations programme with outside consult-ants. One basic rule was:

Only demand what the budget calls for. Do not expect to agree to pay for five projects and then want seven. This area is one I am extremely sensitive about in the Middle East. Many compa-nies believe that when they are approaching public relations consultancies, the same rules exist as bargaining in the local bazaar. Senior executives from other large consultancies have told me they are often turning down offers to pitch for Middle East business in the Middle East as it is too time-consuming and the budgets are often unrealistic.

The situation did improve dramatically in the next decade. But some of the largest clients, especially government organizations, continued to create problems for some PR firms by ignoring their contractual obligation to pay their fees monthly. It was true that they eventually paid, but the long wait between payments meant the PR firm involved had to be financially strong to handle the slow trickle of cash flow.

Even before we opened our local Dubai office, we had already been working for many years for Saudi Basic Industrial Corporation, a government owned chemical company and one of the leading indus-trial companies in Saudi Arabia. I had signed an agreement with them in the US, and the account was headquartered in New York, since the US was their major potential market. But soon an opportunity arose that would dramatically increase our work in Saudi Arabia.

One day I got a call from Harold Burson, who told me that he wanted me to go to Riyadh to meet with a Saudi prince, Bandar bin Sultan. The royal family needed an international firm to handle the public relations for The King Faisal Foundation. The Prince had called someone he knew and respected in California asking him to recommend an American PR firm that would be able to handle their account. He was told about Burson–Marsteller, and it was suggested that he call Harold Burson to discuss the opportunity. The Prince followed this advice and the result was positive for all involved. Harold told the Prince he would be sending me to Riyadh for further discussions.

The King Faisal Foundation is one of the largest philanthropic foundations in the world. Each year it awards the King Faisal International Prize to 'dedicated men and women whose contributions make a positive difference'. The prizes are given in five categories: Service to Islam, Islamic Studies, Arabic Language and Literature, Science, and Medicine. Awards consist of a 24-carat, 200-gram gold medal and $200,000 for each of the winners. These awards have been popularly called 'the Arab Nobel Prizes'.

The Foundation also has a Centre for Research and Islamic Studies, sponsors a private, non-profit university, a library covering the fields of Islamic Studies and Islamic Civilization, and a manuscripts library of more than 23,000 hand-written texts, some of which are more than 1,200 years old, highlighting contributions made by Arab and Muslim scholars.

The Foundation is truly non-political, as are its choices for awards. In 2009, for example, the prize given for medicine was awarded to an American Jew, Professor Ronald Levy, head of Stanford University's Oncology department, for his role in the development of a new revolutionary drug used in the treatment of many types of cancer. Professor Levy was allowed to bring his wife and daughter, both born in Israel, to the award ceremony, even though there were Israeli visa stamps in their passports which can mean automatic refusal of entry to Saudi Arabia. He also attended a dinner with King Abdullah. Professor Levy noted later that he received only the finest treatment while he was in the country.

When I arrived in Riyadh to meet with Prince Bandar, I found that we were not pitching against any other firm, and after a series of discussions I was told that we could start immediately. Prince Bandar and some of his associates explained to me exactly how the Foundation worked, what it had accomplished, and what it really meant to the Arab World. So much of this, the Prince explained, was not known and appreciated.

The Director-General of the Foundation at the time was HRH Prince Khalid Al-Faisal, who is now in charge of Mecca. He is the son of the current monarch, King Abdullah. Prince Khalid is extremely articulate and also an excellent artist. He gained world-wide fame by founding Painting & Patronage in 1999, a prominent cultural and artistic exchange programme between Saudi Arabia and numerous other nations around the world. The programme included exhibitions, scholarships, lecture series and special events.

Painting & Patronage had its first international launch in June 2000, in London's Banqueting House, under the joint patronage of Prince Khalid and Charles, Prince of Wales. The show exhibited watercolours and oil paintings by both Princes and was attended by the Queen and Prince Philip. Both Khalid and Charles have remained extremely active in Paintings & Patronage and exhibitions have been held in many countries. On the tenth anniversary celebration of our working for Saudi Basic Industrial Corporation in Riyadh, I was fortunate to be given a print by Prince Khalid as a gift. Despite my good relations with the Saudis, I never felt it advisable to open an office in Saudi Arabia, although I did send a senior executive to stay there during periods when there was a great deal of activity.

Of all the places I have operated in, the Middle East was by far the region where we had to be the most sensitive and careful about what we said and to whom. The political and religious minefields were everywhere. We rarely knew precisely what the person we were dealing with really thought, to whom he might be beholden, what kind of alliances and connections he had, or how he would take what we were saying. I found it safer to say very little than to make a statement that could alienate someone.

By contrast, in the West we can be openly critical of some aspect of a politician's actions even if we have a high opinion of him generally. Not so in the Middle East. Any kind of criticism of a leader could be dangerous to the critic. Recent events have under-lined how deep and strong the resentment was against many of the authoritarian leaders in the region, in spite of the lack of public (or even private) expressions of it. Once the opportunity for change arose, the hidden unhappiness and frustrations were revealed and people proved willing to risk their lives to effect change. The press in most of the Middle Eastern countries I was familiar with was government-controlled, and all our clients knew this. They did not expect nor did they want us to place stories that could possibly be construed as negative or intemperate in nature.

The only time that I ever turned down an opportunity to work for a client took place in the Middle East. It was basically Burson–Marsteller's philosophy that everyone has the right to tell his story just as anyone on trial has a right to legal representation, even if there might be a great deal of public hostility towards the person. But my only refusal of work took place more than twenty years ago when someone from the *Financial Times* called and said that Libya and Colonel Gaddafi wanted an international public relations firm.

The caller asked if I would be willing to discuss their needs with someone from the Libyan government. I politely declined. But I can't take credit for seeing into the future (this was before the Lockerbie bombing) or knowing just how bad things would get for the people of Libya or, in the end, for Gaddafi himself. I just felt, even at that time, that presenting a favourable image of the Colonel and his government would be too close to science fiction for my tastes.

Meanwhile, Burson–Marsteller Intermarkets showed rapid growth, working for clients such as Coca-Cola, McDonald's, Polaroid, Nissan and Tag Heuer, for whom we helped sponsor a Regional Offshore Powerboat Racing Championship. The Middle Eastern country where I did feel there were great future possibilities for us was Egypt. Hosni Mubarak appeared to have established a general calm. I began to interview PR executives to select someone to move to Cairo and work in our partner Intermarkets' Cairo office. I found Allan Biggar, who greatly impressed me both in knowledge and attitude, and he went to Cairo and stayed there for four years. He later became head of Burson–Marsteller in London and even later started his own international marketing company.

Business came in relatively quickly. We helped to reposition Coca-Cola after they bought Pepsi Cola's regional bottler. We worked for the Agency for International Development promoting the benefit of privatizing state industries. And we helped launch the first business TV programme, called *Indicator*. By 1998, our Cairo office had grown to a staff of six.

Unfortunately our biggest assignment and one of our greatest successes was the result of one of Egypt's greatest tragedies. On 17 November 1997, six terrorists attacked and murdered sixty-two people, including fifty-eight foreign tourists, at a major tourist attraction, Deir-el-Bahri. The place is a popular archaeological site across the Nile River from Luxor, and features the mortuary temple of the eighteenth-century dynasty female pharaoh, Hatshepsut. The assailants were disguised as members of the Egyptian security forces and were armed with rifles and machetes. For forty-five harrowing minutes they systematically massacred men, women, even children visiting the temple. They left a note in the disembowelled body of a dead woman that claimed they were the 'Brigade of Devastation and Destruction' and that their aim was to destroy what they saw as the corrupt Egyptian government.

The murdered tourists came from a number of different countries, so the news of the massacre hit hard all around the world. Tourists in droves began to cancel their Egyptian holiday plans and airlines began to cancel flights. The Egyptian economy, dependent on foreign tourism, began to suffer accordingly.

One of our initial clients in Egypt before the massacre was the country's tourist board. We had originally been hired by an ex-banker who had become Minister for Tourism. Shortly before this tragic event, he had been replaced by Dr Mamdouh el Beltagy, an extremely insightful public official who appreciated the vital need for an intelligent public relations campaign in the aftermath of the Luxor disaster. We began to train his staff in crisis management and how to deal actively with the press. It was clear that perceptions about travel to Egypt would not change dramatically within a week or even a month – or possibly even a year – and that the country would have to live with that.

The act of terrorism, of course, reverberated within Egypt itself. The Egyptian public was so repulsed by the massacre that it became even more pro-government and wanted to do everything possible to promote tourism, which was vital to the country's future. Very quickly though, tourism began to improve. In the long run the attack had a far smaller effect on tourism than the government had originally feared.

After these events, preparedness for crises became a key issue for most tourist boards, and in August 1995, I gave a major address to the World Tourism Organization at its Cairo meeting entitled 'Crisis Management: How to Prepare for the Worst and Handle It Best'.

I stressed that every tourist organization should have a crisis team and that there should be: a crisis manual, one that is continually updated; a key media list, both local and international; a list of organizations affecting the tourism business such as major hotel chains, credit card companies and leading travel agents; internal exercises for staff where a specific crisis is simulated and they plan exactly how it would be handled.

As I've already noted, good PR professionals in the Middle East at the time were scarce – the good ones were few and far between. The sophistication of some clients was also noticeably lacking. Certain PR companies were paid for the number of column inches that appeared in the press with little concern for the quality of the message. Nor was the local press operating at the height of sophistication and ethical values. And, quite often, gifts to journalists ensured the upward swing of column inches. None of this is true today. Both local journalists and PR executives are now highly skilled and well schooled in the use of PR. And with the Middle East being the centre of the world's focus, the need for good and accurate information, especially since information keeps changing rapidly, has risen dramatically. This is the one reason for the success of the Al Jazeera TV network, which continues to grow throughout the world.

As I travelled from country to country throughout the Middle East, I was surprised and delighted by the younger generation and its attitude towards the future of their countries and the region. While I can't claim to have predicted the Arab Spring, it was obvious to me at that time that change was inevitable. I could feel Western ideas and values emerging more and more. Our operating company in the Middle East, ASDA'A Burson–Marsteller, has been holding an Arab Youth Survey for the last three years whereby Penn Schoen Berland, the research company, interviews 2,000 people between the ages of eighteen and twenty-four in the various countries.

For the purposes of the study, the countries of the region are grouped as follows: The Gulf Cooperation Council (Saudi Arabia, United Arab Emirates, Qatar and Kuwait) and the non-GCC (Jordan, Lebanon, Egypt and Iraq). Some of the interesting findings are as follows: for those in the non-GCC, the most important issue was the desire to be living in a democratic country. For the GCC, it was maintaining a close family relationship. The political views of the area's youth are now much more liberal than in the past, with a very small percentage having no political views. European countries are looked on favourably, especially the UK, and are most well perceived in Lebanon and Saudi Arabia. Positive feelings towards the US are also growing.

The need to maintain traditional values in the future remains very strong throughout the whole region. The most trusted news sources are newspapers and TV, with TV rated most highly and magazines at the bottom. Eighty per cent use the Internet daily. Social networking is most popular in Iraq and Egypt (where it was put to widespread use during the protests), and least popular in Saudi Arabia and the United Arab Emirates.

ASDA'A Burson–Marsteller is now the largest PR firm in the Middle East. Headquartered in Dubai, the firm has seven wholly-owned offices with 140 professionals and seven affiliates covering sixteen markets. Growth has been consistent and continues despite all of the political change in many Middle Eastern markets. We have been able to remain constantly aware of the continuing changes in perception – internally and externally – in all audiences, and have made sure our communications efforts take these continuing changes into account. The future for public relations in the Middle East remains very bright but nowhere else is there a greater need for care and sensitivity when attempting to manage perceptions.

10   My Most Memorable Clients: Good and Bad

During my fifty years in the public relations business, I worked with many different types of clients in all parts of the world. That's what made my job so exciting and satisfying. The truth is that there were also times when it was difficult and times when it was frustrating. Usually it was a client who made it so. Even as chief executive, though, I couldn't unilaterally drop a client because I found him or her a pain in the neck.

The only time I have taken a really hard stance with a client and risked losing him was when we felt that the action they were requesting would damage whatever we were trying to accomplish together. Fortunately, this very rarely happened. It was equally rare that I went home in the evening thinking that I'd rather be a teacher or a lawyer.

Obviously there are many things you can't put in a memoir, not because you are afraid there will be a lawyer knocking at your door, but because you have a moral obligation that comes with the job to respect confidences. So while in this chapter I describe some of the most enjoyable and the most difficult people that I have worked with, the difficult ones I have chosen to write about have been long since deceased.

Robert Maxwell

Robert Maxwell, a truly unique figure whose death is still myste-rious, deserves his own book, and a number have already been written. Of all my clients, he was in many ways the most unique and in some strange ways the most fascinating. One story will show that I was not the only one who thought of him in that way.

In 1983, I was invited as a guest to the wedding of one of my major clients, Rocco Forte, then head of a hospitality empire that included 800 hotels and 1,000 restaurants. The nuptials took place in Rome. The day after the wedding, the bride's parents gave a luncheon at a local trattoria for those guests who had come from abroad. Rocco had arranged a bus to take people to the restaurant from their hotels, but since my wife and I were so familiar with Rome – I had started an office there and spent a good amount of time in the Eternal City – we decided to walk to the restaurant.

When we arrived, there were only two guests present – Robert Maxwell and Gerald Ronson, who had arrived together for the wedding on a private plane. I was at that time working for Maxwell, and when he saw me come in, he yelled, 'Bob! Bob! Come here, Bob!' He introduced me to Gerald Ronson, chief executive of Heron, who was then, and still is, one of Britain's largest property owners. He said to Gerald: 'Bob is the only PR man I use.' This was far from the case. 'And you should use him too,' he added.

Gerald's wife Gail, who was extremely nice, said to her husband, 'Gerald, he might be right. I live with you and I know what you are like. You're not like what they say in the papers. Those constant stories in the press just are not true. Maybe Mr Leaf can help you receive a more accurate appraisal.'

Gerald turned to me and said, 'No insult intended, Mr Leaf, but it doesn't upset me what the press says. All that matters to me is what profit I return to my shareholders and that those profits remain

Signing a partnership agreement with the Chinese Government in the Great Hall of the People in Beijing establishing the first Chinese government PR company.

With my client, Lord Forte (centre), who ran the largest hotel chain in Europe.

With Tony Iveson, one of England's 'Dam Busters', meeting the head of the government of Argentina in Buenos Aires.

Making final arrangements with a Japanese partner to open the
Burson-Marsteller offices in Tokyo.

I found no two people better to work with than King Constantine and
Queen Anne-Marie of Greece.

Saying prayers with a Buddhist priest at the opening of our Thailand offices.

In conversation with Prince Charles at wedding of the King of Greece's son.

On the occasion of my 30th anniversary at Burson-Marsteller, the Asian staff thought it would only be fitting if I came dressed as the Emperor of China.

high.' At that point Maxwell wandered off in the direction of the men's room. I turned to Ronson and said: 'No insult meant, Mr Ronson, but considering what you told your wife about your feelings towards PR, I'm quite sure you would be a very difficult client to deal with.' He smiled and replied, pointing to Maxwell in the distance, 'I'm sure I wouldn't be as difficult as he is.' He knew what he was talking about.

When Maxwell hired Burson–Marsteller, he also hired Hill and Knowlton, saying: 'I want to be the only person employing the two best PR firms in London.' Whether we were or weren't the best, in his mind we had to be since he had selected us. I mentioned previously that we had handled Rupert Murdoch's successful fight against Maxwell to take over the *News of the World*. Had Bob known that, I guarantee we would not have been hired or even allowed to pitch for his account. He was still extremely bitter over his loss and angry at Murdoch personally. In a *Playboy* magazine interview he said:

When he got *News of the World* he didn't outbid me. He got it for nothing. For the *News of the World* I put up £47m, and he put up nothing and got it. Simply, Margaret Thatcher [who he also hated with a passion] gave Murdoch everything he wanted and deprived me of what I wanted as long as she could. Rupert Murdoch would be nothing if he weren't allowed to beat rules in Britain.

There is no doubt that if Maxwell was still alive, these would be some of the happiest days of his life watching the current problems enveloping *News of the World* and Rupert Murdoch.

A few years after hiring us, both agencies were still handling different parts of the account, and Bob invited all those involved to a party in a suite at Claridge's. He was the ultimate charmer when he wanted to be, and he told the group that the reason for the get-together was to announce that he had just hired someone to be responsible for the entire account in-house, someone who would now be the liaison to the PR firm. We noticed he used the singular when referring to PR firms, meaning that one firm would soon be fired. Then he named his in-house PR manager, a senior executive from Hill and Knowlton. One of my staff, the senior Burson–Marsteller executive on the Maxwell account, turned to me and said, 'I guess that means we are on the way out.'

I smiled and, knowing Maxwell as I did, replied: 'It means just the opposite.' By hiring a senior man away from Hill and Knowlton, he now had access to that firm's thinking, special skills and contacts. He could still have the best of both worlds, employing the two best PR firms (as he saw it) in London without having to pay fees to both. Soon after, just as I predicted, Hill and Knowlton were let go.

To understand Maxwell, one has to know a little bit about his background. He was born Ján Ludvik Hoch to an Orthodox Jewish family in a town then called Slatinské Doly in the easternmost province of pre-war Czechoslovakia. The area was later claimed by Hungary, and when the Nazis occupied it in 1944, most of his family were sent to Auschwitz, where they died. Maxwell, however, had already escaped from the Nazis and arrived in Britain in 1940 as a 17-year-old refugee. He joined the British Army Pioneer Corps in 1941 and transferred to the North Staffordshire Regiment in 1943. He went on to become a sergeant and fought all the way from the Normandy beaches to Berlin. In 1945, he was promoted to captain and was given the Military Cross by Field Marshall Montgomery. Robert Maxwell showed that he was capable of doing great things and should never be underestimated.

After the war, he moved to Berlin; he spoke fluent German. He decided to publish scientific journals and set up Pergamon Press. Later, after returning to Britain a fervent socialist, he became an MP for Buckinghamshire in 1964, retaining his seat until 1970.

Maxwell was also very family-oriented and had nine children, two of whom unfortunately died very young.

Some of his business practices came under question over the course of his career. When he agreed to a takeover of Pergamon by Leasco, an American financial and data processing group, the deal fell apart when there were claims that Maxwell had falsely stated profits. The Department of Trade and Industry, who investigated the situation, said: 'We regret having to conclude that, not with-standing Mr Maxwell's acknowledged abilities and energy, he is not in our opinion, a person who can be relied on to exercise proper stewardship of a publicly quoted company.'

Such obstacles never deterred Maxwell on his way to building a media empire. In 1984 he purchased the Mirror Group from Reed International, and in 1988, he purchased Macmillan, an American publishing firm, for $2.6bn, a price considered by most well over its real value.

As Murdoch found when taking over *The Times*, Maxwell discovered when taking over the Mirror Group that the unions had dominated the previous owners and that the papers were way over-staffed. Maxwell was not one to play games. He made it quite clear, as Murdoch had at *The Times*, that he wanted only the number of people really necessary to run the paper or he would close it down. His subsequent agreement with the unions resulted in 2,000 job losses. When told that one union leader had said about him that he could 'charm the birds out of the trees – then shoot them', Maxwell responded: 'Well, if I have to shoot the birds, I shoot them. But I get no fun out of it.' A cab driver, who previously worked for the Mirror Group, told me that Maxwell was quite fair regarding termination fees and that his severance pay was what had allowed him to purchase a cab.

People were wary of attacking Maxwell as he was known to bring in his libel lawyers at the drop of a comment. *Private Eye* found this out to their discomfort when calling him 'Cap'n Bob' and 'The Bouncing Czech' – a bit of whimsy among more uncomplimentary things, which ended up costing them around £225,000.

In my dealings with Bob Maxwell, I found that he always had to be on stage and have an audience. He was like Cyrano de Bergerac but it was his ego rather than his nose that was grandiose. He loved his image, as he told one reporter: 'I won't budge and I won't compromise. I'm known for that. And as a consequence many people won't challenge me. They say you get as much pleasure out of chewing frozen gum as you do fighting Captain Bob.'

There was no question, though, that he was fascinating to work with. He always had to make it abundantly clear that he was the boss and that *you* were in a position inferior to him. When I would come to his office for meetings, they were scheduled to take place at 9 a.m. and I always arrived promptly. In turn, he always kept me waiting at least half an hour, often more. That way, I would know my place.

Bob was always willing to listen to ideas or suggestions and would readily adopt them if he felt they might be helpful. But the price you often paid for acceptance of your good ideas, though, was to give up ownership. More often than not he would claim the ideas as his own, declaring that he had been thinking about them already. He didn't always demand that you kissed his rear end, but he liked you heading in that general direction.

When I would arrive with our monthly bill, he would usually look it over, shake his head and if, for example, it was for £6,000, he'd say: 'I like the work your firm's been doing, but what if I gave you a cheque right now for £5,500?' I'd always agree because if I didn't I knew our payment would be a long time in coming. But knowing Bob so well I always had our accounting department add roughly £500 to the amount accrued by our hourly charges before I brought it to him.

One of the great Maxwell stories, and I know it to be true as he admitted it to *Newsweek* in an interview, involved smoking. Bob was a smoker, but he had within his office a no-smoking zone where NO ONE was allowed to smoke. One day he walked by and saw someone enjoying a cigarette. He went over to the felon and angrily asked, 'What is your name and how much do you earn a week?' When the smoker replied, he said to an assistant, 'Get me someone from the accounting department.' When the clerk arrived, he ordered, 'Make out a cheque for six weeks' pay for this man, as he is no longer working for us.' Then he stormed out. He later found out that the man was not in his employ but was actually a messenger making a delivery.

Around 1990, when he was setting up a pan-European newspaper in Paris called the *European*, we decided it was time to end our relationship with Maxwell. It had become a terribly difficult account to work on, and our people had had enough. Soon after, things started to go bad for him. His companies were failing, and it was later learned that in order to shore up his organization and avoid bankruptcy, he had stolen hundreds of millions of pounds from his companies' pension funds. Fortunately these were later replenished by investment banks and the British government.

On 5 November 1991, at the age of sixty-nine, Maxwell fell over the side of his luxury yacht, the *Lady Ghislaine*, and drowned. Then the rumours began: it wasn't an accident, it was suicide; it wasn't suicide, it was murder. After his death, more and more hidden personal information began to surface that I was completely unaware of and that fascinated me. It was claimed that he was an agent for the Israel intelligence service, Mossad, and that for years he had been providing them with extremely valuable information. The *Daily Mirror* later printed that he had been murdered by Mossad as he was trying to blackmail them.

Bob was given a funeral in Israel at the Mount of Olives that would have befitted a head of state. It was attended by six present or former heads of Israeli intelligence and by Prime Minister Yitzhak Shamir, who said at the funeral, 'He has done more for Israel than can today be said.' Interesting.

Many journalists called me and asked if I personally believed that he had committed suicide. At first I thought that he hadn't because the Maxwell I knew was more likely to throw everyone else overboard rather than to jump off himself. And I never felt that murder was a probability. But once it had been revealed that he had been stealing hundreds of millions of pounds from the pension funds of his company, and that he knew the government had gotten wind of it, he must have also realized that there was a strong possibility that he would be spending the rest of his life in jail. The thought of a trial and incarceration could well have caused him to believe ending his life at the bottom of the sea would be preferable. But the manner of his death is still an open question that will probably never be answered.

Dr Armand Hammer

One afternoon in 1971, the phone rang and a voice said, 'Dr Hammer would like to speak to you.' I wondered why. I had never met Dr Hammer and our company had never worked for him. I certainly knew who Armand Hammer was: a millionaire businessman who, in his late fifties, had invested $50,000 in Occidental Petroleum – an impoverished oil company – became its chief executive and major shareholder, and built it into one of America's twenty-five largest companies.

Armand Hammer was already a legend because of his personal friendship with Lenin, a relationship he capitalized on all his life. He had become a hero to the Russian leadership after the First World War by arranging to ship a million tons of grain to Russia at the height of a terrible famine. But even in those days you didn't get something for nothing from Armand Hammer. He became the first Western concessionaire in communist Russia, setting himself up as the sole representative for Ford, US Rubber, Ingersoll Rand, Underwood Typewriter and Parker Pen, among others.

He also amassed a valuable collection of furs, furniture and artwork, which were of little value to their previous owners. Hammer maintained good relations with Lenin, but he was not immortal and Stalin was a different kettle of fish. With Stalin in charge Hammer was forced out, but he kept alive his image and reputation as the friend of Lenin. When Stalin died, Hammer returned to favour in the Kremlin, enjoying good relationships with Brezhnev and Khrushchev. Even now, over twenty years after his death, stories still surface about Armand Hammer, some claiming that he was a spy for the Soviet Union, and others that he was a willing or unwilling dupe for the CIA.

Dr Hammer wasn't calling me to polish his image. He got to the point quickly: 'I have a public relations assignment, and I've been given your name. Can you handle it?' He wanted an answer even before I knew what the job was. He liked people with confidence. But showing confidence can be foolhardy when you don't even know what you are supposed to be confident about. In any case, my reply, long since forgotten, obviously satisfied him. And I got the assignment. Then he told me what it was:

We have made a deal with Holiday Inn to open hotels in Morocco, Casablanca, Fez, Marrakech and Tangier. Since they are so well known in the hotel business, I am afraid that they will get all the publicity, and my company will be left behind. I want to make sure we get at least equal mention in all the press coverage. Can you send someone to Marrakech where one of the royals will preside at the first opening? I want to make sure the Occidental name is prominent in all the coverage.

His tone of voice made it quite clear that this was not just a suggestion.

Now that the assignment was clear, my confidence improved. Occidental was a well-known company. What they did was news, and we had a great deal of experience in the travel business. The assignment wasn't difficult, even though the person giving it to us was. I took it for granted that there would be further briefings, after which we would prepare a written proposal.

'When do you want the man to go to Marrakech?' I asked.

'Tomorrow,' he replied. 'I'll arrange for his ticket, and the executive accompanying him on the flight can brief him. The opening is in a few days, which should give him plenty of time.'

Now that he had accomplished his basic objective, Dr Hammer became quite charming. He asked me questions about myself and the company and intimated that if this assignment were successful there could be a lot more work to do. By the time he hung up it was as if we had been long-time comrades.

The first assignment was a great success. One of our directors, Tony Iveson, who originally thought I was kidding when I told him what I wanted, hastened off to Morocco. To our good fortune, he found that one of Holiday Inn's key executives had, for some reason we were unaware of, inadvertently alienated the Crown Prince who then became an Occidental fan, and we ended up getting extensive coverage.

So, I began my relationship with Dr Hammer on the right side, the only side to be if peace, harmony and more assignments were the goal. He was a fascinating man. Of all the clients I have ever worked with he was the most driven by a desire for publicity. But usually it wasn't publicity just for publicity's sake but for some predetermined goal he wanted and wanted badly, such as getting close to a particular US president, a task at which he usually succeeded, or winning the Nobel Peace Prize, which eluded him.

Three books have been published about Dr Hammer from two extreme perspectives – one favourable, two highly unfavourable. The first was written twenty years ago by Bob Considine, a top notch American journalist, who specialized in biographies. Considine wrote *The Babe Ruth Story*, working with Babe Ruth, *General Wainright's Story* with General Wainright, the hero of the Philippines in the Second World War, and *The Men Who Robbed Brink's* with Specs O'Keefe, who did rob Brink's. In his book *The Remarkable Life of Dr Armand Hammer*, Considine does not claim he worked on the book with Dr Hammer, but the good Doctor's fingerprints are all over it. If there ever was an authorized biography, this was it. All you have to read is the book cover:

> Bob Considine documents the life of one of the most fasci-
> nating and successful private entrepreneurs of all time (. . .)
> Less familiar but equally intriguing are Armand Hammer's
> exploits in other fields including the arts, cattle breeding,
> whiskey distilling and as an undergraduate in medical school.
> The diversity of Armand Hammer's pursuits as well as the excel-
> lence with which he achieves his goals makes for a well paced,
> informative biography.

The book portrays Hammer in a way that makes him a shoo-in for passing through the gates of Saint Peter or the doors of Valhalla, whichever his preference.

The second book, entitled *The Dark Side of Power* by Carl Blumay, paints a completely different picture. Here, too, the cover blurb tells the story:

This is a book that never could have been published while Hammer was alive (...) [He was] a man driven to make money not for its own sake but for the power it gave him over anyone and anything that stood in his way. *The Dark Side of Power* shatters the Hammer myth with startling revelations about his marriages and tormented family relationships, his shrewd and ruthless business deals, his sly manoeuvres to win political favours from five American presidents, his self-serving manipulation of the media, his bribery schemes and his many brushes with the law.

Hardly a flattering portrait, but Dr Hammer did evoke strong feelings.

Much of what Blumay has to say is in all probability accurate. He was the director of public relations at Occidental for twenty-five years. Being so close to the Doctor he had access to much inside information. What surprised me though, was the intensity of Carl's vituperation. Carl Blumay was one of the first people Dr Hammer hired when he took over Occidental. For twenty-five years I am sure he paid him a salary that allowed Carl to live reasonably well. And although the book shows that Carl felt Hammer was the same miscreant from beginning to end, still, it took him twenty-five years to resign. That is a lot of masochism. I often had to work directly with Carl who was responsible for positioning Dr Hammer, so when the book cover also claims that it 'gives us the explosive truth about the man behind the mask that Hammer himself created', you sort of wonder if the word 'himself' is accurate. Possibly he received some help during those twenty-five years from the director of public relations. I do have some sympathy for Carl. I am sure he was treated with disdain during those twenty-five years, because Dr Hammer's references to him when talking to me were often unkind, but that was true about most people who worked for him. The third book came out a few years later, as we will see.

After the success of the Morocco project, Dr Hammer lived up to his word and employed us to handle the company's public relations in Europe, but not in the US. At first, this entailed putting out news releases to the European media that were being written and issued from America extolling Occidental or Dr Hammer. We were not asked to provide input regarding the releases or how best to get coverage for him in our local markets. I would chuckle when the first releases came across my desk, and I began to joke that we'd soon be seeing releases announcing every time Dr Hammer had gone to the men's room. I finally decided unilaterally not to send out to the local press those releases that I knew were of zero interest to them. No one in Los Angeles ever noticed that they were not charged for production and distribution of those particular stories.

I got to know Dr Hammer a lot better as he included us in more meaningful projects. While he took occasional naps to recharge, he was nearly always bursting with energy. And he always wanted immediate action. He had absolutely no qualms about calling associates anywhere in the world regardless of the time. When he once did this from my office, I asked, 'Isn't it three in the morning there?' He replied, 'Waking him up will be good for him.'

For a while, Carl Blumay tried to emulate his boss's calling habits. The time difference between Los Angeles and London was eight hours. Sometimes I would be awakened in the middle of the night. Finally, when the phone rang yet again at three in the morning, I passed the receiver over to my wife who is very easy-going but not always at her best at three in the morning. She spoke in a tone that would have done justice to a hanging judge: 'Do you have any idea what time it is?' After that my relationship with Carl became more of a daytime one.

The Doctor could be especially charming if he wanted something, and what he always wanted were results – results that were always measured on his personal scale of values. If you achieved them he remained charming. However, when you didn't, his anger could often be more extreme than his charm.

He was in London once when an article appeared in *The Times* that included confidential information about Occidental's Libyan operations. The minute I heard his voice on the phone I knew there was a problem high on his Richter Scale. 'Did you see the article in the paper?' He did not say which article or which paper because he took it for granted that if you were doing PR for Occidental, you were aware of everything that was said about them. Fortunately I had seen it. 'Did one of your people leak that story?' he asked. I said that I didn't think so, but that I hadn't had time to investigate, so I couldn't be sure. 'If one of your people did it,' answered Hammer, 'I want you to cut his balls off.'

I knew from his tone that he felt that this was one of my duties as chairman and that he would happily provide the scalpel. I discovered upon investigation that the leak did not come from us, since no one in our organization had any knowledge of the facts involved. The source had to have come directly from Libya. Dr Hammer accepted my word on this, saying he would look into Libya. I still sometimes wonder if someone in Tripoli is wandering around *sans* gonads.

When it came to publicity, Dr Hammer was his own worst enemy. His office constantly released so much material with such inflated claims that he was always suspect among journalists. I sometimes tried to cut down on the euphoria when it came to major announcements, but it wasn't always easy. Having made a very newsworthy deal in Russia, it was agreed to hold a press conference in London where Dr Hammer would personally make the public announcement. When I reviewed the draft of the news release prepared by

Occidental's PR department, I winced a little. It was an important release but by comparison it made the purchase of Manhattan Island from the Lenape Indians for twenty-four dollars pale into insignificance.

I didn't believe I could shift Dr Hammer on my own since his ability to operate successfully in Russia represented an important part of his total persona. I solicited an ally, Sergeant Shriver, President Kennedy's brother-in-law, who was the legal advisor to Dr Hammer on this deal and an extremely nice and sensible man. I asked if he could go over the release with the Doctor and cite some legal reasons for toning it down. He was able to, and the release returned to a semblance of reality. Sarge and I became friends over this manoeuvre. He later asked me to become one of the original signatories required under US law to put him in the running to become vice president of the United States.

There followed a couple of years hiatus in my relationship with Dr Hammer. How it ended and how it resumed tells a lot about the man. Dorman Commons, Occidental's financial vice president, was growing increasingly concerned about Occidental's reputation within the financial community and the financial press in the US. He felt he needed the services of a major PR firm to help patch it up. He asked if I believed our New York office could handle this. I said yes, it could, if the Doctor acquiesced. He said the Doctor agreed but would have to approve the final proposal. He put in place a budget for research so that we could establish just how severe the problem was. Our New York office then did a study of the financial community's attitude to Dr Hammer and Occidental. The results were withering.

Hammer's credibility was south of zero and getting worse. We prepared a detailed report for Dorman spelling it out in realistic terms. He was not in the least bit surprised and said we should present it to the Doctor. We asked if we should tone it down a little bit lest he overreact, but Dorman felt it was important that the Doctor understand the exact situation before we moved ahead to rectify it.

So Buck Buchwald, our executive vice president, and Tony Hughes, head of our financial affairs group, flew to Los Angeles to present the study to the Doctor at his home. Dr Hammer was not amused. 'Did you talk to anyone in Peru about what they thought of me?' he queried. He had recently signed an exploration agreement with the Peruvian government. He asked why we had not spoken to others who would have cast him in a more favourable light. When Tony and Buck left, they knew that they had not made a hit and that we would not be given that assignment. But they underestimated the Doctor's ego. For this major transgression – presenting accurate research results that he didn't like – he fired us in Europe also. I assumed that marked the end of my relationship with Armand Hammer.

About two years later I got a phone call from Carl Blumay in Los Angeles. 'Bob,' he said, in a familiar and friendly tone as if we were still working hand-in-hand, 'the Doctor would like you to see him tomorrow at Claridge's. He has an assignment for you.' I told Carl that I already had an appointment. He responded, 'I'd really appreciate it if you could see him as I promised him you would be there.' I have to admit that I would have broken my other appointment out of curiosity, and because Dr Hammer, even with his many faults, had been one of my most fascinating clients.

When I arrived at his suite in Claridge's, both the Doctor and his wife Frances greeted me and were extremely charming. We talked generalities for a few minutes. Then Frances left. 'Bob,' he said, 'I always liked you. It was your New York people I didn't care for. I have an assignment I would like you to handle. I am going to exhibit my paintings at The Royal Academy of Fine Arts here in London and then at the National Gallery in Dublin. I'd like Burson–Marsteller to handle the press previews in both countries. I would especially like you to arrange for some of the leading art critics from France to attend.' His collection was controversial, because some critics felt that it included too many inferior works by major artists, but it was still significant. It later became the centre of controversy when the Doctor changed his mind as to where it would be finally bequeathed. As a throwaway line he said, 'And you can have the Occidental account back in Europe.'

One nice aspect about working for a very large public relations firm is that no one client or prospect is so large that you are hungry for any sort of deal. I said with a certain degree of frankness, 'What happens if you get mad again and want to fire us on the spot? I'll need a year's contract after which there is a three-month termination notice by either side.' That meant we would have the account for at least fifteen months. The Doctor said, 'Fine, send a contract to me here tomorrow and I'll sign it.' He signed it the next day, and as things went, we held the account quite a bit longer than the fifteen months.

Armand Hammer had great charm and incredible energy. Most of all he had charisma. Any time you spent with him was exciting. Even though Carl Blumay's biography was scripted as Othello might have written about Iago after he found out the truth about Desdemona, he too agrees. One thing Hammer didn't possess was loyalty. People meant very little to him. If we performed well we were part of his team. If any one of the account team messed up according to his personal and usually unreasonable criteria he was expendable. That is why he replaced five corporate presidents in fifteen years.

Dr Hammer lived and worked as if he were immortal, and perhaps he really thought he was. But on 10 December 1990 death finally caught up with him. He was ninety-two years old. The obituary in the *Wall Street Journal*, describing 'one of the most colourful and forceful entrepreneurs in the twentieth century', summed him up perfectly.

Six years later a book by Edward Jay Epstein, entitled *Dossier: The Secret History of Armand Hammer*, made Carl Blumay's book look complimentary in comparison. *Fortune Magazine* headlined its review 'Armand Hammer: Tinker, Traitor, Satyr, Spy'. Epstein argues that Hammer was probably a Russian agent and that one of his skills was pay-offs and bribes. He even wrote that the Doctor, for blackmail purposes, recorded some bribes using microphones hidden in his cufflinks. Epstein went after his personal life as well. He claimed that when his wife learned that he was having an affair with the woman running his art collection, he had his mistress change her name and wear heavy make-up, glasses and a wig – a ruse that Epstein maintains fooled Mrs Hammer for years. I didn't come across these aspects of Hammer while handling his account, but having watched him in action I don't doubt that Epstein's *Dossier* is most probably valid.

Constantine, the Former King of Greece

Some time in the 1970s, an assistant to Stavros Niarchos, one of Greece's wealthiest ship owners, came to see me and said that Niarchos had been very upset by the coverage that one of his children was receiving in the press. I had been recommended to him as possibly being able to rectify the situation, and that the budget, by the way, would not be a problem. I told the assistant I would look into the situation and get back to him. I went to work and studied a number of clippings, mostly from gossip columns, that seemed to be spreading the negative publicity. We met again and I said that I could prepare a proposal but that in reality very little could be done about this, as gossip columnists are skilled at making innuendos that you can't do much about and certainly can't sue over. He thanked me and left.

A few days later the assistant contacted me again and quoted Mr Niarchos as saying that I was one of the few people he had come across who didn't seem eager to take his money. My reluctance to take on the assignment had apparently impressed him. As a result, he had recommended me to General Michael Arnaoutis, the assistant to King Constantine of Greece, who was looking for someone to assist him with a matter that had just come up.

From the moment that General Arnaoutis and I met, I knew that working with him would be a pleasure. He had great charm, humour and intelligence. General Arnaoutis had been the closest advisor to the King from the days when the King was Crown Prince, and he had been appointed to be his instructor. He later acted as aide to the Crown Prince, and when Constantine became King, Arnaoutis became his private secretary. When the King was deposed in 1967, Arnaoutis was the first person to be arrested. He was severely beaten up and sentenced to death by the ruling junta.

Because he was a hero to the people of Greece for his performance in the Korean War, the death penalty was removed and he was exiled to the UK. While serving in the Greek regiment in Korea, he was considered by the Americans one of the greatest heroes of the war and was awarded two Bronze Stars and two Silver Stars. Upon arrival in the UK, he became the King's advisor and continued to expand on his already considerable intellect by studying at the London School of Economics and earning postgraduate degrees in Social Administration, Economics and History. He also spoke fluent German, Russian and English.

Because he held the rank of Lieutenant-Colonel, the Greek military later ordered him to return to Greece to serve the government. When he refused, he was banned for life, not allowed to ever come back for a visit, even to bury his parents. When he died, the government's attitude reversed dramatically. He was brought back as a hero and given a full military funeral complete with eulogies. There is now a General Michael Arnaoutis Foundation established in Greece to do good works in his name.

During our first meeting, the General explained that they needed someone to work with Queen Anne-Marie to prepare a paper launching a Cyprus war relief fund being set up to help Greek citizens following the Turkish invasion. The King and Queen were living in a suburb of London and it was arranged for me to meet them the following day. So began a thirty-year relationship.

Both King and Queen were extremely easy to work with right from the start. While I would show the normal respect that might be expected when dealing with royalty, it was never demanded. And they were always willing to consider my suggestions and were very appreciative of my contributions to their cause. They both had very retentive minds and showed great warmth. When they invited me to their home to have lunch with them, it never seemed like a client–agency relationship. And they approached their missions with professionalism. Both were willing to sit through training sessions before specific interviews. These weren't generally necessary as they were both intelligent, articulate and familiar with the subject matter.

There was one major hurdle that needed to be cleared in my first assignment for them. The paper I was helping to draft had to be approved by Archbishop Makarios of Cyprus who was coming to London to look at it personally and to see what changes he might feel would be necessary. Archbishop Makarios had a reputation as someone you never wanted to find yourself in disagreement with. He arrived with bodyguards at the Grosvenor Hotel and was quite formal and distant with me during our meeting. I imagine that he acted differently with the King and Queen when he was alone with them as they were royalty and I wasn't.

The Archbishop had the most terrifyingly piercing eyes I have ever encountered. When he looked directly at you, you just wanted to say, 'Yes sir, yes sir. I'll do that right away, sir.' The fortunate thing was that he liked the speech and did not change a single word. The launch of the war relief programme turned out to be quite successful, an ideal start to my working relationship with the Greek royal family.

Constantine had become King of Greece in March 1964, succeeding his father to the throne. In April 1967, a month before elections were to be held in which a centrist victory was expected, a group of right-wing army officers staged a coup d'état and surrounded the King's residence in Tatoi with tanks. The King had little choice, facing this show of force, and accepted the inevitable by swearing in the new regime headed by the unelected generals. He immediately began to plan a counter-coup with the help of senior officers in the air force and navy who were traditionally very royalist. But, in December, after flying to the north of Greece where he hoped to lead a counter-rebellion, it became obvious that the controlling junta was far too strong and any military action he might take would result in a great deal of bloodshed with little chance of victory. He wanted to avoid at all costs putting his subjects in harm's way, so he took his family and left Greece for Rome on 14 December for what turned out to be a permanent exile. He never abdicated, but a vote held by the ruling party in 1974 ended the monarchy. The government seized his property, voided his Greek passport, and only allowed him back for a short time to bury his mother, Queen Frederika, in the family cemetery at the former royal palace at Tatoi.

Queen Anne-Marie was of Danish descent, the youngest daughter of King Frederick IX of Denmark and Ingrid of Sweden. She first met the King in 1959 when she was thirteen. They met a few times after that, and they became engaged and married in 1964, a few weeks after her eighteenth birthday. She learned Greek and became an extremely popular queen, even among many of those who did not favour a monarchy. Much of her time was spent working for a charitable foundation known as 'Her Majesty's Fund' which primarily aided people in the rural areas of Greece.

In exile, the royal family established their home in England, first living in Chobham in Surrey and then in the Hampstead area of London. England was not a surprising choice as there had always been a close relationship with the British since Prince Philip, the husband of Queen Elizabeth II of England, was the son of Andrew, Prince of Greece and Denmark. Philip was born in Corfu, which was part of Greece, and is the King's cousin. The relationships have always remained close as the Queen of England is godmother to Constantine's daughter, Theodora; Prince Charles is godfather to his son, Philippos; and Constantine is godfather to a future heir to the throne, Prince William.

The most difficult thing about working for an exiled King, especially one as articulate as Constantine, was that I was constantly deluged with requests from journalists from all over the world for interviews. We had to decide whom he should talk to and what subjects should take precedence. Since the Greek press was then government controlled, it was no surprise that its reporting on the King was usually unfavourable and often untrue. But it usually did not make sense to respond to the coverage, as the response would not appear in the Greek press in any case. Journalists outside of Greece were well aware that the Greek press would not be publishing hosannas to the former royal family and so did not generally spread the stories that appeared less than true. One of the nice things about dealing with the King and Queen was that they were realists and did not expect any miracles from me.

Because our relationship was long and close, I had the opportunity to meet with various members of their families. When the Queen's mother, former Queen Ingrid, was visiting, we sat together on a sofa talking mainly about her love for her grandchildren. It was such a warm and comfortable moment that it was almost like talking to my own mother. I also met King Carlos of Spain, King Constantine's brother-in-law. We were once in the elevator at Claridge's, and I witnessed him chatting with the elevator operator in a friendly and casual way that you just wouldn't expect of a royal.

The main issue that remained constant throughout our professional relationship and that I was continually working on was his possible return to Greece, plus the question of the ownership of the property he had left behind. In 1992, in an agreement with the conservative government of Constantine Mitsotakis, the King ceded most of his land in Greece, then valued at 24-billion-drachma (£77,000,000) to a non-profit foundation in exchange for the 400 acres at Tatoi, including the house, chapel and graveyard of his ancestors, and the right to export to the UK a number of pieces of personal property within the palaces he was giving up.

In 1993 he was allowed to return to his homeland with a small entourage. As he travelled by boat around the country – to very favourable audiences – he was constantly harassed by Greek air force planes, and the government finally asked for an early departure. In 1994, the new government of Andreas Papandreou passed new legislation that cancelled the agreement of 1992 and stripped him of all his remaining property in Greece and revoked his passport. The passport which he had been allowed to keep was issued to Constantine, former King of the Hellenes. The government said it might consider reissuing him a passport if he adopted a new surname, but this he refused, explaining he did not have one.

In his statement to the press, the King noted that while the Prime Minister was entitled to his personal opinion about him, he could in no way claim Constantine wasn't a Greek citizen. 'All my children attended a Greek school which my wife and I helped to found. My wife and children speak fluent Greek. I am Greek. My wife is

Greek. My children are Greek. And nothing the prime minister says can ever change this,' he said.

The response in his favour was overwhelming. In the US Senate, Senator Claiborne Pell called on the Greek government to drop its actions saying, 'This is a clear violation of human rights and I urge the government of Greece to reconsider its actions.'

Pell even went further, noting that the King in London had held a press conference (that we arranged) attended by more than one hundred journalists from around the world, to set forth his reasons for opposing the legislation. He added, 'Mr President, I ask unanimous consent that the full text of King Constantine's statement as well as the draft legislation against him be printed at this point in the *Congressional Record*.' In England, the reaction was the same. Thirty-three members of the House of Commons attacked the action of the Greek government stating:

> This house condemns the declared intention of the Greek government to destroy the rights of former King Constantine of the Hellenes as a Greek citizen. By removing his citizenship and his passport, by appropriating his property without compensation, including his family graveyard, through use of edicts imposed by colonel dictators, and by denying him his basic human right of recourse to the courts of his own country to challenge the validity of these edicts and laws.

In the thirty years that I worked for the Greek monarch, he never once suggested that I should try to place a story indicating that it would be sensible to have a return to the monarchy. He had accepted the will of the people in the referendum that ended it, and as he said in an interview with *Time Magazine*, 'If the Greek people decide they want a republic, they are entitled to that and should be left in peace to enjoy it.'

As time went on, he began to be looked on more favourably by many of the Greek people, not as their monarch, but as an important individual with close ties to their country. In 1993 he gave an hour-long interview on Greek television, his first major TV interview in twenty-five years. Fearing a favourable reaction in the country, the Greek political press absolutely hammered him, causing him to reply: 'I was surprised, possibly even a little flattered, by some of the violent denunciations by segments of the Greek political press, some of which were printed even before my interview appeared.'

As it became more and more obvious that the Greek government would not return the land, the King found it necessary to take the case before the European Court of Human Rights, stating:

> I am first and foremost a Greek and I love my country. I have no quarrel with the Greek people or with the Republican constitution. We have brought this case to protect our home and our land, our Greek nationality and our name; against the misuse of public powers on discriminatory grounds. We seek to vindicate the basic civil and political rights of ourselves and our fellow citizens.

The court ruled in the King's favour, saying that the land was owned privately by the King and his family and was not in their capacity as members of the Greek royal dynasty. But they also said the land would not have to be returned but that there would have to be a financial payment as the European Court of Human Rights only provides monetary compensation. The details of the payment would have to be worked out between the two parties.

The final settlement provided €4m to the King and a far smaller sum to his sister Irene, well below what was asked for. Constantine announced upon receiving the settlement the creation of the

Anna-Maria Foundation to allocate the funds back to the Greek people for use in extraordinary natural disasters and charitable causes.

With all these weighty matters and others pressing upon them, Constantine and Anne-Marie remained excellent, involved parents. I was truly impressed to see how much time the King and Queen spent raising their five children. The children themselves appeared never to try to use the fact that their parents were royalty to gain themselves special advantages. In fact, in some cases, they went to extremes to hide their heritage. Their oldest daughter, Princess Alexia, who mastered her teaching skills at Froebel Education Institute in Putney and later spent many years working for Down's syndrome charities in the UK and Spain, was a teacher at a nursery school in London's East End in her early years. Neither the children in her care nor their parents ever knew her background, a condition on which she insisted so that all the emphasis was on what she was teaching and not who she was.

A good deal of the King's time was, and still is, taken up as President of the Round Square, an international association of similarly-minded schools that share a commitment that goes beyond academics. The association's mission is based on the philosophy of a world famous German academic, Kurt Hahn, who ran a school in Salem, Germany, before he was imprisoned by the Nazis and forced into exile in Scotland. There he founded a secondary school, called Gordonstoun. His basic approach to education is that teaching and learning should focus on six ideals: international understanding, democracy, environmental stewardship, adventure, leadership and service.

In 1967 he held a conference that resulted in the founding of Round Square (the name coming from a building of that shape in Gordonstoun) with seven other schools from three nations. As of 2011, the organization numbered eighty-five schools from around the world, with another twenty-five observers waiting to join. Patrons in addition to King Constantine include Nelson Mandela and the Duke of York. The King presides at yearly meetings, called the King Constantine Round Square Conference, in different parts of the world, and a King Constantine medal is awarded to an individual or group of individuals that has done outstanding service work. Students of the Round Square have become increasingly known for their contribution to relieve human suffering from earthquakes, floods and other disasters.

The King has remained active in projects that have Greek overtones, travelling to Nashville, Tennessee, in 1990 to help unveil a 42-foot statue of the Greek goddess Athena in the Nashville Parthenon. The King's popularity in Greece took a huge boost when the country was awarded the 2004 Olympics. It was well known that he had been actively campaigning for Greece for many years, as an honorary member of the International Olympic Committee. He himself had won a gold medal for Greece in sailing during the 1960 Olympics and, at the 2004 Olympics, he was the official presenter of the sailing medal. He was very favourably treated by the Greek press, which was aware of his contribution.

The King complimented the Prime Minister and the government on the way they handled the bid, and he attended the Olympics as a member of the IOC. For the first time since 1967, the Greek royals visited their former home and were greeted by President Costis Stephanopolis. When he returned he told me he could not have been better treated by both officials and the general public during that visit.

Over the years press interest in Constantine has continued and members of the press have commented that they were always treated extremely nicely and that his responses to their inquiries were always cogent. Even if something appeared in the press from an interview that was unfavourable or even to his way of thinking untrue, he never was upset or sought retractions. He never took me to task for setting up an interview that resulted in unfavourable coverage, nor did he ever admonish me to be more careful in the future.

Now his life has gone full cycle – Constantine is building a home in Greece. His daughter-in-law, Marie-Chantal, has opened two shops in Greece and his son Prince Nicholaus was married in Greece. As godfather to the wildly popular Prince William, he was deluged with TV, radio and press interviews at the time of the wedding. There is no doubt that the Greek royals will be spending much more time in Greece.

In my thirty years working with Constantine, my most challenging assignment by far involved the marriage of his oldest son Prince Pavlos to Marie-Chantal Miller. In reality, because of all the nuances involved, it turned out to be the most exciting and memorable assignment of my entire career. According to *Hello Magazine*, the wedding was the greatest gathering of royal families in fifty years – there were more royals in attendance than at the wedding of Prince Charles to Diana Spencer. All of Europe was involved. The King's sister was the Queen of Spain and the Queen's sister was the Queen of Denmark. There were royal families attending not only from Greece, the United Kingdom, Spain and Denmark, but also Germany, Italy, Yugoslavia, Jordan, Sweden, Austria, Belgium, Bulgaria, Iran, Luxembourg, Netherlands, Romania and Russia. In all, twenty-nine princesses attended.

Such an assemblage alone would have created worldwide interest, and I had four of my staff working full-time dealing with the media. But there were other aspects to the story. The bride's father, Robert Miller, was a billionaire who owned a duty-free shop empire in Asia. An extremely successful businessman and an art patron, he employed me separately to represent him and his family because his public relations needs were completely different from the royals.

Throughout his career he had always avoided publicity. He knew the press would be interested in him, but he did not want that interest in any way to distract the press and divert coverage away from the young couple and the royal family. Yet at the same time he didn't want to make a negative impression on the press that might possibly result in unfavourable coverage for the wedding.

While it was unquestionable that the wedding would generate favourable publicity for the King within Greece, the King and Queen wanted the emphasis to be on the bride and groom. Thirty members of the Greek parliament had accepted invitations to the wedding, but twenty dropped out after Prime Minister Papandreou made it quite clear in no uncertain terms that he was categorically against any attendance by members of parliament. Ten still attended, despite his threats and recriminations.

The problems, including the details involved in the initial planning for all things that had to be considered, were monumental. Constantine was in London. Bob Miller lived in Hong Kong. Prince Pavlos was in Washington DC studying for his Master's degree in International Relations at Georgetown University, and Marie-Chantal was studying in New York. So the four main protagonists were in four different cities on three different continents, not the perfect scenario for putting together a major event like a royal wedding.

Selecting the venue was the easiest. The Saint Sophia Cathedral in London is the leading Greek Orthodox Church in England. The first service celebrated there was Whit Sunday in 1877. The inscription above the door reads: 'The Greek community on this Island surrounded by the sea built this church far from their dear country dedicated to the Holy Wisdom of God during the reign of the great and illustrious Queen Victoria.' It was a natural place for the wedding to be held. The date was quickly established when 1 July turned out to be the day most royals would be able to attend.

Members of the media who desired to attend any of the functions had to be registered. Many newspapers, magazines TV stations and photographic organizations were sending more than one person, so in the end we had 260 members of the media with whom we were in continuing contact. Forty-three of them were representing Greek publications. To handle all the arrangements at each event, Bob Miller had selected Lady Elizabeth Anson of Party Planners. A distant relative of the Queen and friendly with the royal family, she was well aware of problems of security and protocol. Both families wanted to make the wedding a fun occasion, with protocol at a minimum.

The Millers had always planned to give a very festive ball for the young couple two days before the wedding and Lady Anson found the perfect setting – Wrotham Park, a Palladian mansion in Berkshire. Hampton Court was chosen as the venue for the wedding breakfast to take place after the marriage ceremony. And fortunately, the Royal Palaces Commission gave its permission for use of the site.

In order to handle the number of guests expected, these venues required five enormous tents. At Wrotham Park, one was needed for the guests to meet and have cocktails, and a second for a sit-down dinner and dancing. For Hampton Court, three were necessary: one for the gathering, one for the banquet and a third to accommodate guests who would be watching the wedding ceremony on television as Saint Sophia could hold only 450 guests (fortunately my wife and I were to be in that number). The other 750 guests were to watch the wedding on live monitors at Hampton Court. Because this was the time of Wimbledon, Ascot and Henley, tents of the size needed were ordered well in advance, and it was even necessary to have some shipped from Brussels.

When the guests arrived at Wrotham Park for the pre-wedding ball, they entered a 135- by 240-metre tent adorned with a Greek motif which had been kept as a surprise for the royals. What really struck my wife and I was how relaxed and totally informal the atmosphere was. At 10 p.m. the three-tiered central drapery was lifted to expose an even larger tent made up to resemble an ancient Greek garden. It was so beautiful that the guests broke out into spontaneous applause. Twenty Greek dancers brought from Greece performed as the guests entered. Mr Miller welcomed the guests first in Greek and then in English. The guests then sat down to a sumptuous meal followed by Greek and Western dancing.

At 1 a.m. everyone was asked to come outside. A large antique merry-go-round stood by itself in a meadow and kings, queens, princes, princesses and non-royalty took turns riding the wooden horses in a carnival-like atmosphere. This activity was followed by a most dazzling display of fireworks synchronized to music, climaxing with Puccini's *Nessun Dorma*, after which the audience again broke out into spontaneous applause. My wife and I left at about 3 a.m. but those more lively than us stayed up all night.

On the day of the wedding, the area along Moscow Road in Bayswater, where the church is situated, was packed by media and well-wishers. To handle the one-hour commentary for the live transmission, we employed Nicholas Owen of ITN – the station's royal correspondent. He used a research assistant to put together all the background material necessary for an event of this kind, of which there was a great deal.

CTN, which was responsible for the filming, arranged to have five fixed cameras within the church, only one having a live cameraman. There were two screens in the church to help those seated at the side get a clearer picture of the ceremony. Two more camera-men were outside the Church. All twenty CTN staff, whether working in the church or at Hampton Court, were dressed in morning suits to fit in properly with the occasion. Since the press could not attend the ceremony, we set up a press centre at ITN headquarters at Gray's End Road. There, the journalists could watch the ceremony live.

There were weeks of planning meetings and rehearsal for all the technical people involved, and when it was over I received a letter from Nick Owen commenting, 'For myself, it was utterly exhausting – but utterly enthralling.'

The bride and groom were willing to go through media training and both were naturally very relaxed and articulate. Before the wedding we held an individual press meeting for the Greek press and one for the Danish and Spanish press. To make it easy for the entire press corps covering the event, we conveniently provided a set of questions and answers for the kind of facts that we knew would interest them most, such as, 'When and where did you meet?', 'Where and how did he propose?', 'What did your father say?', 'What about going to Greece?', 'Where will you honeymoon?' The last had a very simple answer, 'Even Marie-Chantal doesn't know.' We also had CTN film interviews with the royal couple and with the bride and groom which could be used as background by TV stations.

As would be expected, we were deluged with requests for information about the bride's dress. But no information was allowed to be supplied before the wedding started, not even to the groom or to Nick Owen. Nick was adamant, to be professional, that he had to have the information on the dress when Marie-Chantal entered the Church, so I went up to the bridal suite where the famous designer, Valentino – who made the gown – and his team were dressing the bride and her mother and sisters. I took Valentino aside and made notes for Nick and got them to the church on time.

The dress had been made from an ivory-coloured silk with a tulip-shaped front with two deep pleats forming a long train of three metres. The hem was embroidered with petals and flowers in the same material with opaque beading. Valentino was most ecstatic about the veil which consisted of twelve different old laces embroidered with butterflies to symbolize good luck.

The ceremony, which was attended by Queen Elizabeth, Prince Philip and Prince Charles, was held entirely in Greek. A high point was when Prince Pavlos's best men, his brother Prince Nickolaus and Prince Felipe of Spain, passed crowns over the heads of the bride and groom. What was so nice about this is that the passing of crowns in a Greek wedding service has nothing to do with royalty. The crowns (or sometimes wreaths) are passed over the bride and groom to indicate that on that day they are royalty, regardless of their background. At the end of the ceremony, flowers rained down from the ceiling as a final beautiful touch.

The people watching the whole ceremony at Hampton Court were extremely touched. The quality of the rear-screen projection ensured they had a far better view of the entire proceedings than many of those seated in the church. The person in charge of handling the coverage at Hampton Court told me he was amazed how mesmerized they were – most sat for an hour and a half without moving.

Hampton Court stands majestically on the banks of the River Thames and has been a royal palace since Henry VIII 'acquired' it from Cardinal Wolsey when he fell from favour. It remains the property of Queen Elizabeth II but has been open to the public since 1838. Bob Miller made every effort to ensure it was set up to be the perfect venue to follow the ceremony at the church. One British Royal remarked to me that it had probably never looked better in the days when her ancestors lived there.

Mr Miller welcomed the guests in Greek and English and gave a warm and funny speech about being the father of the bride. The King too blended humour and warmth, quoting lyrics from composers Rodgers and Hammerstein that also underlined the plight of the father of the bride – but first he promised the audience that he wouldn't sing to them. Prince Nickolaus and Prince Felipe of Spain did a double act about their relationship with Pavlos. The whole day, despite the size and grandeur of its setting, seemed like just one big happy family event. My main memory was seeing Queen Elizabeth II smiling happily as she was driven away in a golf cart from the lunch to where her royal car was waiting.

While we could not ensure it, we did expect that the wedding would greatly enhance the King's image in Greece. I was incredibly impressed by the fairness of the Greek correspondents who had come to England to cover the event, even those on the far left of the political spectrum. One said to me, 'This is the best thing that ever happened to the monarchy.'

There had to be an exception, though. One statement that appeared in a Greek paper – that helped me stay humble – was by a Greek journalist who felt he wasn't allowed to get close enough to the King. He wrote: 'Bob Leaf was no help whatsoever. The King should have hired a Greek.'

The Greeks agreed that the event had been a great success. Sales of newspapers covering the marriage increased dramatically. And Antenna, a leading TV channel in Athens which ran the whole wedding live, experienced the highest rating it had ever received for any programme: 75 per cent of the viewing audience. When they reran it a week later it still garnered more than 50 per cent. All the Greek press and most of the major US and European press covered the wedding at length and favourably. Every major TV network carried it in full. Thirty channels took the feed CTN had set up and thirty-eight others took coverage from international networks like Reuters and CNN. CNN played it every hour and Sky reran it at least six times. At least 350 million people saw segments of the wedding. Fortunately, nothing went wrong. Opinion polls after the wedding in Greece showed a significant boost in the King's popularity and the personal attacks on him began to subside. It also proved to me what love and marriage can accomplish, even in the minds that tend to be hostile.

Sam Wanamaker and Shakespeare's Globe Theatre

All through history there have been numerous examples of how one man, whether he was president, prime minister, pope or a general, has made a major impact on society or on an organization. We can often see it happen in companies when an individual CEO such as Jack Welch, Lou Gerstner, Steve Jobs or Warren Buffet is the real key to the organization's success. But in my career, the greatest example of an individual making this kind of an impact, especially an individual who certainly would not have been expected to, was Sam Wanamaker.

About twenty-five years ago, Sir Michael Perry, then the chairman of Unilever, came to see me and said, 'Bob, I'd like you to do me a favour.' Without even knowing what it was, I was sure I'd say yes. Sir Perry had been one of my favourite clients over the last nine years. 'I would like you to take on an assignment pro bono,' he said. 'Pro bono' means you don't get paid one cent because you are doing it for the public good. That should make you happy enough, even if your wallet isn't.

Sir Michael went on to explain that a trust had been set up to help rebuild Shakespeare's original Globe Theatre, and that he was in charge of the trust. But, he went on, 'It's not me you'll be working with but Sam Wanamaker, who has been completely responsible for this whole venture coming to life. I would really like you to be part of the team. I would appreciate it if you would have lunch with him and get to know him and what he is trying to accomplish, and then come to a decision.' He added, with a wink, 'You will probably love him or hate him.'

So I joined Sam for lunch at a pub in Southwark where the Globe was scheduled to be built, and by the end of lunch, I had decided that I loved him. He explained the venture to me in great detail and why he felt it was so important. His enthusiasm was equivalent to what Romeo felt for Juliet. I agreed immediately that I would be happy to provide support in the areas of public relations and fundraising. And I am certainly glad that I did.

Sam Wanamaker's story itself would provide an ideal plot for a movie, which may be made some day. Sam was born in Chicago to two Jewish parents who fled Ukraine to avoid the pogroms. At an early age he became active in the local theatre, and by the time he was twenty-three, he had performed on Broadway. He became quite a success four years later playing opposite Ingrid Bergman in *Joan of Lorraine*. He later produced, directed and starred in Clifford Odets's *Winter Journey*. He acted in or directed over fifty films. Remarkably, he also became a success in opera, directing Prokofiev's *War and Peace* at the official opening of the Sydney Opera House and directing Luciano Pavarotti in his first performance in *Aida* in San Francisco.

But the plays of Shakespeare, which had always been a great love of his, began to dominate his thinking, and in 1957 he became director of the New Shakespeare Theatre in Liverpool. In 1959, he joined the Shakespeare Memorial Theatre where he played Iago opposite Paul Robeson as Othello. By now, he was living permanently in England, but not completely by choice. Sam had always leaned towards the left politically, and his father had been a strong unionist. During the height of the Red Scare in the United States in 1952, Senator McCarthy subpoenaed Sam to appear before his Committee to be questioned about his political activities. It didn't matter that he had had a distinguished army career in the Second World War. Sam was in no way an active communist, but he decided he did not want to tangle with the McCarthy committees and so took up permanent residence in England.

In 1949, during an earlier visit to the UK, Sam wanted to find the spot in London where the Globe had once stood. As fans of the Bard will know, the Globe was Shakespeare's home theatre in London. It was destroyed in 1613 during a performance of *King Henry VIII*. The story goes that a cannon being set off as part of the play was misdirected, causing the thatching in the playhouse to catch fire, completely destroying the theatre.

As a strong advocate of Shakespeare, Sam was surprised to find that there was no replica of the Globe in London. Instead, all he found was a blackened bronze plaque on the wall of the Courage Brewery in Park Street, Southwark, that read, 'Here stood Shakespeare's Globe'. In Sam's mind it was unacceptable that while there were Globe Theatres in the US, Japan and Canada, there wasn't one where the original had stood in London.

He was always questioning the Londoners he met – often to the point of annoyance – 'Why isn't there a Globe? There should be a Globe.' Never having received a good answer, finally, in 1959, he decided, 'I will make it happen,' and he began to bombard anyone who might have any interest in the project with letters and phone calls.

Not everyone was overjoyed with Sam, and as Barry Day notes in his excellent book, *This Wooden 'O': Shakespeare's Globe Reborn*: 'One of Sam's undeniable qualities was the ability to provoke.' I was to find out that he really had that ability. To many of the English he approached, his crusade evoked a simple question, 'Who wants to see Shakespeare reborn under the aegis of an American, especially an American driven out of his own country?'

And Sam's struggle began. And it was a great struggle with ups and downs that went on for many years. Supporters were gained. Supporters were lost. The Southwark Council decided in favour of some specific actions to support the project. The Southwark Council decided against other specific actions to support the project.

When Sam first went to the Southwark Council to ask for a parcel of land upon which to build the Globe, close to where the original had stood, he encountered a group of loony lefties who were then in charge. They dismissed Sam, with one of their members saying to him, 'We want none of your elitist crap here.' Even by loony-left standards, telling an American that Shakespeare was 'elitist crap' was a high or a low for loonies, according to how you look at it.

When a new, more rational Labour council was elected to replace the previous one, they realized what the building of the Globe could mean to Southwark's development. They understood what a Globe Theatre would mean for tourism, jobs and growth in general for the area. They gave Sam the land, which was then a car park, for free. And were they ever smart to do it!

The Globe turned out to be the key to the Southbank's renewal and its becoming one of London's important tourist areas. The Globe was later joined by the Tate Modern Museum and the London Eye. Crowds of tourists pour into the area every day to see the sights, stroll along the river, watch the street performances, eat in the restaurants and spend money. If anyone reading this book had bought property in Southwark around the time Sam got the go-ahead, they would now be living a life of leisure in a villa in southern France – or anywhere else in the world they wanted to be.

Another high and low involved a former client of mine, Armand Hammer. The very thought of Armand Hammer and Sam Wanamaker partnering in anything would in my mind be the equivalent of Hamas and Israel being bosom buddies. But that's what had happened.

By 1974, Sam had set up a North American chapter of the American Globe Centre in Chicago, his home town, and by 1982 there were many other centres around the country. Equally important for Americans was the fact that the Shakespeare Globe Centre had tax-exempt status, making it more advantageous for American donors to contribute as their gifts would be tax-deductible. So in 1982, Dr Hammer, who always wanted to be associated with activities of cultural significance, especially since he was hoping to someday win a Nobel Prize, agreed to head the North American chapter, and made a large donation himself.

He threw a party in which the guest of honour was Prince Philip (who later became a major supporter of the Globe and helped with fundraising). Each guest had to pledge $10,000, and guests included Cary Grant, Elizabeth Taylor and Richard Burton.

But, as I could have predicted, the relationship came to a bitter end. Hammer, by nature, always demanded absolute success and uninterrupted perfection – but his standards were his own, of course. Unfortunately, Sam's skill did not include always the best and smartest use of the funds being raised. He would set up committees and stage events that were not always completely necessary, and so there were times when more money went out than came in. It was in Dr Hammer's nature to avoid any association with any project that might not attain the highest levels of success, and the Globe project was starting to look like it was running out of steam. He wanted no part in a possible failure, so, instead of increasing his efforts to make it work, he pulled out. Sam took Dr Hammer's withdrawal very hard and pleaded with him to stay involved, but there was no chance of that.

Fortunately the key people now involved with Sam and the Globe in London were ideal for the work that needed to be done. Theo Crosby was the official architect and, next to Sam, gets the most credit for the final birth of the Globe. Theo was a major factor in the final construction, but sadly he died before the official opening. Theo did seventeen years of research on the Globe and convinced Sam to establish smaller, workable sections which he designed. These included the main outdoor Globe theatre, an indoor Inigo Jones theatre, a restaurant area and an outdoor plaza. When the Globe's prospects were at their lowest, he convinced Sam to let him design and build some sample bays to show what the Globe would look like upon completion. The results were inspiring, private funding began flowing in, and they never looked back.

Theo had done some work for Unilever, so he introduced Sam to David Orr, then chairman of Unilever, and Orr agreed to become head of the Globe Development Trust, which had replaced the WCSS as the governing body. He was later followed by Sir Michael Perry, who had replaced him as chairman of Unilever, and, as I previously mentioned, it was Sir Michael Perry who got me involved.

They were responsible for monitoring the financing, and there were still periods of ups and downs in fundraising even after construction began. There were times they had to say, 'Sam, have all the builders put down their shovels. When more money starts coming in again the shovels can start again.' And that's what happened.

The more I dealt with Sam, the more he inspired me. He even turned down a lead part in a Broadway show to concentrate all his efforts on bringing the Globe to life. He certainly wasn't doing it for the money. The Globe was a charity and Sam's salary was nothing to brag about. No matter how successful the Globe might become, there would be no personal financial benefit to him. But personal financial gain was not what Sam was about.

Sam had the tendency at times to oversell. At one fundraising luncheon, I was sitting next to him when he got up to speak. When he began to say more, much more, than the audience needed to hear, I poked him and said, 'Enough, Sam, enough,' and he ended quickly, but not before offering a moving conclusion to his speech. Sam was willing to listen to my suggestions because he knew that, like him, I would not benefit financially from the Globe. I was there to help it become a reality because the prospect was very exciting for me.

Construction on the Globe began in 1989. Every effort was made to be sure it would look exactly like the original theatre or as close as possible given modern safety laws. No one wanted to tempt fate by putting up a structure that might burn down again. It was edifying to see Sam in action as he came to realize that his dream was going to come true. As often happens, as success comes within reach, and as the project was no longer considered a crazy pipe dream, fund-raising increased dramatically and well-known actors such as John Gielgud and Judi Dench, among others, became active promoters.

But unfortunately Sam had developed prostate cancer, and he was dying. I, and many others, hoped that he would last long enough to be present when the Globe officially opened, but it was not to be. Sam died in 1993, three-and-a-half years before the opening. But fortunately the importance of his personal efforts had already been recognized and the Queen awarded him a CBE before his passing.

I am sure that if he had lived, he would have found the Globe and what it has meant to London to be even beyond his expectations. As in Shakespeare's day, standing room near the stage was provided for people who could not afford the full price of admission. They were called groundlings. The present Globe has space for 500 groundlings, and the cost of entry is only £5, allowing students and others with limited funds to come and enjoy Shakespeare in the Globe. In spite of inflation, the £5 price has never been raised from opening day.

The Globe project includes Globe Education under Patrick Spottiswoode, who has been there from the beginning. It is the largest theatre education department in the country with twenty-three full-time staff and sixty part-time practitioners holding workshops, talks and courses for more than 100,000 students a year from all nations. In one year, they taught 15,000 German students.

In many of the years since it first opened, the Globe has had the highest attendance record of any London theatre. Much credit goes to Mark Rylance, who was artistic director from the opening day until 2005. Since leaving the Globe, Mark has won acting awards in the UK and the US and was called by one American critic 'the modern-day Olivier'. His performance in the play *Jerusalem* in New York was labelled by the *New York Times* drama critic as 'the performance of the generation' – and he won a Tony Award for it.

Mark directed and starred in many of the productions, even playing women such as Cleopatra, as men playing women was the custom in Shakespeare's day. Being a perfectionist like Sam, he never settled for mediocrity. And as it was in Shakespeare's day, he made sure that the performers and the groundlings interacted with each other.

Peter Kyle, who was chief executive from the time the Globe opened until 2010, also played a key part in making sure all aspects of the whole Globe operation – including an exhibition, a shop and a restaurant – also functioned effectively.

Sam Wanamaker was an extremely appreciative man, especially when anyone did anything to help further his ambition to make the English Globe a reality. After attending his seventieth birthday party I wrote to him, saying: 'I have been incredibly touched by your single-minded drive to make the Globe a reality. As Zoë [his daughter] said at your birthday, there are very few people with your tenacity.'

He was especially kind to me knowing that I was working every year pro bono to promote the Globe because of my strong belief in the project and him personally. Once after I set up a meeting that he was very desirous of having, he wrote me a letter saying: 'Dear Bob: You have opened the golden door. You have confirmed what I have always suspected. You are a genius.' And though what he suspected was not true, I was certainly pleased with his appreciation.

One of the most exciting nights I can remember was attending the unofficial opening of the Globe, held for Queen Elizabeth II and Prince Philip. In addition to the actual monarch, a noted actress, Frances de la Tour, sat on a horse in the groundling section dressed as Elizabeth I. Different, brief scenes from Shakespeare were presented by a number of actors, including Zoë Wanamaker, who played Henry V. Zoë remains very active in promoting the Globe and today is one of the country's leading actresses.

Perhaps the high point of the evening, had Sam Wanamaker been alive to see it, was when a man dressed as Richard Burbage, an original owner of the Globe, came onto the stage and was met by Richard Griffith, a noted British actor, dressed as a modern-day street cleaner. Griffith asked, 'What do you want?' Burbage replied, 'I'm looking to build something.'

'Build what?' asked Griffith.

'Some sort of a theatre.'

'What kind of a theatre?'

'The Globe Theatre,' answered Burbage.

Griffith replied, echoing the Southwark councillor: 'We don't want any of your elitist crap here!'

It was a shame that Sam wasn't there to witness the scene and see the tremendous smiles on the faces of the entire audience, including the Queen of England.

Sam Wanamaker was a brave and dedicated man. One of my fondest memories of him was at an event at the Malaysian Embassy related to Sam's great cause. Malaysia had contributed some of the wood used in building the Globe and was now going to contribute some money as well. Sam was coming to the Embassy to thank them formally for their generosity. I had arrived before Sam, and when I saw him enter the room where the ceremony would take place, I could see immediately that his prostate cancer had taken its toll on him. In fact, he looked so ill that I thought he wouldn't last the day.

After the Malaysian official made a short talk about the donation, Sam got up to speak. He thanked them and talked about how important their contributions were and what the Globe would mean to the world when it was completed. He was like a new man as he spoke. He was suddenly imbued with so much energy and enthusiasm that you would have thought he could walk out of the Embassy and play two sets of tennis. Sadly, that was the last time I saw Sam alive.

11   A Positive Perception of the CEO: A Key to Company Success

One of the greatest changes I have seen in my fifty years in PR has been the role of the CEO and its effect on businesses. When I started, most CEOs ruled the roost and were not to be questioned, usually under any circumstances. This was often made clear to me by the in-house chief of PR when we had our initial meeting. Business in general had a high reputation back then. But this has changed dramatically, especially in the last decade. Everyone – the government, the financial community, customers and issue-oriented non-profits – now look at companies in a critical, often adversarial way. Especially significant, now that company loyalty is dead, is that the same is true of employees. As a result it has become increasingly vital for top management, especially the CEO, to realize this sea change and act accordingly – usually with increasing help from PR professionals, both internally and externally.

A US-based study has shown that the perception of the CEO in the US is responsible for 47 per cent of a company's reputation. In Asia and Latin America the number was even greater. And Warren Buffet made it clear how important reputation is when he stated publicly: 'If you lose money for your firm I will be understanding. If you lose reputation I will be ruthless.'

For some corporations a particular 'name brand' CEO can have even greater importance. While Steve Jobs was chairman of Apple, his company's share prices went dramatically up and down, depending on his health. When Bert Becht – who was chief executive of the Anglo-Dutch firm Reckitt Benckiser for ten years and had been responsible for great increases in shareholder value – announced unexpectedly that he was going to step down, £2bn were wiped off the value of the firm's shares the next day.

The image a CEO projects can be vital to a company's success. No greater example exists than Lou Gerstner of IBM. In a cover story, *Fortune Magazine* said that IBM, once known for its greatness, had become 'a national disaster'. Enter Gerstner as CEO. He decided it was not their technology that was at fault but that they had screwed up relations with customers. He dedicated himself to showing his employees and the business world how IBM was changing. He spent 40 per cent of his time with customers listening to their complaints and plans. He became part of new business presentations. And he made sure that the rest of management became more customer conscious. He transformed IBM into a service organization and moved it back to the top of its industry.

A *PR Week* study showed that 85 per cent of CEOs taking part in the study believed it was either 'very important' or 'important' to be perceived as an influence on their respective industries. As a result, many CEOs are now gaining a greater appreciation of the need to manage perceptions and are starting to act accordingly. For some, though, learning this is coming at a painful cost. Anyone watching the CEOs of various financial and automotive institutions who appeared before congressional committees in the US or government panels in the UK during the economic crisis could see first-hand the damage they were doing to the reputation of their companies, not only in the eyes of government officials, but in those of the public at large.

The image of the banks during the crisis moved in many people's minds from 'the growers of the economy' to the 'destroyers of the economy'. What was even more surprising to me was that, of the many in the banking industry who realized how negative their image had become, very few did anything at all to rectify it. They didn't seem to care.

You didn't need a Master's degree in Public Relations to advise the management of General Motors that to fly down in a private jet to appear before the members of Congress, hat in hand, would not be the best possible image to present while claiming poverty and looking for big government handouts. Fortunately, after the scathing press coverage their plane trip got, they were wise enough to drive down in a car for the second hearings and portray the kind of humility that was expected of them. Then they got their money.

In my own corporate work, I often faced difficulty convincing companies of the exact image they, and especially their CEO, needed to project in particular situations. They just didn't get it. In my view, the image had to realistically take into account the perceptions held by their key audiences. The company needed to understand those perceptions and communicate in a way that would satisfy them. Also, they had to realize that circumstances can change rapidly externally, and even quite often internally. They had to recognize this and understand the need to react quickly.

Ruth Sunderland, editor of the *Observer*, once made this very wise statement: 'CEOs should be presented more as team captains than demigods.' That seems to be happening more and more.

There has been a great deal of improvement in CEOs' understanding of the role of outside PR consultancies; what to expect from them and, even more importantly, what to demand from them. With growing PR sophistication, executives now understand what can and cannot be accomplished, and programmes worked out with outside consultants have become far more meaningful and realistic.

I still remember going to meet with the CEO of a British company who was considering hiring us as his PR consultancy a relatively small budget. He wanted me to tell him why I felt he should employ us. His main question was, 'How do I know I'm getting value for money?' I said it would be difficult to prove it unequivocally, because the cost of employing research to prove exactly what our agreed programme had accomplished would in all probability cost much more than the programme itself. He said, 'I know exactly what is necessary. I'll take all your clippings, measure them exactly and then see what it would have cost me if I paid for advertising to get the same amount of coverage.'

I immediately thought this would not be something difficult to disprove to his satisfaction. I explained that it is not the size or volume of coverage that counts but what is said. I agreed, however, that if that is how he wanted to judge our effectiveness that would be fine with me. I would go to the *Financial Times* and tell them his company was having all sorts of problems with their products, customers and employees and the outlook for the future was very bleak. I would be certain to get significant column inches in the *FT*, possibly even a whole page. He laughed and took it very well, hired us and turned out to be a very nice client to work with.

There is no doubt that companies today are facing far greater image problems than was the case years ago. A study regarding trust made by Penn Schoen Berland, a leading research company, underlined this dramatically. Some results of the study: front line staff were more trusted than CEOs with 72 per cent regarding CEOs as less trustworthy than the average employee. Eighty per cent felt companies were more trustworthy when the respondents were younger than they are today, and two thirds saw companies today as generally dishonest and their communications as lies. These results alone underline how important it is for companies to communicate effectively. As Alan Greenspan said, when he was head of the US Federal Reserve System, 'Competition for reputation is a significant driving force.'

The reality is that some CEOs are not the best choice as chief communicators on all issues. While many feel they are modern-day Winston Churchills, someone listening to them could easily believe otherwise. Often it is the chief operating officer, the chief financial officer or the chief technical officer who should be paraded before specific audiences. It is vital, no matter how good a spokesperson or how knowledgeable about a subject a CEO is, that they undergo training sessions. As *Fortune Magazine* wrote: 'If you want to analyze a corporation, read its financial statements. If you want to plumb its soul, talk to its chief executive.'

CEOs are catching on. An interesting statistic from a *PR Week* CEO survey noted that when questioned as to what they thought was the most effective external activity for getting a company's message across, conducting media interviews was ranked the highest by far – well above advertising, public speaking, or customer forums or events.

Love them or hate them, the media are here to stay. Once a CEO let me know how upset he was by what he considered to be an unfair piece in the *Financial Times*. I agreed with him that this was a rare case where the *FT* really got it wrong. He told me, 'I'm not going to deal with the *FT* anymore.' I explained to him – tactfully of course – that he didn't have that option. One of the things he was being paid to do was deal with the *Financial Times*.

While these training sessions have historically been called 'media training', I have always preferred calling them 'message training'. There are important key audiences besides the media, and deciding what the most important messages are for each of these audiences and how to deliver those messages most effectively are really the point of this kind of training.

I have done a great deal of 'message training' during my career. There were certain fundamentals that I always adhered to. For example, if I was training a chief executive, I always trained him alone. The reason? There were questions I might want to ask him or comments he might want to make that he would be uncomfortable with in front of other executives.

What was and still is important is that companies all have executives who are going to present the company message to various different audiences – press, customer organizations, the financial community, or even internally – undertake 'message training'. Without it, there are no assurances that all messengers will be conveying the right message – or even the same message.

I found that it was never advisable to train more than three executives at one time. This allowed for the necessary discussion time with questions to or comments by each of those being trained. Also attending the training sessions when possible should be the internal head of PR and consultancy executives responsible for the account.

I started each session with an overview of what we all expected to accomplish during the day. Then each person would tell us a little about themselves, their backgrounds and their current roles. We would then have a general discussion on the exact messages that they wanted to get across and to what specific audiences.

If they wanted the message to appear in the *Wall Street Journal* or the *Financial Times*, what exactly would they have to say to the reporter to help accomplish this? We then agreed on four or five key points they would have to get across to make it likely that message would appear in the desired media. It was made clear they had to communicate these points regardless of what the reporter asked them. Because, as one wise pundit said: 'There is no such thing as a stupid question. There is only a stupid answer.' Getting the desired answers across is extremely important in the time of 'bad news', whether you represent an airline that has had a fatal crash or a company about to close a major plant. While neither event is a time for glee, there are ways of presenting bad news, even horrible news, in the most favourable manner.

One of my colleagues with a strong media background, joining me in this session, would then explain the different needs and problems involved with print, radio and TV interviews, and the best kind of approach to take with each. In radio and TV, because of the time factor, you can avoid going into detail about things you prefer to avoid. This is not the case when a print journalist is sitting opposite you and can keep repeating the same question. Also, it is highly advisable you do your homework and try to learn as much as possible about the interviewer — particularly his key interests and what he is hoping to accomplish with the interview. The poor interviewee only sees his own needs and often answers accordingly, ultimately to his own detriment. Also you can ask a reporter in advance what the key questions are that you will be asked as most interviewers will provide them so that you can do the necessary homework to make the interview more effective.

I would then take each executive, one by one, into a studio where I would do a bit of role playing: first as a newspaper reporter, then a radio reporter and then a TV reporter. In each of these roles I would be far more demanding and difficult than the average journalist would be. I often attacked their company for some real or imagined mistake to test how the interviewee responded under pressure. Everything was recorded.

When every executive had been put through his paces, we would return to the conference room and play the newspaper interviews one at a time. After each one was shown we'd question how effectively they felt the right messages had gotten across. Then we'd do the same with the radio interviews and then, finally, with the TV interviews.

What really pleased me in these sessions was that nearly always those being trained were the first to spot the mistakes they made in answering specific questions. They were also the first to realize what they should have said in order to earn the best chance of getting the desired coverage.

I found that these executives, no matter how high up they were in their organizations' hierarchy, were always pleased to learn the lessons we were teaching them. When I trained the head of Coca-Cola in Africa, an extremely bright man, I was particularly tough on him. One question I asked was, 'The only reason that Coke gave you the job is because you're black. Isn't that right?'

He answered in a very modulated manner, explaining that his background and accomplishments were the reason for the promotion, not the colour of his skin. Listening to him talk, you would sincerely believe he would have gotten the job if he was green, blue or pink. He felt the training was so valuable that he later had me train his chief financial officer and his head of human resources.

Once I was training the head of a British company's largest division, an executive who had just been put on the board of the parent company. Acting as a TV announcer, I asked him what he thought was the most important advantage of being put on the board. He replied, 'It gives me the opportunity to learn much more about the whole company and the areas I've not been personally involved in.'

When we played the interview back at the end of his session, I explained why I felt that particular answer was not the best possible. 'The majority of the company's employees have been working for you as head of their division, and it would make far greater sense if they heard you on TV say something along the lines of "My new role will allow me to let the board know in depth the reasons that my staff have been able to accomplish what they have and why the division has been so successful."' He agreed completely and later employed me for other assignments.

While employees will be presenting different information concerning the specific areas in which they are most involved, there are always some key messages about the company itself that must remain the same no matter who is being questioned. I once trained eighty-two executives from Coca-Cola, including the chairman and the heads of Asia, Africa, Europe and the Middle East. Before I began, I had numerous sessions with the then head of Coca-Cola communications in Atlanta, working out what were the exact, important messages that everyone needed to get across regardless of their position or area of operation.

It is advisable for many of the executives who have gone through the training to do so again every few years. In today's tumultuous times, situations can change dramatically very quickly. The company's messengers need to be nimble and ready to respond.

There is an area, which unfortunately remains significant, that CEOs and others in top management must continually be aware of. It was true when I wrote the following for *Atlantic Journal* many years ago, but is even truer today: 'In England and in the United States, the 1990s rang the death knell for a patient that had become terminally ill in the 1980s – company loyalty.'

When I started my career, if you went to work for IBM or AT&T you were pretty much guaranteed a job for life. If you weren't a great success, promotions and salary increases were less likely to come your way, but if you wanted to remain employed by the company you usually could. In Japan 'usually' was replaced by 'nearly always', and loyalty even extended to contributing to the funeral costs for those employees dying while still on the company payrolls.

But as competition became much more intense, the business

climate grew more ruthless and companies had to stay lean – not only to compete, but in some cases to survive. At first leanness meant cutting off unnecessary fat that grew on organizations as they got bigger and more successful. But when this kind of cutting didn't achieve the necessary results, more layers, closer to the bone, had to be excised. Out went employees with one or two decades of service, employees who were looking ten years down the line towards a comfortable retirement.

Job function also provided no protection. Blue collar workers and white collar workers were affected, but so were middle and top management. So the reaction of employees was not surprising. How loyal can someone be expected to be, if, when the crunch comes, they know that that loyalty is not going to be reciprocated? The problem was exacerbated when it was seen that companies like Unilever, once considered one of the most paternalistic and still a very employee-oriented firm, closed its final salary pension scheme to its existing employees. A survey of the National Association of Pension Funds found that 20 per cent of companies with similar plans took the same action as Unilever. These actions had to have an effect on company loyalty.

At the same time, the need for a dedicated workforce is greater than ever. Competition is not slowing down – it's increasing and it's more and more global. Not only local companies but foreign organizations are on the prowl for key people. In addition there is a demographic time bomb. The percentage of people in the workforce in relation to those retired will lower dramatically so the need to keep your key people is even more vital.

But there is some good news. Even though the average employee no longer has an unconditional loyalty to their company, they can still have loyalty to the company's vision and direction, if they believe in it. And here is what CEOs and their top executives must understand: nowadays companies must have a meaningful vision, one that key employees can believe in and feel good about. It cannot result from a few people in management appearing to have come down the mountain with the tablets, like Moses, providing a message for all to obey and follow.

There is now a greater need for human resources departments to be put to the task of really understanding what key employees at all levels feel positive and negative about within their company, what changes they would like to see made and whether they are possible. The task is complicated by the fact that communicating with employees is becoming more difficult now that some companies have large numbers of employees working from home or at great distances from headquarters.

Nokia is one company that claims a lot of its success has been due to employee communications and encouraging employees at every level to say whatever is on their minds. In 2009 Nokia set up an intranet soapbox known as Blog-Hub encouraging employees to feel free to say *anything*.

Because there are specific times when company loyalty is most likely to waver, a well considered internal communications programme is most important when:

1) a new CEO or management team takes over;
2) a company is acquired or makes a major acquisition;
3) reorganization is in the offing;
4) there is a major change in strategy;
5) there has been some particularly bad news such as a heavy fall in the stock value, a government investigation or the failure of some major new product;
6) there are strains within the organization because of salary freezes, a loss in market position or deflection to competitors by some key executives.

The attitude of the chief executive can have a major impact. I've seen that in my own career at Burson–Marsteller. I was extremely fortunate that Harold Burson, the founder and chief executive of the only company I ever worked for, stayed active from the firm's inception and was still working full-time at ninety years of age.

The perception of Harold, and one that was completely true, was that he cared for all his employees, regardless of how low down the management chain they were – that would include secretaries and junior executives. When I ran all of our international offices, employees, regardless of the country they worked in, felt that he headed a company that cared for them as individuals. As a result, we went through a number of periods when we had very little staff turnover, which contributed greatly to our growth and success.

If anything underlines the growing desire of CEOs and the companies they run to manage perceptions it is CSR – Corporate Social Responsibility. The concept first came alive in the sixties and has mushroomed dramatically ever since. In somewhat clinical terms, it was defined as the economic, legal, ethical and discretionary expectations society has of organizations. In simpler terms, you are not there just to enrich yourself and your shareholders. You also have ethical, moral and philanthropic responsibilities.

The message has struck home as more and more organizations add CSR to their agenda, and those already involved expand their activities in this area. As *The Economist* once noted: 'It would be a challenge to find a recent annual report of any big international company that justifies the firm's existence merely in terms of profit rather than service to the community.' On a similar theme, *Fortune Magazine* claimed that, 'Today more and more organizations are awakening to the fact that corporate social responsibility is key to their long-term success and cannot be overlooked.'

Not everyone agrees. A noted economist, Milton Friedman, has said that a company's ONLY responsibility is profit. He was backed by the dean emeritus of George Mason University who said: 'Corporate social responsibility is bunk.'

Where I feel their argument falls flat is that more and more consumers feel that they are helping society when they buy from a company that is showing corporate responsibility in some way. When consumers feel that way, the company sells more and profits move up. A study by *Citizen Watch* said that four out of five US citizens consider a company's reputation when buying a product. As CSR strengthens a company's reputation, sales go up.

Even before CSR was as dominant as it is today, Coca-Cola was a major adherent. From the time they first entered the Chinese market, they were a major supporter of schools and local sporting teams. Many years ago they started working with the China Youth Development Foundation to improve education opportunities for underprivileged students, and by 2011 had built one hundred Project Hope schools in some of the poorest regions of China. They have been by far the greatest contributor of any company to the fight against AIDS in Africa, even taking an active role when the then chancellor of South Africa, Thabo Mbeki, declined to consider the illness a serious problem within his country.

There is probably no greater example of a company seeing the need for CSR and actively undertaking it than Walmart. The largest American company, Walmart was under continuous attack for its supposedly anti-social activities both in the US and abroad. At first the attacks did not seem to concern the company, as business as usual was providing more than generous profits and growth was continuing. Then both the quantity and impact of the attacks began to increase dramatically. Some of the big retailer's practices were even attacked by vice president candidate Joe Biden during his primary campaign as a way to appeal to the union vote. A group called Boycott sprang up on the Internet announcing that Walmart was their primary target. They said:

'We have chosen Walmart as the target of our primary call for a boycott because of the company's unfair labor practices around the world. Not only does this chain mistreat many employees that work for them, it also sells goods made by suppliers that grossly violate the rights of their workers around the world. Despite protests and a law suit they have refused to correct these problems.'

They then put out a thirty-eight-page document that made the Nazis under Hitler look loveable in comparison. One area that they used as a focus was a factory in Saipan where Chinese women brought in from the mainland were making clothing for sale in Walmart stores in the US. They listed the following reasons the women, who they claimed were being paid $3 an hour, could be fired and deported, they:

- fell in love;
- got married;
- became pregnant (terminate pregnancy or be deported);
- participated in political or religious activities;
- failed to meet their daily production quota;
- refused to work overtime, including unpaid 'volunteer' hours;
- participated in any activities which lessened their energy for work;
- refused to lie to inspectors regarding safety conditions at work, the number of hours worked, the true number of women living in each barracks room;
- asked for a higher wage;
- tried to organize a union.

And this was only one of a number of other charges that made Walmart appear equally unappealing, by one of several websites attacking the corporation.

Whether such claims were completely accurate or not, Walmart took appropriate action. At a gathering of more than 1,000 suppliers, Chinese officials and advocacy groups in Beijing Walmart revealed a new supplier agreement that would require manufacturers to allow outside audits and adhere to specific social and environmental criteria. Walmart said that it would keep close track of factories from which its products originated, and by 2012, would require suppliers to source 95 per cent of their production from factories that receive the highest rating in audits of environmental and social practices. The agreement included a ban on child labour, forced labour and pay below the local minimum wage.

But Walmart didn't stop there. The chief executive Lee Scott announced the intention of transforming Walmart into a company that runs 100 per cent renewable energy. It wasn't an empty gesture – they are making remarkable progress in that area.

After a competing company was widely criticized for banning Salvation Army bell-ringers from the front of their stores, Walmart ran TV ads with Antonio Banderas, featuring the bell-ringers in front of their stores. And they announced that instead of being allowed to have their charity drives at just a limited number of stores for fourteen days, the company's previous rule, they could now operate at all stores for twenty-eight days.

And that wasn't all. In a great shot in the arm for what is known as e-health, Walmart began to digitize employee records so that they would spend less time filling out forms in doctors' offices. They can now log on to the company's Intranet to download and print any medical records their physicians require, including allergy information, prescriptions, blood tests – and their entire health history if necessary. Thousands of employees signed up, making this initiative one of the greatest uses of digital medical records or e-health by any US company.

Companies are also using CSR as a sales tool. Jones Lang LaSalle, the global property management company, created a twenty-page document signed by the chairman of the board and the CEO entitled 'Corporate Social Responsibility at Jones Lang LaSalle', and set forth the following on the cover:

'As part of our commitment to create value in a world that is constantly changing, we are determined to be a good corporate citizen in every corner of our global community.' Inside, the document went into great detail on how they were leaders in CSR in their industry and their belief that 'the best clients want to work with such companies'.

The Public Relations Society of America outlined how a successful CSR programme would benefit companies by:

1) Building brand loyalty.
2) Attracting and retaining high quality employees.
3) Strengthening partnerships with stakeholders.
4) Enhancing credibility with various publics.
5) Burnishing the organization's public image.

But CSR is not universally accepted. A study showed that 29 per cent of CEOs were not convinced of a return on income through CSR, and 58 per cent said they did not have enough resources to divert any to CSR.

And there is no doubt in recessional times that CSR is going to be hurt. The art and theatre community in England found this out when the British government cut its contributions dramatically causing some organizations to fold.

Jack Welch, ex-chairman of General Electric, summed up the case for CSR succinctly in *Business Week*: 'Even in these uncertain times CSR belongs in every company. But every company must face reality. You have to make money first to give it away.'

Crisis Management

By the 1960s, one area that corporations were beginning to pay far more attention to was crisis management. We expanded dramatically into this new area of public relations. Martin Langford, who worked for me as managing director of our London office, was our expert, and the *Daily Telegraph*, in a major piece about him, called Martin 'The Master of Disaster'.

Martin once wrote: 'Managing a crisis is fundamentally different from normal management. Rather than system, there is chaos. Rather than order, there is lack of control. Rather than confidentiality, there is a fishbowl. Rather than decision-making based on information, there is intuition based on fragmentary and often unreliable data.'

Crisis management is not new – crises have always existed. It really started on an industry-wide basis with the airlines. Aeroplanes will crash – not exactly a tragedy you can hide. Some airlines in the early years did not plan carefully enough for the inevitable. In some countries, when questioned by reporters about a plane that had crashed in a field for all to see, the official response was, 'What aeroplane?'

But over time the airlines became expert at getting information out quickly and accurately, and to the right audiences. And some can even go beyond that. *Business Week*, in an article about the conduct of US Airways after its flight 1549 with 149 passengers aboard made an emergency landing in New York's Hudson River, said: 'For a company that's not known for its customer service, its handling of the near-disaster has cast a halo around its brand. The airline's care of Flight 1549's passengers may become a model for crisis management.'

The airline, like most others, has a manual for such happenings. And it runs emergency exercises at least three times a year and has a special 'Care Team'. When informed of the accident, the company activated a special Freephone number for families to call. They sent one hundred employees from headquarters with cash for passengers, and credit cards for employees to buy any medicines or personal items they needed. They also made prepaid mobile phones available, as well as sweat suits for anyone who had a need for dry clothes. Each passenger was put on a new flight or personally brought to a local New York hotel where they were entitled to round-the-clock buffets. They arranged train tickets or rental cars for those who didn't want to fly and went so far as to arrange locksmiths to help passengers who had lost their keys get into their cars or homes.

But even today it is amazing how poorly some, and I emphasize some, companies handle the inevitable. Oil spills are not new. Thirty years ago we held crisis management seminars for Gulf Oil in the US, Europe and South America. In order to create a realistic situation in the US, we invented a mythical city, Crisisport. Each participant in the seminar received material about Crisisport before he arrived. This included the physical, economic and political make-up of the city, Gulf's position, and information about the company's friends and adversaries. In the US, we photographed backgrounds with the name Crisisport on street signs and public transportation. In South America, one of our people was nearly arrested for putting up these signs in one of the cities.

The day began with the delivery of a newspaper we called the *Crisisport Post* that we had prepared for the different groups – different editions for each group. Each paper had a news item involving Gulf. One covered how environmentalists were launching an attempt to block a Gulf application for offshore drilling. Another said Gulf would lay off a large number of workers and close an installation. Another said the company would be the target of union organizers at a facility that had no union. Another talked about

Gulf's firing an employee who leaked some news about Gulf being involved in a cover-up. Every story had a mixture of fact, innuendo and untruths.

Each group had to report back on how they would have handled each situation. This was followed by a discussion with a panel of experts from Gulf and members of our company. Later in the day participants had to meet with various adversary groups such as civil rights leaders, irate city councillors and union leaders. These roles were played by professional actors. The final exercise was a true disaster module. The US audience was watching a US football game where a touchdown had just been scored. In Europe, it was European football and Pele had just scored. Then came a newsflash and they were shown actual films of a refinery fire.

The Gulf executives were then told which among them were in charge, and they were told to head to the refinery to meet with local print, radio and TV media. There we had professional journalists with microphones and cameras ready. They bombarded the executives with questions. At the same time, the executives were continually handed up-to-date information from company people. As is the case in real life, they were given incomplete and conflicting reports.

One group was told that everyone in a specific building had been killed, and they were given a list of everyone working there. They decided to give the list to the press. After it had been sent in for publication, they were told that one employee had not come to work that day but his relatives would read in the paper he was dead.

This was probably the most detailed crisis management training programme we were ever involved in, and the response from the client executives underlined how valuable it was for them. Obviously there is no way that most companies could undertake this degree of training, but the more that employee spokespeople are faced with these kinds of drills, the better off their company will be when a crisis finally arrives.

Even today companies sometimes don't follow the most basic approach to handling crisis situations. Ten years after Crisisport, Exxon had a serious oil spill in Alaska that had worldwide ramifications. Surprisingly, the chief executive would not even travel there to review the damage and explain in a positive way to the local community what actions they were preparing to take to lessen the overall damage. Certainly we would have advised him or another senior executive to go and be prepared with all possible answers. The result was that the *Wall Street Journal* and the *New York Times* criticized Exxon, not just for the oil spill, but also for their poor public relations handling of the crisis. And this criticism continued for a long while, causing major problems for Exxon. I'm sure that seared into the memories of those Exxon executives are the press pictures of customers tearing up their Exxon credit cards in disgust.

You would not need to take a poll today to determine what people think of the way BP handled its PR following the oil spill disaster in the Gulf of Mexico. It was a spill disaster followed by a PR disaster. Just one statement by CEO Tony Hayward, 'I want my life back,' made it twice as difficult for BP to get its life back.

Any company, no matter what industry it is in, can and will possibly face a crisis. It will not always be a major one, but it is just as advisable to be prepared for minor crises. Salmonella lurks around the corner, benzene can get into bottles, chemical lines do leak, and toys have sharp edges that can cut children. And as Toyota found out, recalls, if not handled well, can create a major crisis. The sudden death or resignation of a popular chief executive or the departure of a number of key executives can also create a crisis.

The hotel industry is another that is crisis-prone. When I was training executives from a major hotel chain, they gave me access to their crisis manual. It was ninety-one pages long with the table of contents taking up three pages. In addition, there was a twenty-six-page appendix of supporting documentation with emergency planning forms, detailed checklists and report forms to cover the various events that might take place.

Among the individual listings with instructions on how to handle each type of crisis were: bomb threats, terrorist threats, riots, food poisoning or food contamination, a sudden death in the hotel, kidnapping, fire or explosion, rape, robbery, suicide, infectious diseases, and still others. I am sure most other hotel chains have similar manuals, even if they are not quite as detailed.

The greatest example of how to turn a crisis from negative to positive still remains with Tylenol. Universities throughout the US still teach it as the best recorded example of crisis management.

In the autumn of 1982 someone, for reasons unknown, went into a store in Chicago and injected some extra-strength Tylenol tablets with sixty-five milligrams of cyanide. Five to seven milligrams is sufficient to kill an individual, and seven people who had purchased the product died after taking it.

This was a crisis of major proportions for the parent company, Johnson & Johnson, as Tylenol was one of their best known and most successful products. Though the company was in no way responsible, the possible short- and long-term damage was immeasurable.

The company immediately acted in the best interests of its customers. Using the media, they notified audiences throughout the country not to use the product. Then the CEO of Johnson & Johnson, James E. Burke, made a decision which not everyone in J&J's management or legal team agreed with at the time, but which made him a legend. Even though the company in no way bore responsibility for what had happened, Burke recalled thirty-one million bottles of Tylenol from the market at a cost of $100m. He said that the company's first loyalty was not to profits but to the customers, who were the reason for J&J's success.

The press throughout the country lauded Burke's action. The *Washington Post* wrote: 'What Johnson & Johnson executives have done is communicate the message that the company is candid, contrite and compassionate and committed to protecting the public.' As the PR firm handling the Tylenol crisis, we arranged for an appearance by James Burke on *60 Minutes*, a major news programme, which created a highly favourable impression of the man and his company. We also organized a press conference televised in thirty-five markets across the US announcing that the product was tampered with on the shelves and not during manufacture. We also held a nationwide poll that showed the majority of the country still had confidence in J&J.

At the same time as the recall was taking place, the company began a programme to regain its market position. Less than six weeks after the deaths were announced, we arranged for simultaneous press conferences in six cities when the company announced that Tylenol capsules were to be introduced in a new triple-seal tamper-resistant package. McNeil Consumer Products, the J&J company that produces Tylenol, gave special deals to consumers, and a totally new advertising campaign was launched. And 2,250 sales people from the company's domestic affiliates took part in presentations to people in the medical community.

Within a year the company had won back 90 per cent of its previous market position. What J&J had done was not only of interest in the US – I was interviewed in depth about the 'Tylenol Crisis' while travelling in Asia. To this day, whenever a crisis comes up, and, whether they feel it was handled well or badly, the press refers back to J&J and Tylenol as an example of perfection when it comes to crisis management. On the Internet, the Wikipedia encyclopaedia says the Burson–Marsteller handling of the Tylenol Crisis is called 'The Gold Standard' for crisis management. And James Burke is remembered as a legendary chief executive whose ideas and actions helped to save a major company.

Chief Executives and all other key executives must come to realize that we now live in an environment where crises and how they are handled, however major or minor, can be the most important issue that a company faces. As crises become more frequent, more wide-spread and more damaging, the manner in which they are dealt with will be an increasingly important factor influencing a company's success or failure.

At a conference on crisis management where I spoke, I told the audience: 'There are certain rules about answering questions regard-less of what the crisis is or who the group you are facing is.' I outlined the rules as follows:

1) A good answer answers the questions. Avoiding the answer shows you are either unprepared or else afraid of the truth.
2) A good answer is stated positively.
3) It is expressed in layman's terms.
4) A good answer is specific.
5) A good answer is concise.
6) The main point is up front.
7) It does not include more than is necessary.
8) A good answer does not repeat loaded or slanted words used by the interviewer.
9) It recognizes opportunities in the questions to present your point of view.
10) It doesn't sound defensive or antagonistic.

I have no doubt that if Rupert Murdoch and the staff of News International had followed these guidelines they could have decreased the overall hostility built up against them dramatically. Elton John once sang, 'Sorry seems to be the hardest word.' But had Murdoch used it earlier, he certainly would have benefited. But 'sorry' alone is not enough. What is important is to explain what steps you are taking to remedy the thing you are sorry for.

It constantly amazes me that senior politicians and corporate leaders from all over the world, when questioned about a crisis, show no realization of what impact their answers will have on an audience. Nor do they understand how difficult it is to build back confidence once it has been lost. In Rupert Murdoch's case, his initial statements alienated not only the media but shareholders, governments, employees and the British public. The statement that did him the most damage was when he said he wasn't going to appear before the parliamentary committee even though they had requested it. Later he changed his position and appeared, but the damage was already done. Pandora's box was now opened and even Pandora would have had a tough time closing it.

One point I always tried to convince client companies of is that the time to prepare for a crisis is before it happens. Once it happens, you are always on the back foot. So advance planning and a crisis manual are vital. The manual should make it very clear who does what during the crisis. A study we conducted in 2010 showed that at that time only 44 per cent of the companies interviewed had a crisis management plan. But since then we know that the numbers are improving.

Another study showed that the most effective way for a company to communicate with consumers in a crisis is through the company website. Word of mouth and customer service representatives come out as a distant second and third, with paid advertising way down at the bottom.

Chief executives living through a crisis must also understand that the media is not perfect – far from it. You can be questioned by someone who is rude, uncompromising, even seemingly prejudicial. What they print might be unfair and, even in some cases, untrue. But such is life.

Also, crises have great impacts internally, at all levels of an organization. Your employees are an audience you have to pay special attention to when a crisis occurs. Human resources departments should be made well aware of this necessity.

As the world continues to change, so does the role of the chief executive. He no longer sits on the top of the mountain sending commands to his minions below, expecting his orders to be implemented immediately and without question. He now must listen as much as talk. He must be aware of all the key audiences, what their needs are, and how best to meet those needs. He must understand that in today's digital world, response time to any question is very limited, and the whole world is watching. Staff loyalty is dead to a large degree and employees are just as important an audience as customers and shareholders. Most importantly, the CEO must understand that the perception of him as a man and as a leader that is held by his key audiences is make or break for him and his organization. It's not the job it used to be.

12 Managing Perceptions: The Key to the Future for Communicators, Politicians, Church Leaders, Doctors, Lawyers and Even Jobseekers

On the day I joined Burson–Marsteller in 1957, my mother asked me, 'What will you be doing for a living?' I answered, 'Public relations.' She replied, 'Exactly what is that?'

At that time it was very easy for me to explain. 'Public relations is handling client relationships with various publics or audiences,' I told her. 'And the main publics are the government, the financial community, the local community, employees and most important (which it was at that time) customers or potential customers. We help our clients keep their publics informed of their latest news, happenings, products and services.' All of this was easily digested and understood by her. She now was confident her son had a future.

But times have changed dramatically, and so has the practice of public relations. As I opened offices around the world, serving clients who had many different important audiences, I came to see that the very nature of PR was changing dramatically. In reality it had become 'perception management'. A primary role for us was to help our clients create the necessary perception with key audiences to ensure their success. In turn, effective perception management has become the real key to success for all practitioners of PR.

According to Wikipedia, 'perception management' is a term originated by the US military as a euphemism for information warfare. It has become a synonym for the word persuasion.

But in reality, perception management is not new and existed long before the US military coined the phrase, if in fact they did. Though it might have been described in different ways in different times, managing perceptions has been a fact of life as long as life has existed. As I've already noted, the ancient Egyptian people didn't need a PR firm to tell them they should be on the good side of the pharaohs, priests and generals. During the Spanish Inquisition it didn't take a high IQ to understand that you should stay on the right side of Torquemada. Moses managed the perceptions of his followers when he convinced them he knew the best escape route out of Egypt, even though it seemed an odd choice to many of his followers.

Jesus and his disciples created a whole new set of perceptions for potential followers, telling them what the Lord really wanted from them, and how to live up to them and make them central to their lives. And who better to get Jesus's message across to the waiting public than Peter and Paul. Likewise, Saint Thomas Aquinas helped to develop the persuasive nature of religious communications, writing the Apologetics to get his message across. Martin Luther reached his audience by posting his ideas on a church door, a perfect placement.

What has really changed today is the level of sophistication with which perception management is now practiced – just look at the incredible growth of corporate social responsibility, which we discussed in the last chapter, as companies came to realize that customers will gravitate more to organizations that are not only making products they enjoy but that are also perceived to be doing something beneficial for the public.

Public relations practitioners themselves are becoming increasingly sophisticated. They would know if Torquemada read *Inquisition News* and would arrange for favourable client interviews to be placed there for him to see. They would know if the pharaoh planned to attend seminars on 'How to Build the Perfect Pyramid' and they would make sure their client became a speaker at that seminar. And Moses would have found it much easier to galvanize his followers if he could have used Facebook, Twitter and LinkedIn.

To many, the term perception management has a manipulative ring about it. But any type of persuasion is manipulative by nature and that includes advertising, public relations, selling or merchandising.

We are all aware that there are manipulative aspects to most things in life. We are always 'manipulating' others to some degree. Parents manipulate children. From a young age, children manipulate parents and sometimes do a better job of it than their parents. Ministers manipulate their flocks, especially during collection time. Husbands manipulate wives, and wives do the same.

There is nothing inherently wrong with managing perceptions. It is not illegal and it is not immoral. Doing it well can be essential at times for the future well-being of those being manipulated – for example, when parents tell their children why they are splitting up or when a doctor tells his patients about a recent test revealing their cells are malignant. Or when a statesman, such as Winston Churchill, explained to the British public in 1939 the sacrifices they would have to make and why they must make them.

There is no question that perception management can be used

for the completely wrong and even evil reasons. Who was one of the great perception managers of the century but Bernie Madoff? In his guilty plea he explained he knew exactly what he was doing. He created a perception of untold riches for those who would invest their money with him. And invest they did, and many headed right into poverty.

Joseph Goebbels created an image for the German populace of a nation led by Adolf Hitler that would return the country to the position it held before the First World War, a position that all the people were eager to see again.

Perception management cannot do the impossible. Not even P. T. Barnum could have convinced the American public that Bill Clinton was shy by nature and no PR man could have changed the image of Attila the Hun to Attila the Honey.

Corporations, countries, executives and even individuals face situations where it is necessary to change perceptions to achieve certain goals. What counts, whenever a problem must be solved or an opportunity maximized, is how the facts are presented and how they are perceived.

Equally important, it is necessary to understand that different audiences are going to perceive things in different ways. Many years ago this fact was spelt out most engagingly by Janet Street Porter in a London *Times* review of the book, *The History of the Breast*, by Marilyn Yalom when she noted, 'The breast means food to babies, sex to men, disease to doctors and a commercial opportunity to the clothing industry.'

The key, of course, is to know in advance what factors are shaping the perception of the audience you are trying to reach. This often calls for a great deal of research. And for some organizations, if the perceptions are deeply rooted, the cost of trying to change them might not be worth it.

Perceptions can change dramatically. In 2008, young people voted overwhelmingly for Barack Obama as they perceived him as a man who understood them and could be the one who would fulfil their most important needs. But their major needs did not include health care, which is where he has put in the most effort. He did not remember the words from Bill Clinton's winning campaign against George H. W. Bush: 'It's the economy stupid.' As a result, so many young people without job opportunities deserted Obama and the Democratic Party in the 2010 election. They did not feel that Obama was doing enough to solve the problem that was most important and most immediate for them.

Before you are really able to manage perceptions, you need to know:

1) Who are the audiences you want to reach, and in what order of importance?
2) What are their current perceptions on the subjects most important to you?
3) What are the best ways to create or reinforce the perception you would like them to have?
4) Are the finances available to accomplish this? And, if so, are the potential results worth it? If funds are not available to reach all objectives, which should be given priority?
5) Who is best in the organization to deliver the necessary messages most effectively, and do they need any training to ensure they can accomplish this?
6) Is there a time factor involved?
7) Will the results be measurable?

When it comes to perceptions, regardless of who the audience is, you face four basic conditions:

1) When those you are trying to influence have absolutely no perception about what you are trying to promote, it is necessary to create one, for example, when launching a totally new product. In many ways this is an excellent situation to be in because you are facing less possible controversy.

2) If the perception is already favourable, obviously you want to reinforce it and add new elements, as is the case with many charities.

3) If the perception is negative, you want to change it but you must be aware of what caused the negativity and make every effort to change that. A good example is the case with the Egyptian Tourist Board after the Luxor massacre took place. They had to change the perception that Egypt was now a place to avoid for holidays.

4) If the negative perception is very deep-seated and in all probability unalterable to any real degree, you have to decide what might be done to modify the situation. That's true with Israel in its dealings with Hamas, which is not going to change its perception of Israel. Bigotry, whether individual or collective, aimed at individuals, organizations or countries will always exist. But great strides can be made in modifying even these kinds of perceptions, as Lyndon Johnson, then president of the United States, found as he shepherded his historical Civil Rights legislation by convincing previous recalcitrant congressional members from the South that there was no other direction for them to take.

With the right message, mass perceptions can change quickly. Nobody learned this to his own detriment to a greater degree than Thomas E. Dewey when he ran for the presidency of the United States against Harry Truman in 1948. Every poll had Dewey way ahead, and even members of Truman's own party had written the president off. Believing he was a shoo-in, Dewey ran a lacklustre campaign, just waiting for the counting of the votes. But Truman and his advisors felt that if he could get a simple message across about what he stood for, he could change the perception of the electorate, and they would gravitate to him. He rode trains all around the US, and at each stop he talked to the crowds in simple terms they understood and found believable. He won re-election in what is considered by many to be the biggest upset in American political history.

Sometimes a single fact can change a perception and alter a response. Let me explain this on a simple personal basis. Let's say you have a close single male friend and you know a nice woman, and you believe they would enjoy each other's company. You tell your friend that she is very pretty because that is what you think will interest him. You introduce them at a party, but later your friend tells you that he isn't really interested as she didn't exactly live up to the lovely picture you painted of her.

Obviously you are not going to be able to change his impression of her looks. But there is another way that you can shift his impression of her and why he should go out with her. You explain they have very similar interests. She loves travel, tennis, the theatre, eating in good Asian restaurants – all of which are important to him. He then decides that he will definitely ask her out because looks have now become relatively unimportant in his perception of the better reasons to go out with her. He realizes that there are other qualities that make her someone whom he might enjoy spending time with.

It is not only communicators and PR practitioners like myself who have to worry about managing perceptions. It can also be an important success strategy for professionals like lawyers and doctors, and also for people *trying* to become professionals – I'm speaking about job candidates.

Lawyers

When I started in public relations, it was rare to find PR practitioners, whether in-house or at a company's external consultancy, working closely with the company's legal department. Quite often there was an unexpressed hostility, as both were fighting for the chief executive's ear. Lawyers felt their role was simply to win a case or advise a chief executive on the potential legal liability of a proposed course of action. At that time, very little thought was given to the public relations ramifications of a case or action. This has changed dramatically, and the legal department and corporate PR people now work hand in hand with a strong appreciation of each other's role.

And lawyers now understand very well that winning a case is not all that really counts. At a legal conference I attended in the US, the chief lawyer for a major American energy company said that he now never thinks of the possible results of litigation that he is seeking without also considering how the results would be perceived by the public when announced on the front page of the *New York Times*.

At no time was this made clearer than when McDonald's in London sued two young people from Greenpeace, won the case but lost thousands of customers. I was working for McDonald's in four European countries then, and the chief executive in every one of those countries told me that they could not understand why the company lawyers were allowed to file suit.

In some cases, lawyers actually become PR men. No better example exists of the lawyer's expanded role than that of my client, Robert Amsterdam. A partner in the law firm of Amsterdam & Peroff, he acted as one of the legal counsels for Mikhail Khodorkovsky in his legal battle against President Putin of Russia. A two-page profile of Amsterdam in *Business Week* stressed the public relations role he undertook, as he told his client's story around the world, because of his strong belief in his client's innocence.

According to Amsterdam, there are two factors that have now had a major impetus in marrying law with public relations. The first is increased activity for many companies in emerging markets, from China and India, to smaller countries in South America and Africa. Amsterdam explained:

> It is vital for lawyers to be aware of the public relations ramifications of what a company does in an emerging market and this can differ greatly from the home market. In today's rapidly changing world and its constantly changing political emphasis there is a far greater chance that a company in an emerging market or their staff can end up in a criminal litigation, which obviously has a PR impact.
>
> The other area binding PR and law concerns corporate social responsibility. During the planning and implementation period, many legal questions can surface. At the same time the public relations aspect remains primary as this is a major reason for launching CSR campaigns. So this is an area I get involved in with nearly all my clients.

It is not surprising that once when I finished my message training of a chief executive, he told me that he wanted me to train his legal counsel also, which I did.

A member of a law firm once told me that they were seriously considering developing a close relationship with a PR firm so that – for certain potential clients at least —they would pitch for the business jointly.

And having your PR keep you constantly in the public eye can be very good for business. No one is better at this than Gloria Allred, who represented two of Tiger Woods's mistresses and who has become nearly as famous as Tiger, not for her golfing skills, but for her abilities in the court house and, just as important, in press conferences.

She uses PR to build cases for her clients in the court of public opinion, before she even enters the courtroom. And her legend has grown so great in her efforts on behalf of wronged women that she is referenced in popular entertainment programmes. On *Saturday Night Live*, for example, a character representing Justin Bieber tells a character representing Tina Fey that because she fantasized about him, he was going to contact Gloria Allred. In the TV programme *The Simpsons*, she counsels the character Lisa and is captioned as 'a shrill feminist lawyer'. In the popular TV series *Glee*, one of the main characters, Will, is told by someone that she is planning to sue and will be contacting Gloria Allred. There is no doubt in my mind that Allred does not have to spend her spare time hunting for clients.

Doctors

If there is any group of professionals who should see the importance of perception management it is doctors. They cannot change the terrible facts that they must often communicate to deathly ill patients or their patients' relatives. But how they do it – their choice of words, their tone, their body language – is of paramount importance and can have a lasting impact. What do you say when the tests have proven that the chances of survival for your patient are minimal at best? Or that a child has a mental malfunction that will continue throughout their lifetime?

Doctors are also in a position of having to treat unpleasant or very unlikeable people in the same professional manner as they handle patients they have a personal regard for. But many don't. The medical profession in general has been aware of this problem for some time. In 1978 the *New England Journal of Medicine* published an article, 'Taking Care of the Hateful Patient', and in

2005, the *Journal of the New Zealand Medical Association* printed a piece about 'Reflecting on the Difficult Patient'. In 2005, in the *American Family Physician*, an article appeared with the title, 'Management of the Difficult Patient'. All of these articles spelt out that doctors have to carefully manage the perceptions of ALL their patients.

But one of the clearest descriptions of the problem as it exists was written by Doctor Monica Lalanda, in the United Kingdom Casebook. Lalanda wrote:

> Some of the most intrinsic feelings and inner thoughts that we have as doctors live hidden in our own personal Pandora's boxes. There are certain things that we find difficult to acknowledge, even to ourselves. Becoming aware that we have feelings of dislike toward some of our patients or that we find them really difficult to cope with can make us feel uncomfortable. As doctors, we usually expect medical encounters to constitute a source of mutual satisfaction.
>
> Challenging patients are not those who have difficult medical problems; we have the knowledge, the training or the resources to deal with those issues. Such patients are those that engender in us a negative emotional response; patients who trigger strong feelings of frustration, hopelessness, exasperation, sadness or even anger. This is all part of the daily practice of being a doctor. However, as you know, traditional medical training has in the past failed to properly prepare new doctors for dealing with such sensitive situations.

I can give three personal examples of where doctors desperately needed a course in perception management. A close friend of mine was dying, and his wife had to decide whether to keep him at home or send him for assisted aid at a hospice. A doctor came to speak to her about her husband going into a hospice before he spoke to my friend. The wife asked one thing: 'Please do not at this particular time use the word, "hospice". He doesn't know his condition is incurable and that word would tell him he has no hope. It will make his last days filled with even greater suffering.' The doctor said he had no choice but to use and explain 'hospice' to the patient. The wife ended the visit and kept her husband at home with her until he died about a month later.

A very close widowed friend of mine who lives in England was visiting her brother in Sweden. She woke up on a Friday to find out that she had turned completely blue. She called the British National Health Service and was told that she could have an appointment on Monday morning and that she would have to take blood tests, which she well understood. 'The reason,' she was told by the anonymous voice on the phone, 'is that you might have cancer.' This phone diagnosis caused my friend considerable anguish over the entire weekend as she wrestled with the possibility of cancer. It turned out that she didn't have cancer and her condition was cured in a relatively brief time.

My brother was diagnosed with a brain tumour, but it was initially declared benign. His wife and I were sitting with him in his hospital room when the phone rang. His wife picked up, listened for a short time, and then hung up and ran out of the room without saying anything. She came back after a while and when my brother questioned her, she replied, 'It's nothing very important.' But, of course, neither of us believed her.

What had happened was that the doctor, with very little consideration, had told her further tests had proved the tumour was malignant and that there was no hope of any cure. This was a cold way to deliver such bad news and certainly was not meant for a phone conversation, especially not to the patient's room. It had a devastating impact on my sister-in-law that lasted for a long time.

A study at Duke University underlined the serious consequences of not managing perceptions effectively. Researchers taped 398 conversations between fifty-one oncologists and 270 patients, all with advanced cancer. The researchers were looking for empathy. If patients said something that showed they were sad or scared and doctors ignored the comment or shut it down, researchers named this a 'terminator response'. Or if doctors tried to show some empathy or become involved in a compassionate conversation, researchers called this a 'continuer response'. The oncologists responded with empathy to the patients' negative feelings only 22 per cent of the time. As one commentator wrote about the study, 'In other words if the patient was going to be depressed, he better do it somewhere else.'

A Harris poll of 2,267 patients found that respondents cared more that doctors listened to their concerns and questions than they did about doctors being up-to-date on the latest medical research and treatment.

There is no question that segments of the medical community attempt from time to time to improve the situation but accomplishing personality changes with certain doctors won't be easy. One London clinic even hired actors to play the role of difficult patients to help train the doctors. And in the University of Texas and Columbia University medical schools, a stage actor ran a class called 'The Craft of Empathy'. The course showed doctors-in-training how to use their bodies and facial expressions during emotional encounters with patients.

In the US more and more doctors themselves are turning to acting classes to improve their bedside manners. Also in the US, some private health care companies offer rewards to medical centres that are rated highly by their patients.

At Virginia Tech Carilion School of Medicine in Roanoke, Virginia, the newest medical school in the US, students now go through a series of mini interviews aimed at testing their social skills.

The National Health Service in Britain issued an edict recently instructing hospitals to make their patients happy. The Health Secretary wanted to link budgets to bedside manners, saying that the amount of funding a hospital received could be linked to how happy they keep their patients. 'Sometimes hospitals are missing the point,' he said. 'How you are spoken to, how you are dealt with, whether you are treated in a friendly way – these things can be as important as your medical care.'

We can only hope that more and more doctors will realize the importance of managing their patients' perceptions as well as providing effective medical treatment. They will benefit as well: I have no doubt that if this happens, there will be a significant drop in medical malpractice suits.

Jobseekers

Nowhere does perception count more than in a job interview, no matter what level job one is looking for, whether it be as a dish-washer on a night shift or as chairman of a board. It continues to surprise me to observe how often jobseekers do not really under-stand this and prepare accordingly. I once was hired by a leading headhunting organization to interview the heads of all their European offices. In our discussions they too expressed amazement at the number of job candidates who came to see them with no understanding of what their interviewer would be looking for, or how to present effectively the necessary information, or how to make the best impression.

Over my fifty-year career, I've received thousands of résumés and have personally interviewed thousands of job prospects. Whenever I received a résumé and a letter, I looked them over very carefully and already had a definite perception of the potential candidate and whether I wanted to interview them.

One mistake that many people make is that they send the exact same letter and the exact same résumé to dozens of companies. No two companies and no two jobs are exactly the same with the same needs – so it calls for homework to understand and differentiate these documents before applying.

One detail, though, that might not seem important and is often overlooked is making sure the names of the company and the recipient of the letter are spelt correctly. I've received letters addressed to Bob Leak, Bob Leap and Bob Leech. (Maybe they had checked up on me.)

And this is no joke: I once received a letter at Burson–Marsteller addressed to Bursting Marshmallow. The résumé and the letter were serious, so I can only conjecture that someone was playing a practical joke on the petitioner and recommended he send it to us and gave him the ridiculous company name he put on the envelope.

I received more than a hundred letters where Marsteller was spelt Marstellar. While this might seem insignificant, it isn't to me. If someone applying for a job in communications can't take the time to check carefully the spelling of the company's or person's name he is communicating with, my perception of him or her has dropped even before the first interview.

The more homework jobseekers do in advance about the company and the job on offer, the greater the chances are that they will be given an interview and that it will go well.

If anyone wrote to me, 'I read in the paper that Burson–Marsteller has just opened an office in the Middle East. I lived and worked in Dubai for two years and speak perfect Arabic, and believe I could be helpful,' even if we didn't have an immediate opening, I would definitely have that person interviewed for possible future employment.

Here's what always interested me about any candidate: how much have they learned about the company, its history, and myself in particular? What has been written about us recently that they were aware of? What do they know about the competition we are facing in the area they are applying for?

The kinds of questions they asked were also important because that gave me a clue to their insights. You should never go to an interview without a list of questions in mind that you are prepared to ask.

Once the job is secured, the need for perception management doesn't end. In fact, it becomes even more important. Reasons for getting a promotion vary greatly, but the perception of the boss or bosses about you as an employee and what you are expected to accomplish in your new role are often the key. It is surprising how many employees don't understand or make a real effort to find out what current perceptions are being held about them, and take action to shore them up or change them if necessary.

So it makes no difference whether you are a communicator, a politician, a churchman, a lawyer, a doctor, a jobseeker or simply a parent – just having basic intelligence or basic skills will not always ensure the kind of success or results you are seeking. There is the need to have an in-depth understanding of the perception of the audience or audiences you are trying to influence. Surprisingly enough, and happily enough, this is not always so difficult. The answers are usually right there in front of you.

13 How Has Public Relations Changed in the Last Fifty Years and What Does the Future Look Like?

During any fifty-year period, change is inevitable – sometimes for the better, sometimes for the worse. This is true for countries, economies, religions, businesses, and each and every one of us. Fortunately for me, my wife – who has been with me throughout these fifty years – says I've changed for the better. So I certainly have been using the right perception management at home. I just hope my writing has also changed in this direction and that you're not overjoyed that this is the final chapter.

PR has changed dramatically during my time in the industry, mostly for the better. The future looks even brighter. It will undoubtedly make even greater contributions to the overall success of companies, organizations, charities and individuals during the coming years.

Whether you accept my belief that public relations is primarily perception management or not makes no difference. No matter what you call it, its role is still the same: to convince key audiences that the messages that are being delivered are completely true, and that it is to their benefit to react to them accordingly. Whether you want an audience to vote, purchase, invest, join or, in the case of families, behave in a certain way, makes no difference.

Throughout this book, I have been pointing out as we've moved along changes I've seen in the business over the years. Here's a more focused and deeper set of observations.

The greatest change I've witnessed is PR's increased importance to many groups or individuals. When I started, the primary aim for most clients was to get a favourable mention for a company or its products in the media. PR was a baby industry. It didn't have a real track record. It was more open to questions about what exactly it could really accomplish and on what scale. Budgets were relatively miniscule, as were the objectives.

Except in very specific cases, PR was not high on a chief executive's agenda. The in-house PR man was usually of minor consequence to the company. In most, if not all companies, the individuals holding that job were neither inspired nor inspiring.

These days, there are very few companies or organizations that do not have public relations high up on their agenda. They appreciate the fact that the way they are perceived by their important audiences is the real key to their success. And they acknowledge that PR holds that key.

The same is true of politicians. Even in Russia, Putin and Medvedev are increasingly trying to manage the perceptions of the Russian people; sometimes with the same message, sometimes with conflicting messages. Now, in the Middle East, we find the greatest need and greatest attempt to manage perceptions both within national boundaries and globally. There are many parties located outside the Middle East wanting to affect what is happening inside.

Because PR is now so important, there is a far greater realization that it must be done right. Practitioners have to know exactly what they want to accomplish and how to go about it most effectively. To that end, far more research is being undertaken than ever before.

What do your key audiences really think at the present time? And what messages have to be developed to ensure their thinking is favourable? In nearly all its pitches, Burson–Marsteller presents potential programmes that are evidence-based and the result of research undertaken in advance, all in an effort to create the most realistic approach possible to the mission at hand.

PR professionals and clients alike must still face the realization that even with all the most sophisticated PR support in the world, one cannot accomplish the impossible. No programme to support the banking industry and the vital role of bankers in our society will be able to convince the average British or American citizen that there has never been a greedy bone in any of their bodies.

No greater example of a perception that has changed so dramatically that even the most highly focused PR programme would not be able to change it back to its previous state is that of the Catholic Church in Ireland. There, the church from time immemorial was the major force, and no group would have wanted them as an opponent in any way. The average Irish Catholic family usually hoped for four children, one to be a priest, one possibly to be a doctor and the other two depending on whether they were boys or girls just to be successful and raise a happy family. Three out of those four wishes still exist. But the child abuse problem, and the way the church ignored or mishandled the issue, has led it on a very steep downward path in the public's perception. Many parishes are now unable to find the number of new priests they need among the locals, so they have begun to bring some in from Africa. Now, the church has little influence over the younger generation in Ireland. Even the government has been conducting serious investigations into past activities, something that would never have happened in the past.

As I've said earlier, the quality of people choosing PR as a career has also gone up dramatically. Highly capable individuals with backgrounds in government, business or the media are now joining communications companies. Young people setting out on career paths have also found the PR industry an attractive place to work.

When I first moved to England, if a bright student told his advisor at Oxford or Cambridge that he wanted to go into public relations, he would have had to run for safety. Now PR firms often get letters from leading universities recommending top students who would like to work as interns in the industry.

The training programmes offered at all major public relations firms have expanded dramatically. Burson–Marsteller made an early start on this type of professional education programme with Burson–Marsteller University, where employees could get grounding in our business. Education should never stop. Now, more than ever, it applies to people not only when they start, but even after they've been in the profession for quite a few years. There are always new things to learn and new approaches to take. The digital revolution alone calls for a lot of ongoing training.

Clients have become far more knowledgeable about the benefits of PR. They know that the need for PR is greater than ever and are willing to pay more. But the flip side is that they are more forceful in demanding that they get value for money. From the very beginning of the relationship, PR programmes have to be more carefully thought out so that they are measurable. That is also why the use of carefully-planned research to really be sure what is being suggested is valid has increased dramatically. Times can change, so needs can change, but firms have to be able to show the client why these different approaches or new initiatives are necessary and what can be accomplished by the changes being recommended.

The quality of the corporate in-house staff has also changed dramatically. When I began in the PR business, it was extremely rare for someone to leave a major consultancy to join a client or other business organization. The salary was usually lower and the role of the PR executive within the company was not at the highest level. Now the exact opposite is true. Many senior people leave consultancies to join their clients or other companies for a higher salary and benefit package, and for a more significant role as well, as they often will sit at the right hand of the chairman.

Chairmen are well aware of the importance of their own and their company's image. A major client of mine went from chief executive of one large company to another and the first person he hired at his new company was the PR director of his previous company, for whom he had great respect. And because they acknowledge the reality of PR and perception management, chairmen are much more willing to accept being trained to ensure they will present the necessary image. And the increased training has resulted in far better handling of problems such as crises.

When I started, major companies usually hired one firm only to handle their total public relations. That rarely happens now, especially in companies in fields such as health care, where it is more typical to have three or four agencies handling different products. Today there are a lot of small or even larger agencies that are specialists focusing only on very specific areas such as health care, public affairs or financial PR. In addition, there are now many specialist freelancers available for companies or even consultancies to bring in at different times to handle specific assignments. Francis Ingham, the chief executive of the UK's Public Relations Consultants Association said, 'using freelancers has become a prime method for giving agencies a greater degree of flexibility, allowing them to speedily assemble teams with the skills and experience to fit a specific brief'.

Some of the high level PR consultants are beginning to see a change in their role. Max Clifford, probably the UK's leading publicist said his PR business, 'has become less focused on promotion in recent years and more about protecting high profile clients from the excesses of British media'.

I have already discussed in detail another major change in PR – corporate social responsibility and its growing importance. As more and more chief executives began to realize CSR could not only be the key to reputation but also to sales it became a major factor in their planning.

By far one of the most significant changes in public relations has been the dramatic transformation of the media and the arrival of the digital revolution and its world dominance in the gathering and distribution of news and information. While the leading newspapers are still important to PR, depending on what you are trying to accomplish, they don't dominate as they once did. Because of the speed that news travels, word often appears on the Internet, Facebook and Twitter before it appears in print, and so the papers are publishing less news-breaking stories and are more likely to print articles commenting on what has already happened or filling in the details.

Because of the world's difficult economic situation and the rise of digital media, newspapers can no longer afford large staff. Ironically, this development actually benefits PR people. When I started, the leading papers had personnel whose sole role was to check up on potential stories we might suggest to them and to research the key facts to ensure accuracy. Now they don't have the staff to do that. Newspapers have to rely on us to a greater degree and are far more willing to talk to PR people and work with them on potential articles.

Today the hot spot is the world of social media, even for reporters, as a study showed 92 per cent of reporters use the Internet, Facebook and Twitter when developing a story. The technological revolution has made it easier to have information at your fingertips. In addition, mobile technology has made it possible for *anyone* to be a citizen journalist.

Digital technologies allow you to engage personally and create a one-on-one relationship. Obama realized the power of digital technology early during his first campaign, and it freed him from dependence on wealthy donors alone. By using the Internet to reach out to potential supporters he attracted more than three million donors with an average donation of $86.

In a survey of shoppers, 92 per cent said they had far greater confidence in information they found online than from a sales clerk or other source. Another survey had 62 per cent of those questioned stating they spend at least thirty minutes online every week to decide what and whether they should buy. For those under the age of forty-five the number went up to 73 per cent.

In light of these changes, companies today must treat the whole digital area as professionally as possible in order to maintain or change perceptions of itself or its products. The goals should be to create awareness, deepen interaction, convert potential customers from expressing interest to actually buying, and building loyalty that motivates people to buy again.

It is not surprising that more and more companies are hiring social media directors. A study by *Fortune Magazine* of their global 100 corporations found that 79 per cent of them were using social media such as Facebook, Twitter, YouTube and corporate blogs – with Twitter the most commonly used. While the figure was 77 per cent for European companies, it was only 50 per cent for Asian companies, but it is starting to move up.

It is very rare now for any consultancy pitching for a major client not to have a digital element in their proposal and an outline of their skills in this area.

Websites continue to take on more and more importance. In many cases it is the website that gives potential customers and other key audiences their first real perception of the company. Still, many companies do not give enough thought to their websites. When developing a website they've got to consider branding, content, design, ease of use, functionality, issues management and its impact on staff.

In today's world, things change quickly and dramatically, and a company website must take this into consideration and be changed whenever necessary. It must continually meet the company's objectives and respond to the issues of the moment.

Websites also give companies the chance to see what the competition is claiming and to act accordingly. Since a website can be changed easily and dramatically, continual monitoring is absolutely necessary. You'll never know what you'll find that might affect your operations in a very negative way. What you do find might even give you a heads-up concerning critical issues that need to be addressed. A leading London law firm recently gave seminars about how to react if something on the web is defamatory, breaches confidence or breaches copyright and might call for legal action.

While social networking provides numerous possibilities to affect positive perception management, we have to be aware of and prepared for the negative. The magazine *Communicate* wrote: 'The digital grapevine is teeming with untruths, flaky misconceptions and malicious fibs.' It used as an example a completely untrue story that was spread claiming that the coffee chain, Starbucks, had stopped supplying donations of coffee to the military because the company was against the Iraq War and anyone involved in it. Starbucks was able to reach the source of the story, who admitted that he was wrong and made a retraction. But considerable damage had already been done. Starbucks now has a rumour response page on its website.

There are plenty of good examples of companies taking the social media world seriously and using it to their benefit. Dell established a Social Media Listening Command Center where they monitor more than 22,000 Dell-related-topic posts per day on average.

Average daily mentions of Dell on Twitter alone have a greater reach than the combined circulations of the top twelve daily newspapers in the United States.

In a room filled with flat-screen monitors in 2010, Gatorade established its own Social Media Mission Control. The team has had more than 2,000 one-on-one conversations with consumers while the brand's mention on Facebook reached 1.2 million and is still growing dramatically.

Companies are increasingly trying to get all their employees in sync when it comes to social networking. Coca-Cola established its own set of social media guidelines which their digital communications director distributed in a memo to all employees. The memo outlines the company policy emphasizing the need for transparency and encouraging employees to use common sense when discussing the brand online.

Companies have to think digitally and at the same time they must act globally. Over the years, as I sat in on more and more international planning sessions, I began to see how far PR has come in its ability to get things done on an international scale. More and more PR projects are being undertaken by people from a number of different offices spread out in different countries, all working together in a tight collaboration. This is even the case with smaller PR firms which are increasingly working with other, unrelated companies around the world in temporary joint collaborations. Of course, all this means that great consideration must be given to the fact that many of the key messages for selling a product can differ in various countries. It's a challenging but invigorating environment in PR these days.

When you have been in the business as long as I have, you have got to accept that not everything that happens will be satisfying or happy. The saddest moment in my career came when a serial killer, out to punish Burson–Marsteller for an imagined wrong, murdered one of the most outstanding people who had ever worked for us, a good man named Tom Mosser.

Tom had been vice chairman of Burson–Marsteller and was then promoted to a senior role in the then parent company, Young & Rubicam. He was fifty, and there was no job he would not have been capable of undertaking in the future.

During Christmas 1994, he was preparing to take his wife and two children to purchase a Christmas tree, when he decided he would open the Christmas packages the family had just received in the mail. One of the packages addressed to him was the size of a hardcover book. When he opened it, it exploded, blowing a large hole through the kitchen counter and killing him instantly. Tom's wife and children were in the next room and, hearing the explosion, rushed in to find him dead.

The package had been mailed to Tom by the infamous Unabomber, Ted Kaczynski. In a letter to the *New York Times*, the Unabomber declared he had selected Burson–Marsteller because the company had helped Exxon clean up its public image after the 'Exxon Valdez incident' and, more importantly, because 'its business is the development of techniques for manipulating people's attitudes'.

He obviously had gotten Tom's name from an old directory as Tom no longer worked for us having moved to Young & Rubicam. In effect, the bomb was addressed to the wrong person. And we weren't even handling the Exxon account.

The impact on the company and on me personally was overwhelming. The funeral took place in New Jersey, where he and his family were living. No one attending could believe this had happened – we are all in shock – and especially to a man like Tom. When I left the church, I was interviewed by the local ABC TV station, and I said this was by far the saddest funeral I had ever attended, including those of my parents. The feeling is still with me. I think I've included this terrible event in the book to remind myself of how lucky I am. My life and career have given me everything I have ever hoped for, but it all could have gone wrong in one terrible moment, as it did for Tom. I still think of him often.

When I look at where public relations and its role in managing perceptions is going, I see few negatives. Nations, NGOs, professions and individuals will increasingly appreciate the need to communicate effectively. With the increased skills that those entering the industry now possess, there is no doubt in my mind that the services and the results our industry provides will continue to get better and better. Budgets will go up. Salaries will go up. Obviously there will be recessional periods affecting various clients in different parts of the world, but these will be short-term.

If you have a son or daughter, sister or brother, grandson or granddaughter who is trying to figure out what to do in life, I can recommend without hesitation that they seriously consider a career in public relations.

It certainly worked for me. I saw and did things and met people that I never dreamed possible. And to prove it was all worthwhile, upon returning home from a recent trip to New York, I found the following letter waiting for me:

Dear Mr Leaf,

I am delighted to inform you that the faculty of Missouri School of Journalism has voted to award you the 2011 Missouri Honour Medal for Distinguished Service in Journalism. The medal, given since 1930, is the highest honour the School of Journalism bestows. You will join an elite group of recipients including Tom Brokaw, George Gallup, Walter Cronkite, Christine Amanpour, Craig Claiborne and Winston Churchill.

Index